LITERATURE AFTER FEMINISM

Rita Felski

LITERATURE
after
FEMINISM

THE

UNIVERSITY

OF CHICAGO

PRESS

Chicago and London

RITA FELSKI is professor of English
at the University of Virginia. She is the
author of *Beyond Feminist Aesthetics:
Feminist Literature and Social Change,
The Gender of Modernity,* and *Doing
Time: Feminist Theory and
Postmodern Culture.*

THE UNIVERSITY OF CHICAGO PRESS, CHICAGO 60637
THE UNIVERSITY OF CHICAGO PRESS, LTD., LONDON
© 2003 by The University of Chicago
All rights reserved. Published 2003
Printed in the United States of America

12 11 10 09 08 07 06 05 04 03   1 2 3 4 5

ISBN: 0-226-24114-9 (cloth)
ISBN: 0-226-24115-7 (paper)

Library of Congress Cataloging-in-Publication Data

Felski, Rita, 1956–
    Literature after feminism / Rita Felski.
        p. cm.
    ISBN 0-226-24114-9 (cloth : alk. paper)—ISBN 0-226-24115-7 (pbk. : alk.
paper)
    1. Feminist criticism.   2. Feminism and literature.   3. Women and liter-
ature.   I. Title.

    PN98.W64 F353 2003
    801'.95'082—dc21

                                                                        2002153271

♾ The paper used in this publication meets the minimum requirements
of the American National Standard for Information Sciences—Permanence
of Paper for Printed Library Materials, ANSI Z39.48-1992.

For Maria, with love

CONTENTS

Acknowledgments
ix

Introduction
1

1 • READERS • *23*

2 • AUTHORS • *57*

3 • PLOTS • *95*

4 • VALUES • *135*

Notes
171

Index
187

ACKNOWLEDGMENTS

IN WRITING THIS BOOK I have accrued numerous debts.

I want first to express my warm thanks to Cornelia Klinger and the Institut für die Wissenschaften vom Menschen in Vienna for a generous residential fellowship which allowed me to write much of this book. I am also grateful to the Edgar F. Shannon Jr. Center for Advanced Studies at the University of Virginia for a Sesquicentennial Fellowship.

When I was first starting out on what seemed like a daunting project, various individuals were kind enough to offer advice, recommend relevant books, or pass on samples of their own work, including Candace Caraco, Donna Heiland, Clare Kinney, Deborah McDowell, Patricia Meyer Spacks, and Cynthia Wall. I owe a great deal to friends and colleagues who were willing to read chapters: Susan Andrade, Michael Bérubé, Kim Chabot Davis, Eugene Goodheart, Cornelia Klinger, Janet Lyon, Bruce Robbins, Caroline Rody, and Jennifer Wicke. And I am especially grateful to Alison Booth, Eileen Boris, Susan Fraiman, Susan Stanford Friedman, Gerald Graff, Heather Love, Toril Moi, Deborah Nelson, and Aiobheann Sweeney for detailed and very helpful comments on sections of the manuscript. I would also like to thank Alan Thomas for his support of this project, Susan Olin for her expert editing, and Rivka Swenson for her able work as a research assistant. My biggest debts, as always, are to Allan Megill and Maria Megill Felski, who gave me plenty of time in which to write but who were always very pleased to see me when I stopped.

I HAVE BEEN READING A LOT ABOUT MYSELF LATELY, and most of what I read is not very flattering. Although I'm a lapsed Catholic, I've seen myself described as a "remorseless Puritan" or even, in one gloriously overwrought phrase, as a "destroying angel." When I'm not ushering in the apocalypse, I am being cast as a hatchet-faced harridan and paid-up member of the thought police. I am told that I indoctrinate my students, ruthlessly crush any expression of dissent, and execrate anything written by a dead white male. Neither my motives nor my personality have anything to recommend them; I am bitter, hostile, resentful, and, it appears, utterly irrational.[1]

I am not being personally attacked in this avalanche of invective, just collectively damned as one of a scribbling horde of feminist "critics." I place the last word in quotes, for the writers I cite are all convinced that the feminist critic is an oxymoron, a mythical creature, as impossible as a unicorn. All literary critics worthy of the name, they insist, share a deep and abiding love of the works they read. Their response to a great work of literature is one of overpowering awe and almost painful pleasure. Feminists, however, are conspicuously lacking in any such higher emotions. They are mean-spirited malcontents who only know how to debunk and denounce, who are importing sterile ideologies into a sphere that was once blessedly free of political wrangling. Along with other members of the School of Resentment (Harold Bloom's choice phrase), they are philistines and whiners who have made careers out of belittling and besmirching great works of art.

Feminists, that is to say, do not only hate men; they also loathe literature. They distrust all pleasure and passionate engagement. They are deaf to the siren call of beauty and oblivious to the enchanting play of language and form. Their ears are closed, their hearts stony and unyielding. They read books with pinched, disapproving lips, zealously scanning the pages for the slightest hint of sexism. Feminist critics, we are told, are dour, humorless ideologues who reduce complex works to one-dimensional messages and crude expressions of an author's social biases. They are conspiracy theorists and purveyors of victimology with absurdly antiquated views about all women as doormats and all men as brutes.

As a job description, this hardly sounds appealing. If this were really the sum total of feminist criticism, surely a great many scholars would be running in the opposite direction. Yet this does not seem to be happening; feminist approaches to literature are successful, popular, and widely practiced. Perhaps, then, the truth is to be found elsewhere. You would never guess from reading such tirades that many feminist critics nowadays are wary of any general claims about women, femininity, or the female condition. That some of the most respected feminist scholarship takes a hard and critical look at women's use and abuse of power. That much-anthologized articles talk frankly about the difficulties of squaring aesthetic value with political value. That feminist critics have found much to appreciate in the work of very dead, very white males from Sophocles to Shakespeare and beyond. That there is a large and flourishing body of feminist work on women's pleasure in literature, popular fiction, and even pornography.[2]

Feminist criticism, in other words, is a very broad church, espousing a wide range of theories, approaches, and methods and including all kinds of dissenters and arguers. In fact, there is not much agreement about the best way to explain the links between gender and writing. When I teach feminist criticism, for example, I lay out half a dozen different frameworks rather than preaching one true gospel. And yet recent reports often make it sound as if all feminists spoke in one bullying, stentorian voice. One of the most diverse, many-sided, and often contentious forms of scholarship is portrayed as an ideological boot camp where students, like Soviet critics of yore, are taught en masse to denounce sexist art and demand Positive Images of Women.

That such an approach has had little credibility among feminist literary scholars for at least twenty years seems to escape the notice of the authors of these reports. They usually make their case against feminist criticism in one of two ways. Some dig up a quotation from the fledgling days of a rapidly growing and changing field and hold it up as an example of what all feminist critics think today. This is a bit like doing a survey of contemporary music by talking about the Beatles. Others simply conflate feminist literary studies with any form of writing or activism that is carried out in the name of feminism. Hence the bizarre spectacle of seeing Andrea Dworkin and Catharine MacKinnon wheeled out again and again to represent the feminist perspective on how to read texts and images. That these figures are controversial even among feminist activists and have had virtually no impact on the study of literature is simply ignored.

It is not particularly surprising that such caricatures regularly appear in the media. A story about a women's studies student who feels offended by a Goya nude is a newsworthy item that can launch a thousand editorials on the lunatic excesses of identity politics. Who wants to read about feminists discussing the difference between a real and an implied author, or pointing out to their students that the sexism of a fictional character is not necessarily that of the writer? Exaggeration always sells better than nuance, extremes are more memorable than the day-to-day work of feminist scholars. Still, writers who claim to be informing the public about the state of the humanities should know better. Of course, presenting feminism as a field with many voices rather than as a single, doctrinaire ideology would seriously weaken many an author's polemical point. Who stole literature? Why, feminists did!

I want to make it clear that I have no desire to defend every claim that has been made in the name of feminism. In fact, one of my aims is to sift through various feminist approaches to literature and to look at their flaws as well as their merits. But the recent attacks on feminism by Harold Bloom, John Ellis, Alvin Kernan, and others ignore a cardinal rule of scholarship. If you want to make a persuasive argument against a particular school of thought, you need to tackle the work of its strongest thinkers, not its weakest ones. It is not very difficult to show that complaining about the sexism of the Western canon is not an especially sophisticated or fruitful idea. In fact, some feminist scholars did a good job of dismantling this kind of argument a long time ago, though you would never know this fact from reading the conservative complainers. No writing is immune to criticism, but a serious engagement with feminist scholarship requires more than bluster and invective.

Feminist criticism, I should point out, is not entirely free of blame for the ways it is being presented. Its arguments, like those of most literary critics, are often carried on in specialized languages and are published in professional books and journals read only by like-minded scholars. These arguments assume an audience that is already in the know, that is familiar with debates about Lacan and Foucault, essentialism and *écriture féminine*, parody and performance. Furthermore, in contrast to the stereotype of the dogmatic feminist, many scholars are nervous about making any general claim about women and literature. The field of feminist criticism is ever more fragmented; many scholars focus on a specific genre, field, or subgroup of women, or alternatively spend their time deconstructing or endlessly qualifying the concept of woman. Judith Butler's wary statement, "if one 'is' a woman, that is surely not all one is," pretty much sums up the tenor of much contemporary feminist work.[3]

I have some sympathy with such caution. In two of my previous books, I looked at specific examples of women's writing while arguing that it was a mistake to try to define a "feminist aesthetic" or general theory of women and literature. And yet the low level of public debate about feminist criticism cries out for a book that spells out key ideas and arguments as clearly as possible. Pausing to take stock and to look back at thirty years of scholarship may also be a useful exercise for those in the field. What are the basic tenets of feminist criticism? How has feminism changed the ways we think about literature? In hindsight, which of these ways do we still want to defend, and which do we want to modify, refine, or discard? And while there is nothing wrong with feminists using specialized language when writing for their peers, they should also be able to explain what they do to a broader audience. There are plenty of good popular accounts of feminist thought, but I cannot think of a single recent book that explains current feminist ideas about literature to a general readership.[4]

This, then, is a book aimed at those curious to know more about what is currently going on in literature departments. I hope to give such readers a rough idea of how feminist critics talk about books without getting mired in hairsplitting distinctions and internecine disputes. But this book is an argument as much as a survey; in fact, it makes a double-sided argument that is difficult yet also necessary. On the one hand, I want to defend feminist criticism against ignorant, careless, or calumnious attacks; on the other hand, I also want to question certain feminist assumptions and distinguish between stronger and weaker feminist arguments. Feminist scholarship, like any other field, is a mixed bag, and not all of its claims are equally worthy or defensible.

Some writers are worried that airing such criticisms in public makes feminism vulnerable and that its defenders should therefore try to keep up a united front. This view might have made sense when feminist critics could still think of themselves as a tiny, embattled band surrounded by hostile patriarchal forces. But those times are long past. Feminist criticism is a widespread and well-known field of study that, according to one Modern Language Association survey, has had more impact on the teaching of literature than any other recent school of criticism. It has generated innumerable books, conferences, and articles and has its own phalanx of superstars. Feminist criticism is an established institution, not a fragile and delicate seedling. It is surely time to sort through this vast archive and think about what is worth keeping and what is not.

In any case, jumping to the defense of every feminist critic would very soon lead to tying oneself into knots by trying to leap simultaneously in multiple directions. Feminist scholars do not just differ, they actively disagree; there are serious conflicts of opinion about the links between gender and writing. Refusing to make distinctions, claiming that all feminist approaches, however dubious, should be given unconditional support, can only lead to a serious loss of credibility. Of course, arguing against certain ideas should not take the form of name-calling, personal attacks, and the like. Furthermore, when we are discussing approaches with which we do not agree, it is often helpful to try to figure out why they seem compelling to others, if not to us. But ultimately, each of us needs to be clear about where we stand.

I am also skeptical about the resort to the notion of "backlash" to explain any substantial criticism of feminist ideas. This phrase assumes, in peremptory fashion, that all those who question such ideas are inspired by base motives. Unless you believe that feminism is Holy Writ and that its supporters are infallible, however, such a view is highly implausible. In fact, it reeks of defensiveness. By dismissing criticism in advance, it cuts off any chance of intelligent dialogue. Yet feminism cannot hope to remain a vital force unless it is willing to engage in criticism and self-criticism, to scrutinize, question, and, if necessary, discard old ideas. And if it is to talk to the skeptical, the indifferent, and the ignorant rather than to preach only to the converted, it must be willing to make its case in public and to talk to those who do not share or indeed who actively reject its most heartfelt beliefs.

Admittedly, this is not always as easy as it sounds. I often find myself seething and spluttering when I come across another supposedly objective account of my field that depicts all feminist scholars as hysterical harpies or grim-faced zealots.[5] But there is little to be gained by stooping to this level of argument. It is also a mistake to respond negatively to criticism simply because it comes from a man. The issue, ultimately, is not who makes an argument but whether it is a good one. If a criticism of feminist ideas is either ignorant or incoherent, it should be easy enough to refute. If it scores some telling points, then feminist scholars need to take them on board and think about them seriously. In either case, we do better to deal with the substance of what is actually being said, rather than trying to impugn the desires or motives of the person who is saying it. To accuse someone of sexism or misogyny is not to begin a dialogue but to end one.

Either / Or

I begin by tackling the most glaring flaw in recent attacks on feminist criticism. This is the belief that you cannot do two things at once. You can either look at literature as literature or you look at it as politics, the argument goes, but you cannot do both. Feminist scholars are, by definition, interested in the social aspects of the books they read; as a result, they cannot do justice to literature as literature. They are doomed to miss much, even most, of what is important in the books they read.

Let us start by looking at John Ellis's *Literature Lost*, a recent, widely reviewed jeremiad against the "race-gender-class" critics that have taken over the American university. In his chapter on gender, Ellis claims that the current state of literary criticism is a testimony to the widespread corruption of knowledge by feminists. Feminist criticism, he argues, is a deeply misguided enterprise that has seriously damaged the scholarly study of literature. "Typically," he writes, "work by feminist critics is shaped so completely by the notion of patriarchy that an intelligent contribution to the understanding of literature becomes impossible."[6]

What relevant evidence does Ellis marshal to support this claim? He offers one three-sentence paragraph on exactly one book, Sandra Gilbert and Susan Gubar's *The Madwoman in the Attic,* admittedly an influential work, but already close to twenty years old when Ellis's own book was published. In fact, much of the history of feminist criticism in the last two decades could be plausibly described as a series of extended arguments with Gilbert and Gubar's theses. Furthermore, Ellis does not seem to realize that many of his own objections to *Madwoman in the Attic* were voiced by feminist critics not just recently but at the time of the book's first publication.

One short paragraph on a book published in 1979 and three other scattered sentences are the only references to feminist criticism in a twenty-eight page chapter that claims to deliver a decisive rebuttal of thirty years of feminist literary scholarship. What fills the remaining pages? Invocations of Catharine MacKinnon and a review of a women's studies anthology that has almost nothing to do with literature. We also get a caricature of feminist views of science, which consist, according to Ellis, of the view that "women's ways of knowing are nice and men's are nasty." (The work of Donna Haraway, which questions all the assumptions about science that Ellis finds so objectionable, is nevertheless dismissed without explanation as an example of "intellectual vacuity.")[7]

It is astounding that a critic claiming to be so concerned with literature has virtually nothing to say about the vast archive of feminist work on literature. Nowhere does Ellis seriously engage the work of a feminist literary scholar or show any knowledge of the main trends in the field. Indeed, many of his comments reveal an astonishing level of ignorance. Back in 1975, feminist critics were arguing that looking for sexual stereotypes in men's writing did not yield much intellectual insight.[8] Twenty years later, Ellis triumphantly brings out this same idea as if he had invented it. Again and again, Ellis claims to refute feminism by repeating what are commonplace ideas of feminist scholarship.

Let me give some more examples. In an early chapter, having established to his own satisfaction that feminist criticism means carping and complaining about a sexist canon, Ellis sets out to defend Shakespeare against his detractors. Not only are Shakespeare's male characters far from perfect, but, we are told, "strong women are everywhere: Portia, Lady Macbeth, Cordelia."[9] Ellis seems blithely unaware that, as Jane

Gallop puts it, "most feminist criticism of Shakespeare . . . is laudatory rather than critical of the bard."[10] Feminist scholars have explored the richness and complexity of Shakespeare's female characters at great length, though they might well feel that Ellis's reference to Lady Macbeth as a "strong woman" is about as insightful as describing Hamlet as lacking in self-esteem.

At another point, Ellis reminds us of the role of women as authors and readers of the novel in the eighteenth century and notes that "contrary to feminist dogma, women have often had a marked influence on the production of literature."[11] This comment is breathtaking in its lack of familiarity with the field. Does Ellis really not know that feminist argument turns on precisely this point and that most of its efforts in the last thirty-odd years have been devoted to demonstrating women's importance in literary history? Similar howlers occur when he turns to the work of scholars of race and sexuality.[12] Ellis wants to cast himself in the role of a knight-errant saving literature from the evil machinations of race-gender-class critics. To achieve its full dramatic effect, such a story requires a large cast of dastardly or doltish villains as well as an unblemished hero. Caricature and melodrama, however, are not a promising basis for an account of the state of literary studies.

I want to look more closely at an especially revealing statement in Ellis's book. Having devoted his energies to discrediting the entire project of feminist criticism, he makes the following grudging concession in an endnote. "This is not to say that some feminist critics do not sometimes read some texts appropriately, but to do so, they have had to respond to what the text says, not measure it against race-gender-class expectations. That is, they have had to behave like critics, not feminists."[13] This comment is an excellent example of the power of either/ or thinking. Real critics, according to Ellis, simply respond to what a work of literature says, reading without assumptions, biases, or prejudices. Feminists, by contrast, impose their own obsessions on the text and hence they are not literary critics. The two projects are mutually exclusive: any feminist critic who appreciates literature cannot really be a feminist.

Ellis does not deign to give us any examples of these female paragons, so it is hard to know exactly whom he has in mind. I suspect, however, that these feminist-critics-who-are-not-really-feminists may well notice aspects of literary works that other scholars did not pay much attention to. Might this difference of view have something to do with their feminism? Do good literary critics, male or female, really check all their beliefs at the door when they walk into the library? Can politics and literature be severed as absolutely as Ellis suggests? And are we really imposing alien and irrelevant ideas onto literary works when we think about how gender shapes character, plot, and language? Could Faust be a woman? Could Emma Bovary be a man?

As I see it, there are several obvious flaws in Ellis's argument. First, he often writes as if the ideal critic were a blank slate, someone who approaches a work of literature in a state of untarnished innocence. Yet as a professor of German, Ellis is well aware of its most influential and long-standing theory of interpretation: hermeneutics. Scholars of hermeneutics have long insisted that such innocence is impossible. Readers *always* come to a work equipped with beliefs, assumptions, and prejudices. This mental baggage comes from a variety of sources: their immersion in a particular culture, their literary training, and what they may have already heard about a particular work or author. It is, in other words, both social and aesthetic. Furthermore, such a predisposition is not just negative but necessary. Without desires, attitudes, or beliefs, we would have no starting point, no motive for reading, no way of connecting to a text, no way of trying to sort out what is meaningful and what is not. There would simply be randomness and chaos.

The phrase "hermeneutic circle" sums up what is supposed to happen next in the interaction between reader and work. We approach a work already saddled with beliefs, but these beliefs may shift and change as we read. Ideally, there is a dialogue between the reader and the work. We may begin what we think is a love story, for example, only to find out that the book in question is actually a postmodern pastiche of romance. The experience of reading such a book may in turn influence the way we think about falling in love. Thus we are always checking, readjusting, and changing gear. Such a dialogue between reader and text calls for a certain amount of risk; we must be willing to entertain new thoughts and strange ways of seeing, to have our own taken-for-granted beliefs put on trial. Asking questions of the text, we must also be willing to let the text ask questions of us.

In this long-established theory of reading, then, it does not make

sense to distinguish between a critic who is already equipped with beliefs, desires, and prejudices and one who is not. The latter does not and
cannot exist. Claiming to possess a non-ideological viewpoint is thus a
deeply ideological act. Robert Hughes shrewdly comments: "It is the
habit of neo-conservatives to claim, when attacking 'politicized' readings of literature, that they themselves represent *un*political readings, a
view of history, novels, drama and poetry that is not contaminated by
ideology. 'Disinterested' is the code-word."[14]

Still, even if no one is completely disinterested, there are obviously
degrees of bias. We *can* distinguish between a reader who is willing to
rethink her views while reading and one who is not. For Ellis, of course,
all feminist critics fall into the latter camp. That is to say, they never
modify their views or respond to the nuances of literature. They are incapable of reassessing their beliefs when reading a book that calls these
beliefs into question. They continue to project their own obsessions
onto texts even when these obsessions are clearly inappropriate. They
always read literary works as either misogynist tracts or feminist
tracts. They are simply bad readers.

I agree with Ellis that riding roughshod over what a text is saying in
order to impose one's own views on it is not a good idea and that some
feminists do read in such a way. (I discuss this question in the next
chapter.) Yet, as Ellis concedes, there is nothing especially new about
such a practice. Critics have often insisted that all literature is really
about irony and ambiguity, or mythical archetypes, or the workings of
the unconscious, or man's place in a godless universe. They have a habit
of imposing their own obsessions on literary works without always listening to what a specific work is saying. Why should feminist critics be
more or less susceptible to this than anyone else? A good feminist
critic, presumably, approaches a work with a series of questions about
gender, not answers.

This, however, will not satisfy Ellis. In his view, the mere belief that
a work of literature is about gender is already a very bad sign. Those
who talk about race, class, and gender are, Ellis insists, excessively narrow in their focus, inflating minor and peripheral issues to a grotesque
level of importance. Analyzing literature for what it tells us about gender is like reading literature for what it can tell us about trains. It is possible, but singularly pointless. Ellis's own analogy is that of hunting. He

describes an imaginary critic who goes through the corpus of medieval literature looking for hunting references. "He would have decided in advance of seeing each poem that the most important aspect of its content will be hunting, regardless of how important or trivial hunting turns out to be to the meaning of the particular poem." Any critic worth his salt will agree, according to Ellis, that such a person has no real understanding of literature.[15]

There is, however, an obvious flaw in this analogy, at least when applied to feminist criticism. Most literature is not about hunting but all of literature is about gender in the minimal sense that it deals with people who are either men or women. (One might, I suppose, make an exception for certain works of the avant-garde.) I would argue, moreover, that a great deal of literature is "about" gender in a much more deliberate and self-conscious sense. What are the great novels of the eighteenth and nineteenth centuries—the works of Austen, Dickens, Balzac, Eliot, Flaubert—if not serious and sustained reflections on the question of what it means to become a woman or a man? These novels pinpoint in dazzling detail the passions, yearnings, perceptions, and ways of being and acting in the world that come to define each sex. The familiar stories of courtship and *Bildung*, of adultery and adventure, would make no sense to the Martian visitor with no knowledge of the differences between women and men.

Thus gender is not just a political concept in Ellis's sense, that is to say, a subject best left to the experts over in the political science department. Rather, it cuts across the very distinction between public and private worlds. Our sense of what it means to be male or female is deeply anchored in our thoughts, perceptions, and emotions, guiding our relations with others and shaping our most intimate, inchoate sense of self. It is hardly surprising, then, that modern literature has focused with such passionate intensity on the gender divide. Many of the urgent questions of modern art, questions about the sources of the self, the nature of desire, the possibility of connecting with others, are also questions about the power and the permeability of the male/female distinction. And last time I looked, gender also seemed pretty important in deciding what kind of part you got to play in *The Odyssey*, or *Paradise Lost*.

Again, to beat what is by now a very tired drum, this is not to claim that literature either causes or simply reinforces the oppression of women. It is to argue that ideas, symbols, and myths of gender *saturate* literary works. Of course, gender is not the only thing that matters in literature, nor is it always the most important thing. Nevertheless, it matters. (And not just at the level of content, either, as Ellis invariably assumes, but also as literary form.) When critics—good critics—read through a feminist lens, they are not projecting trendy but irrelevant ideas onto a hapless work of art. Rather, they are illuminating important things that were there all along.

For example, when I was an undergraduate studying French and German literature, a popular topic for discussion was the conflict between the individual and society in nineteenth-century novels. But no one, myself included, seemed to notice that all the individuals we were talking about belonged to one sex. If we had, we could have asked some new and interesting questions. How is such conflict represented in novels about women? Does it take different forms? How is it muted by the demands of the romance and marriage plot? What possibilities of rebellion or refusal are available for women? What stories, what metaphors, what fictional scenarios come into play? These are not just political questions but *literary* questions, ones that help to explain what a text means and how it holds together as a work of art.

In other words, trying to hold literature and the social world apart is a Sisyphean task: however valiantly critics try to keep art pure, external meanings keep seeping in. This is because literature is double-sided. It is not *either/or* but *both/and*. One face is turned toward the history of conventions, symbols, rules of genre, and styles of language that make up what we call "literature." In this sense art is, as critics like to say, relatively autonomous. For this reason it can never be equated with reality in any simple way. We need, as Wendy Steiner points out, to be wary of literalists who want to reduce works of art to factual propositions or simple acts of advocacy.[16]

Yet literature is also saturated with social meanings. It hooks up with other ways we have of understanding and making sense of the world. This is not a question, I should stress, of trying to adjudicate whether literature reflects or fails to reflect reality. Such a way of putting things no longer makes sense to many humanists, who tend to be wary of the claim that there is a single overarching reality out there about whose essential properties we all agree. Rather, our sense of how things are comes from diverse and sometimes conflicting sources: science, religion, art, politics, the media, and the various and varied contingencies of our own lives. Literature is one of the cultural languages through which we make sense of the world; it helps to create our sense of reality rather than simply reflecting it. At the same time, it also draws on, echoes, modifies, and bounces off our other frameworks of sense-making. No text is an island.

Another critic unwilling to confront the doubleness of literature is Stanley Fish. In *Professional Correctness: Literary Studies and Political Change,* he suggests that "bringing" politics into literature will destroy the traditional practice of literary criticism. "One might think that it would be possible to pay a double attention," he writes, "at one moment doing full justice to the verbal intricacy of a poem and at the next inquiring into the agendas in whose service that intricacy has been put." But our hopes at this apparent willingness to concede the logic of both/and are soon dashed. On the contrary, concludes Fish, such double attention is *not* possible. "One must recall the difficulty of serving two masters; each will be jealous of the other and demand fidelity to its imperatives."[17] Fish, like Ellis, believes that the critic can do only one thing at a time.

Perhaps the problem lies with the alternatives that Fish lays before us. Neither of them looks very promising. A critic who looks at literature in terms of the "agendas" to which it is being put is relying on a rather crude understanding of the social dimensions of art. There are real problems with trying to flatten literature into a mere tool or instrument of political interests. Yet Fish's desire to spend all his time talking about linguistic intricacy seems equally impoverished as a vision of what literary criticism should be. Of course, paying attention to how language works is an indispensable aspect of literary analysis, but it is hardly enough. A critic who thinks that the most exciting thing about *Medea* or *Middlemarch* is the author's use of metonymy or catachresis is surely missing a great deal.

Universals

In fact, many scholars have not followed the path laid out by Fish and have paid a great deal of attention to how writing meshes with the social world. This is certainly true of such traditional critics as Matthew Arnold, F. R. Leavis, Lionel Trilling, and George Steiner, whose response to literature is inseparable from a sustained moral and political vision. Furthermore, in the classroom the logic of both/and is pretty much a necessity rather than an optional extra. Teachers of literature have always talked about changes in worldviews, historical context, and social structure. The Romantics make no sense unless one fills students in on the French Revolution and the experience of industrialization. And how can one discuss modernism without talking about war and mass culture, the growth of cities and the death of God, the expansion of commerce and the increasing social isolation of the artist? These things are there "on the page," an essential part of the subject matter of much modern art. Fish is willing to concede that the author's intention may be an acceptable topic, but one can hardly talk about the views of Shelley or Dickens or Zola or Brecht without mentioning society and politics.

Yet if bringing in social contexts and meanings is part of business as usual in literary criticism, why is there so much fuss about expanding this framework to include gender? One reason, I think, lies in the current challenge to the universality of art. This is the sticking point, the place where traditional critics and feminist critics often seem to be speaking different languages. While scholars have often looked at the social conditions that shape literature, they have also believed that it transcends those conditions. Great art speaks beyond its time and place, and, what is more, it speaks to everybody. Defying details of history and context, gender, ethnicity, or creed, it embodies quintessential truths. Literature is universal because it speaks to a common, shared humanity.

Feminists, however, often have a hard time with this notion of universality. They point to a very long history of equating the male with the universal and seeing the female as the special case. This history can be seen in the most sublime contexts—religion, philosophy, art—as well as the most banal ones—the male body in the anatomy textbook, the use of "man" to include everyone. Images of the male can, it seems, embrace both men and women, while the female can only represent herself. She embodies difference, particularity, the limits of her sex rather than the infinite potential of the human species. And if male experience and the male perspective have a universal reach, then why do we need women's input at all?

Decrying the universal, feminist critics have often sought to demote man to the same modest, particular state as woman. Hence, to take one telling case, they have argued that the traditional heroes of American literature—Huck, Ahab, Gatsby—are a reflection of male fantasies, experiences, and anxieties. Rather than being universal, this literature is highly specific. Furthermore, not only do such works not speak to women, but they often present them as an obstacle and threat to man's pursuit of transcendence. In the strongest version of this scenario, the universal canon dwindles to a male-centered tradition that has nothing to say to women.

I am not at all persuaded by this view of readers segregated by gender and huddled together into tight clusters of particularity, unable to appreciate or to learn from an experience that is not their own. And yet I also share some of the feminist suspicion of the language of universalism, the insistence that underneath the superficial differences of race, gender, and the like we are all pretty much the same. When anyone deigns to describe this essence of the human, it often ends up sounding like a preppy white male from Yale. Feminists and multiculturalists are right to point out that such views reveal a real unwillingness to confront differences. These differences are not minor, trivial, or superficial; they go all the way down.

And yet it is also obvious that art does speak across social boundaries. Readers who may have little in common with a specific author can be enthralled by the literary worlds that author creates. At the University of Virginia, for example, I often teach "The Metamorphosis" in an undergraduate survey of literary theory. And each time, Kafka blows many of my students away. Kafka's own obsessions are carved out of a particular moment in European history, and he is also a writer singularly uninterested in getting inside the heads of women. And yet my students, whatever their background, are often fascinated and perturbed by the matter-of-fact nightmare that is Gregor's transformation. Years ago, when I was teaching in Australia, one of my students, a working-class, single mother of four, told me that reading "The Metamorphosis" was a revelation: Kafka had nailed her psychic life down flat.

How, then, do we account for this spark of connection? Of moments of recognition across the chasm of different worlds? The idea of *analogy* offers an appealing alternative to the fruitless zigzagging between universality and difference. In a suggestive discussion, Barbara Stafford describes analogy as a creative act, a wresting of sense from the world rather than a simple record of what is. To make an analogy is to argue that "this," in certain respects, is like "that." It is a process of finding similarity in difference, of tracing partial echoes and blurred reflections. Analogy speaks to the need to make connection, to our experience of feeling "near, even interpenetrated by, what is distant, unfamiliar, different."[18] It is a way of spanning boundaries and weaving particulars into a partial concordance.

Stafford stresses the visual logic of analogy, but it also strikes me as a powerful model for thinking about reading. "Only by making the past or the remote or the foreign proximate can we hope to make it intelligible to us," writes Stafford. "Analogizing has the virtue of making distant peoples, other periods, and even diverse contemporary contexts part of our world."[19] Analogy, in other words, plunges us into an active process of extrapolation; it involves sorting, distinguishing, and linking. To be successful, a work needs to connect to us in some way. But this does not have to mean a faithful reflection of our own social statistics any more than it requires some universal essence of the human. Involvement can be triggered by many different aspects of a literary work: suggestive constellations of events or persons, a skillful rendering of feelings or perceptions, the rhythms and sonorities of a particular style. We do not need the experience of being a petit-bourgeois white male in Prague between the wars to feel ourselves addressed by Kafka's story (conversely, this is not to say that Kafka speaks to everyone—a claim that is demonstrably false).

Because analogy is an act that readers perform rather than an internal property of a work, it reminds us of the vagaries and uncertainties of interpretation. Some texts are undoubtedly more suggestive than others, better at inspiring readers to connect and translate. But no work can resonate without someone willing to do the work of extrapolation. Literary texts, unlike allegories or works of philosophy, do not spell out their broader resonance. Their meaning derives from the heft and weight of concrete examples, the patient piling up of telling details. A shapeless hat, a meaningful look, a seedy boardinghouse, a pair of tramps; it is out of such minutiae that literary worlds are born. Writing is a painstaking act of carving bodies, movements, spaces, and rhythms out of an amorphous flux of words. Literature gives us a world that is profoundly particular, that is utterly *this* and not *that*.

Yet there is a lack of symmetry in the way we learn to analogize from such particulars, to extract general meanings from concrete detail. For example, we are accustomed to finding broader resonances in male bodies, to glimpsing the sublime in stories of heroic struggle and drawing existential metaphors out of images of male solitude. We are less used to endowing female bodies with this kind of authority and reading female lives as rich in general resonances. I suspect this is true of men and women, who both learn to think of woman as the embodiment of her sex rather than as a symbol of the human.

Of course, one can always find exceptions to any such dictum. For example, George Steiner shows in a fascinating study that Antigone was the most feted tragic figure of the nineteenth century, her sublimity outstripping that of Oedipus. Thus Hegel paid tribute to "the heavenly Antigone, that noblest of figures that ever appeared on earth."[20] For women to possess this kind of import, however, it helps if they, like Antigone, can be slotted into a recognizable tradition of male heroism. By contrast, other aspects of women's lives—motherhood, romance, the love or friendship of other women—are often seen as lacking in literary and philosophical glamour. They have been deemed minor, not major, a sign of women's mooring in the particular rather than the universal. Lionel Trilling captures this view very well when he writes, "women in fiction . . . most commonly . . . exist in a moonlike way, shining by the reflected moral light of men. They are 'convincing' or 'real' and sometimes 'delightful,' but they seldom exist as men exist—as genuine moral destinies."[21]

David Denby touches on much the same question in *Great Books*, his fascinating description of his return to Columbia as a middle-aged film critic to retake its freshman surveys of canonical works. Denby is a dyed-in-the-wool humanist who wants to believe that great works speak to all people for all time, and his book marshals a stirring defense of the canon. Yet in his often engagingly personal account Denby also ruefully acknowledges moments of baffledom and boredom as well as illumination, describing his failure to make much headway with such writers as Goethe and Dante.

Remembering his own distaste for Virginia Woolf as a young man, Denby realizes that gender bias played a role in his response. "She was too . . . *feminine*. She wrote at the edge of her nerves all the time, and was obsessively devoted to states of feeling and sensibility. Novels, I told myself sternly, had to be about something more than that." Confronting this past blindness to a writer he now finds momentous, Denby writes: "my earlier misreading was more than a personal failure, it was, as I now knew, a cultural failure." For, as he goes on to record, "many of the most prominent male literary critics of the century had ignored or dismissed Virginia Woolf."[22] It was feminist critics, he notes, who had to make a case for a greatness that now seems "inevitable," even though Denby also has some harsh things to say about those same critics.

Denby detects his own earlier discomfort among the young men in his class who complain about being made to read *Pride and Prejudice*. Those female students who object to certain male authors make their case on political grounds, but the discomfort with women's writing among some of the male students seems deeper and more inchoate. "Their dismissals came with a frosting of contempt. . . . It was a waste of their time, this trivial girls' stuff."[23] Angry at their obduracy, Denby delivers a passionate defense of Elizabeth Bennett's heroism and of Austen's deeply modern scripting of emotional and psychological nuance. Ultimately, *Great Books* is as much about the experience of reading as it is about the content of specific works. And here Denby shows not only the power of entrenched ways of reading but also the ever open possibility of learning how to read differently.

It is impossible not to be struck, in this context, by the role of the black woman writer in debates about the canon. Almost every writer resorts at some point to framing these debates as requiring a choice between Shakespeare and Alice Walker, or Shakespeare and Zora Neale Hurston, or Shakespeare and Toni Morrison. The mind-numbing repetitiveness of this motif is extraordinary. If Shakespeare is a cultural icon of universal, transcendent, aesthetic value, then the black woman writer must be yoked to serve as his opposite. If Shakespeare stands for the sublime and disinterested gaze of literary genius, then the black female must embody the ideological, blinkered perspective of group grievance.

My point here is not to condemn any individual act of artistic judgment. I agree, with Anthony Appiah, that one should be able to express one's dislike of a writer's work without being labeled racist or sexist.[24] But the monotony and ubiquity of this opposition suggests that something broader is at stake. It is as if some critics cannot conceive that the work of a black woman could speak across the barriers of race and sex, could resonate with general significance and importance. In *The Culture of Complaint*, Robert Hughes suggests, in an evocative turn of phrase, that the growing importance of literature by women and minorities allows readers to learn "how other kinds of cultural consciousness can occupy the speaking centre of literary forms."[25] The authority of being a "speaking centre" is, it seems, more easily and gracefully relinquished to some kinds of writers than others.

Part of the problem, I think, lies in the attitude that I have just described: the conviction that literature and politics are irredeemably opposed and that writers and critics interested in social issues therefore cannot do justice to the demands of art. This idea is a relatively new one—it would have made little sense to the Victorians—but is often invoked by conservative critics as a sacred and timeless truth. Feminist critics have not done as much as they might have to challenge this view of the essential antagonism of art and politics. Indeed, some feminists have actively endorsed it. For example, one distinguished art scholar writes: "so long as feminism also tries to be a discourse about art, truth and beauty, it can only confirm the structure of the canon, and by doing so corroborate masculine mastery and power."[26]

My disagreement with this statement could not be more profound. If feminist criticism does not think seriously about such questions, I believe that it is ultimately doomed to irrelevance. A questioning of transcendental grounds for artistic judgment should not be confused with a rejection of all talk about beauty, value, or pleasure. Such talk is essential to any nonreductive account of aesthetic experience that wants to explain why people actively choose to read books, look at paintings, or watch films rather than engaging in other activities. It is also crucial if feminist scholars want to talk to others who are interested in aesthetics but do not necessarily share their politics. Otherwise, feminism risks turning into a sectarian enclave, while the "main" business of literary criticism carries on unperturbed.

For this reason I have chosen to organize my argument around four key aspects of literary study: readers, authors, plots, and the question of aesthetic value. How, I ask, does feminist criticism change the way we think about readers? Does plot have a gender? How have feminists talked about female authors? What is the role of value in feminist scholarship? My aim is to clarify how feminism has changed the way people think about literature. By framing things in this way, I hope to show that feminist criticism is not just something that feminists need to think about. Rather, it affects everyone with expertise or interest in the study of literature, because it raises questions that are central to the field. It alters our vision of literature *as literature.*

Still, I have no doubt that all this talk about literature will baffle those readers who believe we are now in the age of cultural studies. What makes literature so special? Why do I not say more about feminist approaches to music, fashion, or film? In fact, most of my previous work has dealt with noncanonical and, in some cases, nonliterary texts from a sociological perspective. My writing is thus a prime example of the precipitous decline of literary studies into cultural studies that conservative critics are always complaining about. And, as such, I may look like a highly implausible candidate for the job of defending the literary value of feminist scholarship.

I believe this contradiction is more apparent than real. Unlike some of my colleagues, I see literary studies and cultural studies as related rather than opposed fields. In any event, my decision to focus on literary criticism is pragmatic. First of all, this is the terrain of many recent attacks on feminist scholarship. As we've already seen, a popular complaint leveled at feminist critics is that they hate literature and want to do away with aesthetics. It is time to address this criticism head-on rather than simply laughing it off as a travesty of feminist work. The longer it is ignored, the more deeply this caricature of feminist scholarship settles into popular consciousness. Finally, it simply becomes received wisdom, something that everybody "knows."

Second, most people who come across feminist criticism still do so in the context of studying literature. In spite of the occasional ruckus about students deconstructing Madonna videos rather than reading

Milton, the number of English majors who take classes in popular cul-ture remains small. Cultural studies, in the United States, is only estab-lished in a handful of universities and remains, for the most part, an exotic and often misunderstood import. As someone with a strong commitment to cultural studies, I think this is a pity.[27] But one of my goals in this book is to talk to readers who may have taken one or more literature classes in college and want to find out how feminism has changed the way people talk about books.

Of course, the boundaries between the study of literature and other kinds of texts are often porous. Nowadays, approaches to film, popular culture, and the like often feed into the way feminist critics think about literary works. And, as I hope to show, feminism has also changed our sense of what counts as literature, even as "good literature." But this is not a reason for simply lumping together sonnets and soap operas un-der the general rubric of "text." Analyzing films, for example, calls for skills and techniques that are quite different from those used in literary study. Rather than trying to talk about "everything" and botching the job, I prefer to take on the specific task of surveying feminist ap-proaches to literature.

Like many short books, *Literature after Feminism* is a modest affair; it is limited not only by the format of a concise survey but also by my own knowledge, competence, and interests. I do my best to convey something of the range of feminist criticism as well as explaining its most well-known ideas. By interweaving theory and literary example I hope to show how feminism has influenced our view of literary works and how those works, in turn, speak back to feminism. But the reader will learn far more about the twentieth century than about earlier peri-ods and much more about novels than about poetry or drama. This is also a book that deals with feminist literary studies as it has developed in the United States. Even within these self-imposed limits, it is impos-sible, at a time when feminist criticism has expanded to include a myr-iad of ideologies, methodologies, and perspectives, to mention them all. I urge those who are aggrieved at my oversights to respond by writing another, different, survey. One book cannot provide the full picture; my hope is that more feminist scholars will be inspired to explain the work they do to a broader audience.

What follows, then, is best described as a plea for double vision.

Against those conservative critics and feminist scholars who believe we have to choose between politics and art, society and literature, I argue that any decent critic cannot help but pay attention to both. Double vision means holding art and society together in the mind's eye. It means tracing the ways they inform and shape each other without in any simple sense being "the same." Eugene Goodheart gets it right when he says, "literary experience is not a pure thing: it is an amalgam of interests that includes the political, the historical, the ethical, and so on, but not necessarily at the expense of the aesthetic."[28] So does bell hooks when she warns against prescriptive aesthetic theories and talks of "criteria for creating and evaluating art which would simultaneously acknowledge its ideological content even as it allowed for expansive notions of artistic freedom."[29] Some feminist scholars, as I hope to show, do not scant aesthetics in their attention to politics.

Of course, double vision is a thoroughly ambiguous figure of speech. To see double can also mean to see badly and wrongly, to have the discomfiting and unpleasant experience of watching a once solid outline dissolve into a fuzzy, confused blur. Double vision is often a precursor of blindness, insanity, or delirium tremens. It can be a sign that one is losing one's grip and going over the edge. That it need not have such disastrous consequences, that double vision can help us to see more rather than less clearly, is the premise of the chapters that follow.

1

READERS

What is reading for if not to bring the embodied imagination to these unsettling connections, these dreams? These other spaces we inhabit and these other identities who inhabit us?

MINROSE GWIN

THE most famous readers in Western literature are surely Don Quixote and Emma Bovary. The eccentric nobleman who dreams of valiant quests and battles imaginary giants may seem far removed from the sultry doctor's wife pining away in the French provinces. Yet these two figures from very different times and cultures are bound together by a common thread. They are both foolish readers. Their stories remind us of the perils that await the intemperate lover of fiction. As readers ourselves, we are asked to think of our activity as both a poison and a cure: through the act of reading we will discover the dangers of certain ways of reading.

A number of critics have talked about the parallels between these two figures, but no one has paid much attention to the fact that Don Quixote is a man and Emma Bovary a woman. This point may seem too obvious to be worth mentioning, yet it is a vital clue to how readers and reading are portrayed in these two novels. Critics sometimes refer to Emma Bovary as a female Quixote, but they do not pause to elaborate on what this idea might entail. Yet Emma's gender is not a mere afterthought, a minor variation on a universal theme; rather, her status as a middle-class woman shapes what she reads, how she reads, and the kind of salvation she awaits from fiction. It steers her toward a destiny that is very different from that of Cervantes's hero.

These two well-known readers are a useful starting point for thinking about the larger theme of gender and reading. What do they tell us about how male and female readers are portrayed in fiction? What light do they shed on the perils and pleasures of reading? And how have feminist critics responded to these images? How do they envision the female reader? What are her traits, her attributes, her desires, her dreams? What exactly does it mean to read as a woman?

Reading and Romance

Don Quixote is a fictional character who has made the transition from literature to myth. He is a cultural icon, an easily recognizable figure in a pantheon of popular heroes. During my teenage years, pictures of Don Quixote by Daumier or Picasso were a staple decoration of many student bedrooms. The 1960s musical *Man of La Mancha* is still performed in high school auditoriums; its most well-known song, "Dream the Impossible Dream," recasts the theme of Cervantes's novel in a distinctively American idiom. Don Quixote remains a resonant symbol of unquenchable idealism, a comic-tragic hero familiar to many people who may never have read a word of the book in which he appears.

Emma Bovary is, of course, one of the most memorable tragic women of nineteenth-century fiction; like her celebrated counterpart Anna Karenina, she has intrigued and fascinated many readers. A complex amalgam of boldness and banality, of ennui and eroticism, Emma inspires passionate and often conflicting responses from each generation of literary scholars. Feminists, too, are deeply divided; some decry Emma as a male-authored stereotype, others acclaim her as a complex, many-sided, even subversive heroine. I count myself among those who value Flaubert's novel and who also believe that it gives us powerful if partial insights into the dynamics of gender.

Both Don Quixote and Emma Bovary are led astray by their reading of romances. This very coincidence, however, alerts us to the changing meanings of a word. In Cervantes's novel, the romance is synonymous with the familiar arc of the heroic quest. This quest may include the ceremonial courting of a fair lady, yet its primary purpose often lies elsewhere. The ideal and goal of the romance are the hero's attainment of manhood through a series of grueling tests. His idealized love for an unattainable woman is subordinate to this greater theme of a quest for glory that is both worldly and spiritual.

By the twentieth century, romance acquires a very different meaning. Manly striving and heroic achievement fade into the background. Instead, romance focuses ever more intently on the ebb and flow of feeling, on protestations of love and the awakening of female passion. The elaborate choreography of pursuit and retreat, of courtship and seduction, is now often recounted through a woman's eyes. Romance, in other words, becomes a distinctively feminine preoccupation; stripped of all extraneous detail, it caters to fantasies of emotional fulfillment and blissful erotic surrender. At the same time, its cultural status dwindles dramatically. The adjective "romantic," like its cousin "sentimental," is substantially diminished; it loses all sublimity. Romance now evokes the treacherous terrain of female feeling rather than the heroic myth of male transcendence. From Arthurian romance to Harlequin romance: could there be a more telling illustration of the changing fortunes of a word?

Let us look more closely at the diverging fates of our fictional readers. *Don Quixote* is usually regarded as the quintessential antiromance that marks the birth of the modern novel. The hero's fierce attachment to works of medieval chivalry only underscores the absurd anachronism of such fictions in a disenchanted world. Don Quixote's delusions are directly attributed to his excessive reading; in other respects, we are told, he is a shrewd and able man. It is books that inspire him to take the mundane for the heroic and to confuse the pedestrian with the sublime. It is books that are the cause of his deranged quest, his constant brawling with strangers and his ecstatic appeals to the fair Dulcinea. The repeated clash between the conventions of knightly romance and the everyday life of seventeenth-century Spain exposes the patent foolishness of reading works of fiction in too literal a fashion.

Yet there is continuity as well as change between the medieval romance and the modern novel. Cervantes does not simply poke fun at Don Quixote's love of romance but weaves aspects of the romance tradition into his own novel. One powerful link between the old fiction and the new is the freedom that is afforded the male hero. Both the romance and the novel are structured around a journey and a series of tests. Don Quixote, of course, finds that his path is constantly hampered by his faulty expectations. Castles turn out to be dingy and disreputable inns, fair maidens are really disheveled prostitutes, and his stirring appeals to codes of knightly honor merely inspire puzzled head-scratching from those he meets along the way. Cervantes's novel thus translates the male quest into a new key, that of mundane disappointment rather than heroic achievement.

Nevertheless, Don Quixote still has the freedom of the traditional hero of romance. He is able to abandon home and family, to travel alone across treacherous terrain, to engage in combat with those who threaten him. And the ambitions that are inspired by his reading remain unflinchingly bold in their public reach: "to undo endless wrongs, set right endless injustices, correct endless errors, fix endless abuses and atone for endless sins."[1] In this sense, his dogged devotion to an anachronistic tradition springs from a perverse heroism that is noble as well as comic. Don Quixote's extravagant idealism points to the limits of a world that has been stripped bare of transcendental meaning. Critics often describe him as a Christlike figure, whose attachment to the absolute values of chivalric romance is absurd but also often poignant and even sublime.

When Emma Bovary finds out that she is pregnant, her first reaction is apathy and indifference. Gradually, however, she begins to hope for a male child, reflecting on how life stories are shaped by the constraints of gender.

> A man, at least, is free: he can explore all passions and all countries, overcome obstacles, taste of the most distant pleasures. But a woman is always hampered. Being inert as well as pliable, she has against her the weakness of the flesh and the inequity of the law. Like the veil held to her hat by a ribbon, her will flutters in every breeze; she is always drawn by some desire, restrained by some rule of conduct.[2]

As is often the case with Flaubert, it is hard to know how much of this voice is Emma and how much the narrator, how seriously we are to take such musings. Yet Emma's reflections are largely borne out by the unfolding plot of *Madame Bovary*. The novel takes over large chunks of the gender script of medieval romance and leaves them unchanged. Emma does not do battle with real giants, but, unlike Don Quixote, she does not do battle with imaginary giants either. Both her imagination and her field of action are constrained by the fact of her femaleness.

Reading thus serves a very different role in the two novels. For Don

Quixote reading is a trigger for action; his love of books catapults him into the outside world in search of adventure and excitement. It connects him to a glorious heroic tradition and moral vision that he strains, however comically, to emulate in his own deeds. For Emma, by contrast, reading is a substitute for action; it offers a temporary refuge, an inner escape from the dreary, stale confines of a milieu she despises but cannot leave. As the walls of her home press in relentlessly around her, she turns to books for compensation and distraction. Flaubert's heroine seems to confirm the thesis that women's peculiarly intense attachment to reading stems from the restrictions they encounter in the real world. Thus Emma Bovary and Don Quixote both persistently confuse the real world with the world of books, yet in each novel the reality and the books are of a different order.

Here is Flaubert's description of the books that Emma reads as a fifteen-year-old schoolgirl.

> They were all about love, lovers, sweethearts, persecuted ladies fainting in lonely pavilions, postilions killed at every relay, horses ridden to death on every page, sombre forests, heart-aches, vows, sobs, tears and kisses, little boatrides by moonlight, nightingales in shady groves, gentlemen brave as lions, gentle as lambs, virtuous as no one ever was, always well dressed and weeping like fountains.[3]

This dry list underscores the formulaic nature of Emma's reading. The books in which she delights and which fuel her fantasies are filled with the stock figures of historical romance. There are still residues of danger, heroism, and adventure in these stories, but they are overlaid with a thick layer of sentiment. Romance is becoming synonymous with the sovereignty of love and the mutual confession of intense feeling. These stories become the yardstick against which Emma measures the erotic and emotional impoverishment of her later life. The radiant passions of romance throw into cruel contrast the drab, grinding emptiness of her days. In a sense, her real betrayal of her husband Charles takes place in the realm of literature. She commits adultery with novels.

The fictional illusions that sustain Emma are thus of a very different kind from those inspiring Don Quixote. She does not dream of saving the world through heroic acts but of the redemptive power of love. All of Emma's ambition, aggression, and stifled energies are channeled into an erotic script. She yearns for passionate embraces, whispered endearments, dimly imagined acts of erotic pleasure. Against a backdrop of Oriental palaces and exotic lagoons, Emma is swept off her feet by a bold and sensual hero. In her fantasies, the active role is assumed by a man whose passion will redeem her by transporting her into another world. Her desire takes the form of ecstatic surrender to a transcendent sexual force. Here is Flaubert describing Emma as she writes to her lover, Léon:

> it was another man she saw, a phantom fashioned out of her most ardent memories, of her favorite books, her strongest desires, and at last he became so real, so tangible, that her heart beat wildly in awe and admiration, though unable to see him distinctly, for, like a god, he was hidden beneath the abundance of his attributes. . . . She felt him near her; he was coming and would ravish her entire being in a kiss. Then she would fall back to earth again shattered; for these vague ecstacies of imaginary love would exhaust her more than the wildest orgies.[4]

Clearly, Emma's faults as a reader are very different from those of Don Quixote. Her errors of interpretation are not factual but psychological and emotional. She does not mistake windmills for giants but commits the much more banal error of confusing a bored and indifferent lover for a passionate one. Don Quixote's madness distances him from the rest of his milieu, causing mirth and astonishment among his compatriots. But Emma's confusion of the men in her life with the heroes of romantic literature results in a much more familiar story of imagined love, seduction, and abandonment.

The romantic yearnings of men and women, we might conclude, have very different meanings. Men's desire to place women on pedestals harks back to the codes of chivalry and the pure and unblemished heart of the courtly hero. The passive yet conveniently unattainable heroine is the perfect expression of this fantasy, allowing it to remain intact. By contrast, a woman who idealizes her male lover often comes across as sentimental and foolish; she merely underscores women's gullibility and propensity to self-deception. And yet Emma Bovary can never fully achieve Don Quixote's triumphant solipsism, his unshaken conviction in the reality of his imaginary world. Because she must look to her lovers to play the active role in the romance script inside her head, she is doomed to find her hopes disappointed and her fantasies shattered. Oblivious or indifferent to her yearning, they cannot bestow upon her the recognition and validation for which she longs.[5]

There are, of course, a number of reasons for the more somber and pessimistic coloring of Flaubert's novel. But one way of measuring the distance between Cervantes and Flaubert is by looking at changing conceptions of gender and reading. From the eighteenth century onward, middle-class women were an important part of the reading public, and reading for pleasure came to be seen as a distinctively female province. The novel was attentive to the nuances of psychology and the delicate delineation of feeling; this made it well suited to women who were increasingly seen as experts in emotion and guardians of the private sphere. When essayists or novelists wanted to address the potential dangers and corrupting influence of fiction, they increasingly chose to portray the gullible reader as a woman. The history of the novel is littered with heroines who confuse literature and life and expect their own destiny to echo the radiant trajectory of romantic fiction. Emma Bovary is merely the most visible and notorious example of a long list of foolish female readers.

There was something more than a little unseemly about women's love of the printed word. This theme crops up repeatedly in Kate Flint's survey of attitudes toward the female reader in nineteenth-century England. Almost as interesting as her actual argument are the images that Flint has collected of women reading. Stretched out languorously on a sofa or surreptitiously skimming forbidden books in the library, these women radiate prurient curiosity and sensual abandonment. As a solitary activity that can be compulsive and guilt-ridden, women's reading conjured up the specter of auto-erotic pleasure. Popular images of the female reader often conveyed a distinct sexual charge.

Novel-reading, writers agreed, was an occupation that offered particular pleasures and dangers to women. As one British writer from the 1840s expressed it, "The great bulk of novel readers are females; and to them such impressions (as are conveyed through fiction) are peculiarly mischievous: for first, they are naturally more sensitive, more impressable, than the other sex; and secondly, their engagements are of a less engrossing character—they have more time as well as more inclination to indulge in reveries of fiction."[6] We can see from such comments how beliefs about middle-class women readers expanded to embrace the entire sex. First of all, the author writes as if all women have ample time in which to explore the seductive byways of fiction. Such images of the leisured reader dreaming away her days in the pages of novels would of course have been quite foreign to the harried shop girls, scullery maids, and factory workers of Victorian England. Second, the writer takes it for granted that women possess a particularly sensitive and malleable nature. Women have a greater capacity for sympathy, for entering imaginatively into the thoughts and feelings of others. This capacity renders them ideal readers of novels, which often take as their subject the delicate delineation of sentiment. Yet it also makes women particularly vulnerable to the blandishments of fiction, which can so easily seduce them and lead them astray.

Such assumptions about the impact of fiction on women were not always false. Some women of the period agreed with these accounts of the perils of reading and testified to the ways in which their own lives had been harmed by an uncritical enjoyment of novels. Here is the voice of one female writer criticizing the fictional portrayal of romantic love: "I was prepared to believe that one deep and lasting love could make anyone completely happy, could even fill all the interstices caused by complete lack of any useful occupation or purpose in life. All the novels I read told me that—most novels did tell one that in those days—and I supposed it must be true."[7] The view of women as eager and uncritical consumers of books receives some support from women's own stories of how they read. Well-known female writers such as Mary Wollstonecraft and George Eliot added their voices to this chorus, warning women of the perils of being led astray by vapid and sentimental forms of fiction.

Yet, as Flint shows, this image captures only one facet of women's varied and complex relations to reading. Books fulfilled a variety of roles for women in Victorian England. They were often turned to for guidance, as valuable sources of moral advice and religious instruction. They could serve as useful bodyguards, helping to ward off importune advances from strange men when traveling alone. They formed the backbone of women's home schooling and their projects of self-improvement, which often included a formidable reading program that might extend from Homer to their own time. The periodicals that sprang from the suffragette movement, for example, placed great value on acquiring knowledge from books and encouraged alert and critical ways of reading. Books could become a means of access to a community of like-minded readers as well as a way of experiencing the pleasures of solitude.

In other words, women in the nineteenth century read for many reasons. They read for instruction and for escapism, they sought pleasure and solace in stories of love, but they also turned to books for a sense of moral purpose and social identity. Why, then, is Emma Bovary our most popular image of the female reader? Why do so many people still think of the archetypal woman reader as a housewife dreaming away her days in the pages of romantic novels?

Perhaps the answer can be found in later attitudes to literature, which consolidated the view of women as sentimental, undiscriminating readers. For many male writers of the twentieth century, such a reader came to symbolize the worst aspects of mass society, with its ugly, sordid culture and its vulgar tastes. They recoiled at the prospect of shop girls and servants, secretaries and housewives poring eagerly over lurid novels, true confession magazines, and sentimental stories of star-crossed Romeos. Many modernists saw themselves as embattled heroes struggling to hold their heads above water as this commercial flood of feeling washed over modern society. Creating artful, difficult, self-conscious works of literature was a way of creating a new kind of reader and a new way of reading. If ordinary readers were credulous and sentimental, confusing art and reality, then the truly modern reader would be guarded and critical, always aware of the distance between the carefully laid out words on the page and the distracting buzz of everyday life.

This view is clearly laid out by the Spanish philosopher and critic José Ortega y Gasset, one of modernism's most polemical champions. "All modern art is unpopular," he insists, "and it is so not accidentally and by chance, but essentially and by fate." Ordinary individuals, according to Ortega y Gasset, prefer novels that echo their everyday experience and that appeal to their emotions. Modern literature is, by contrast, dehumanized: that is to say, it intentionally distorts reality, stylizes it into art, and keeps the reader at arm's length. For Ortega y

Gasset, this distinction between elite modern art and popular art is also a division between the intellect and the emotions. Expressing his distaste for what he calls "psychic contagion," he declares categorically, "art ought to be full clarity, high noon of the intellect. Tears and laughter are, aesthetically, frauds."[8]

Modern art is, for Ortega y Gasset, best understood as the play of abstract form, as a kind of higher algebra. This trend toward purity and abstraction is, he contends, linked to the triumph of youthful and masculine values. In the modern era we are witnessing the sons' revolt against tradition and the authority of the fathers. Modern art also expresses a rejection of emotion ("psychic contagion"), bodies, nature, and femininity. "Why is it," Ortega y Gasset asks rhetorically, "that the round and soft forms of living bodies are repulsive to the present-day artist?"[9]

Ortega y Gasset's energetic but crude polemic does not begin to do full justice to the many shades and varied ambitions of modern literature and art. Nevertheless, he voices with great clarity and verve a mental schema that has exercised a powerful impact on the modern imagination. In this schema, as Andreas Huyssen points out in an influential essay, mass culture is embodied in the figure of a woman. The realm of popular art comes to be associated with intense emotion, mindless absorption, and sensual cravings—in other words, with stereotypical feminine traits. The image of a bored and frustrated housewife gobbling up romance novels like Valium remains our most familiar symbol of the insidious effects of mass culture, itself a deeply etched and ubiquitous cultural cliché.[10]

Conversely, to read literature with the seriousness that it deserves requires a sober and detached mode of appreciation. To become a professional reader of literature is to learn what *not* to say. It is to internalize a sense of the inappropriateness of certain ways of talking and certain kinds of value judgments. Scholarly readers do not talk enthusiastically about suspense-filled stories and gripping plots, reminisce about their experience of identifying with favorite characters, or confess to being moved to tears or laughter by the works they read. And they certainly do not rhapsodize about the pleasures of losing oneself in a love story. Such responses do not accord with the common definition of what it means to be a scholar of literature. To be a reader, it seems, is to be either critical, judicious, and masculine, or susceptible, emotional, and feminine.

Resisting and Identifying

Many representations of female readers were fashioned by men. The figure of the reading woman was often a titillating mystery: what was she reading, what was she thinking, what were her dreams and fantasies? To leaf through the documents of the past is to discover images of women reading but also to come across many instances of men trying to read these images of female readers. Thus women themselves were seductive enigmas, mysterious hieroglyphs, asking to be deciphered and interpreted by the male observer. The female reader, oblivious to her surroundings and engrossed in an imaginary world, was a particularly intriguing puzzle.

Feminist critics turned the tables by directing this analytical gaze back on men. In her discussion of a Hollywood cliché—the mousy librarian who takes off her glasses and is transformed into a ravishing beauty—Mary Ann Doane suggests that this motif points to a deep-seated discomfort with women's active looking. "The intellectual woman looks and analyzes, and in usurping the gaze she poses a threat to an entire system of representation."[11] How did feminist readers look back at male spectators? How did they respond to common images of women reading? And how did feminism transform our sense of what it meant to read as a woman?

An early and influential contribution to this debate was Judith Fetterley's *The Resisting Reader*, published in 1977. The polemical flair of Fetterley's introduction had a powerful impact on later directions in feminist criticism. "I see my book," she writes, "as a self-defense survival manual for the woman reader lost in 'the masculine wilderness of the American novel.'" American literature, according to Fetterley, poses fundamental problems for the female reader. "To read the canon of what is currently considered classic American literature is perforce to identify as male. . . . The female reader . . . is required to identify against herself." In describing the experience of such a reader, Fetterley draws liberally on the language of exclusion, powerlessness, and oppression. Women do not find their own lives reflected in art but are required to read as men, to adopt the male point of view. Even worse, this point of view is based on an active repudiation of the female. In most of the classical works of American literature, from Rip van Winkle to the novels of Norman Mailer, the hero achieves an authentic identity as an American man by fleeing the gossiping, claustrophobic, realm of women. Fetterley concludes: "Women are taught to think as men, to identify with a male point of view, and to accept as normal and legitimate a male system of values, one of whose central principles is misogyny."[12]

Fetterley's book was written at a time of renewed interest in the role of the reader. Scholars of literature began to explore how the act of reading helps to fill in the contours of a fictional world. Was it possible, they wondered, to think of the reader as the coauthor of a text? Perhaps readers did not passively consume the words on the printed page but fleshed out the meaning of those words in creative and often idiosyncratic ways. No longer just a necessary but peripheral accessory to a work of literature, the reader began to take center stage in discussions of literary meaning.

The issue of whether a reader was male or female did not, however, enter into these discussions. Drawing up elaborate schemes of different types of readers, critics did not pause to think about how gender might affect the way people read. Feminist scholars were the first to address this question. They rebutted one common view of readers as sexless angels by insisting that men and women brought very different perspectives and experiences to the act of reading. Indeed, the foundational act of feminism was often seen as one of re-reading, or re-vision, in Adrienne Rich's famous phrase.[13] It involved looking at the world from a new perspective, from what seemed at first like an oddly skewed standpoint. The goal of such a rereading was to make the familiar seem unfamiliar, to question our taken-for-granted views about women and men and to make them seem newly strange and open to change.

For Fetterley, then, the feminist reader is a resisting reader. She could not be further removed from the dreamy female figure curled up with a book on the sofa and oblivious to her surroundings. She does not surrender herself to the ebb and flow of feeling and the sentimental pleasures of reading. She cannot afford to lose herself in the pages of a book. Rather, she is constantly on her guard; her goal is to identify and to resist the designs of the literary work. She must strive to outwit the work of fiction and expose its ideology so as not to drown in its assumptions. She is, in a sense, at war with the text, struggling with it to ensure her own survival.

Feminist criticism would surely not have come into being without this first gesture of defiance and refusal, as scholars showed how literature and literary criticism often took for granted the primacy of the male viewpoint and the secondariness of women. The feminist reader was she who said no, who rebelled against the position allotted to women in art and life. In a famous essay, Laura Mulvey showed how women were reduced to objects of the male gaze in Hollywood movies and concluded with an obituary for traditional forms of cinema. "It is said," she writes, "that analysing pleasure, or beauty, destroys it. That is the intention of this article."[14] Aesthetic pleasure was the enemy of feminism because it helped to make sexism palatable, even appealing, and hence reconciled women to the status quo. To lose oneself in the pleasure of reading a book or watching a film was to surrender all capacity for critical thought. It was to bow down to the insidious power of a patriarchal culture to mold women's identities, fantasies, and desires.

In this vision of reading as resistance we can recognize a feminist reworking of a well-known tradition of interpretation. The essence of this tradition is well summarized in Paul Ricoeur's term "hermeneutics of suspicion." To read a work of literature, or philosophy, or art, in this way is to read with skepticism. A text cannot be taken at face value but must be interrogated for its underlying assumptions. It has a hidden agenda; it presents a misleading or distorted account of the world; it glosses over matters of great importance. As a result, what a piece of writing is silent about is often as revealing as what it actually says. It must be interrogated, diagnosed, and rendered accountable. Rather than submitting to the power of a text, the reader asserts her own power to challenge its authority.

It is not difficult to understand the appeal of such a way of reading; in fact, it is hard to see how any form of critical commentary could exist without it. Questioning the literary and cultural heritage was an essential starting point for feminist work. More generally, learning how to read skeptically is surely an essential part of any scholarly training. Martha Nussbaum, for example, speaks of the value of a Socratic education that is based on critical and searching engagement with the works of the Western tradition rather than a deferential endorsement of them.[15] The stakes for feminism have been particularly high in this regard, given the long tradition of seeing women as naive and uncritical consumers of fiction. The resisting female reader is a powerful antidote to the legacy of Emma Bovary.

Yet there are also obvious limits to reading as resistance. Such an attitude locks the reader into a negative stance, requiring her to react against what she reads. By refusing to let down her guard, she cuts herself off from ever being affected, inspired, or changed by her encounter with a book. Instead, her engagement turns into a one-sided skirmish, which she always wins. In this model of reading, the reader is the one who knows, who is able to outwit a text by exposing its errors. This victory does not come without a cost, in reinforcing the reader's solipsism. She reads only to have her original views confirmed, to discover once more that she is right. Instead of a dialogue between reader and work, there is only a monologue, in which the reader admonishes, berates, and corrects the text but is unable to learn from it. Such a monologue in turn makes the act of reading redundant. Once a reader knows in advance that every work she encounters is a mouthpiece of patriarchal ideology, interpretation is no longer necessary. It is nothing more than a tautological exercise that proves the same point over and over again.

A few years ago, I taught a course on the literature of the fin de siècle that included *The Bostonians*. James's novel was particularly good at inspiring vigorous class discussion. I remember being struck by the vehemence with which one or two students condemned what they saw as the novel's complicity with patriarchal values. These students sided passionately with the character of Olive, a genteel Bostonian feminist who forges an intimate friendship with the younger Verena and takes her under her wing. Conversely, they saw Basil, the impoverished southerner who adamantly pursues and ultimately wins Verena, as a stalker, a sexual predator, and a thug. They read the novel, in other words, through the lens of a certain brand of feminism that celebrates the nurturing bonds of female friendship and condemns the violent brutality of men. Here was a particularly telling example of reading as resistance.

The problem with this view was not simply that it failed to account for many of the details of *The Bostonians*. It was also that these students seemed unaware that the novel had anticipated their own reading and presented it in a highly ironic light. Indeed, it is precisely this kind of Manichean feminism that Olive herself embodies. Her own friendship with Verena is forged around a sense of solidarity created through endless retellings of the story of male cruelty and the eternal suffering of women. Yet *The Bostonians* suggests that such a narrative of injured innocence is not to be taken at face value. Olive offers a perfect example of what Wendy Brown calls wounded attachments; she is a person who has an intense psychic investment in the experience of injury.[16] This passionate attachment to an image of female martyrdom in turn veils the manipulative aspects of her own intimate relationship with Verena. The power Olive seeks to exercise over her female friend is more covert than that of Basil's confident pursuit of Verena, but it is a form of control nonetheless.

What these students missed, in my view, was the chance for a dialogue with James's novel. They were so eager to impose what they saw as the correct feminist reading on the text that they were oblivious to what the text might say back to them. Resisting the novel's designs, they failed to realize that those designs were more complicated than they thought. To recognize the nuances of James's portrayals of motivation is not, by any means, to abandon a feminist reading of the novel. In fact, *The Bostonians* explores in depth the differing social constraints that are placed on men and women and portrays with sympathy the precarious nature of female unions that lack legal or social sanction. But it also asks searching questions about the motives of those who divide the world into brutish villains and persecuted innocents. By resisting the designs of James's novel with such vigor, these students cut themselves off from the chance of ever reflecting on their own ways of reading.

In offering this example, I am not suggesting that resisting reading will always result in willful misreading. Nor do I share the view that the ambiguities of great works of literature allow them to elude all forms of sociopolitical analysis. Whatever their complexities, such works are always steeped in the ideas, symbols, and beliefs of a particular world. In this sense, they *do* have designs on the reader. As Wayne Booth has shown, a work of literature is never completely open and indeterminate. Rather, it tries, in varying degrees, to persuade its readers to see things in a certain way.[17] Why shouldn't these readers decide to answer back, to question rather than obey?

And yet to denounce a text is to cut oneself off from any serious engagement with it and hence to fail to do it justice. It is pointless to berate works of literature merely because they do not seem to endorse one's own opinions. To be worthwhile, a critical response, no less than a sympathetic response, must draw the reader in, implicate her, encourage her to get under the skin of the book she is reading. In this sense, she cannot help but be touched by the very thing she seeks to question. Reading in this way demands both rigorous attention to what a text may be saying and openness to the unpredictability that may attend this encounter. Otherwise, we are left with a self-righteousness that reveals a great deal about the reader but not much about the work that is being read. "Can reading be truly subsumed by *self-defense*?" asks Shoshana Felman. "Does not reading involve one risk that, precisely, cannot be resisted: that of finding in the text something one does not expect? The danger with becoming a 'resisting reader' is that we end up, in effect, *resisting reading.*"[18]

So far, of course, I have only told one part of the story. From the early days of feminism, critics often drew a contrast between "reading as resistance" and another kind of reading. The crucial distinction here was between literature by men and literature by women. When they turned to women's writing, many feminists felt they could let down their guard. Rather than constantly fighting the text's designs, they embraced these designs with a sense of relief and gratitude; literature was no longer an adversary but a sustaining resource. In works by other women, feminist critics saw the reflection of their own lives, desires, and experiences. The act of reading became an act of solidarity with other members of an oppressed community.[19]

Such a vision drives the argument of an influential essay by Patricinio Schweickart, published in 1986. Schweickart concedes that a few male-authored works may be of value, but her main aim is to endorse Fetterley's account of the insidious designs of the male canon. By causing women to identify against themselves and hence to experience a form of self-division, she claims, men's writing is responsible for wreaking "grave psychic damage" on female readers. Schweickart's discussion of this process draws analogies between the act of reading and a forced seduction or rape. The male text *does* things to the female reader; it seeks to manipulate, control, or hurt her. However, the reader can choose to take control of her own reactions and inclinations. She can read against the grain rather than submitting to the male text and allowing it to invade her psyche.

By contrast, feminist readings of female texts are inspired by a yearning for intimacy and connection. Looking at women's writing brings, as Schweickart puts it, "a shift in emphasis from the negative hermeneutic of ideological unmasking to a positive hermeneutic whose aim is the recovery and cultivation of women's culture."[20] The task of the female critic of female texts, Schweickart declares, is much more heartwarming. It is about creating positive visions of women's point of view, about celebrating the joys as well as acknowledging the pain of the female condition. An encounter with a female text is like having an intimate and pleasurable conversation with another woman.

Schweickart's words pay tribute to what is clearly a powerful and moving experience for many feminist critics: discovering the words of other women. In a world where cultural authority has so often been assigned to men, female readers may be enormously heartened and encouraged by examples of women's creative power. In some cases there may be a powerful shock of recognition, a sense of delight and gratitude that crucial yet unnoticed aspects of women's lives have finally been recorded. At other times, it is enough that the words carry a woman's signature, that women have seized the authority of authorship. The female critic thinks of herself as bound in kinship and solidarity to the female writer.

Schweickart's account of female textual bonding is, nevertheless, starry-eyed. Projecting psychological stereotypes onto works of literature, she assumes that male texts are violent and predatory while female texts and female readers are nurturing and nice. Like my students responding to *The Bostonians*, she sees hierarchy, conflict, and the struggle for power as a purely male problem. Furthermore, in this description of women as readers, the shifting and many-sided involvements of reading are subsumed within a monochromatic picture of sisterly recognition. Schweickart is careful to suggest that the feminist critic respect the difference of other women's work rather than simply impose her own views upon it. Yet these differences are, it seems, minor

and benevolent variants in a harmonious chorus of female voices. Trot-
ting out some hoary assumptions about gender (men value autonomy,
women prefer relationships), Schweickart describes a highly polarized
literary world.

This argument typifies a once popular mind set among feminist critics: that men's texts are bad and women's texts are good until proved
otherwise. Thus, for Schweickart, any work by a man is "an enemy" or
at best a "symptom of a malignant condition," whereas works by
women, it appears, exist in a state of grace. Some of the problems with
this viewpoint have now been thoroughly canvassed, while others have
been barely touched upon. One of the most forceful challenges has
come from feminist scholars who are also women of color. Why should
the shared fact of femaleness, they ask, be the overriding factor shaping
the act of reading? Perhaps racial affiliation has an equally powerful
and compelling impact on how people read. Perhaps the differences of
racial, ethnic, and cultural background cut across the bonds that are
supposed to connect and unify women. In fact, alienation rather than
affinity may be the overriding emotion defining a black woman's response to a white woman's text.

bell hooks, for example, talks about black female viewers as a problem for feminist film theory, with its armature of psychoanalytical
ideas about phallic power and female lack. To explain how women and
men respond to films by invoking the eternal verities of the Oedipal
story is to deflect attention away from many other crucial factors that
shape interpretation, including race, class, and education. hooks talks
about the history of African American women's fraught relationship to
television and film.[21] Whether a particular story was man- or woman-
centered was often less important than the ways in which blackness
was either caricatured or ignored in the mass media. Conceding that
some black female viewers are seduced into identifying with Hollywood images of the perfect woman, hooks argues that many others
have responded critically and with skepticism.

Black female readers, in other words, are often resisting readers of
texts by and about white women. These texts have included the canon
of feminist criticism itself, which has often assumed, too easily and confidently, that women share a common psychology and a common identity. The last few years have seen an explosion of women's voices

protesting this assumption. In the United States, such challenges to
feminist orthodoxy have centered on race and sexuality. As women of
color have rejected many of the stories about female selfhood circulated
by white women, so too have lesbians forcefully questioned the common and careless assumption that all readers are heterosexual.

For example, feminist literary critics often focused obsessively on
stories about women's enthrallment to male erotic power, depicting
male-female romance as the defining plot of all women's lives. They
subsumed the lesbian reader within a theory of the female reader, without pausing to consider that sexual preference might influence how
people read. Alternatively, they celebrated the lesbian as the ultimate
symbol of female solidarity while evacuating her of her sexuality,
averting their eyes from what Terry Castle calls the "incorrigibly *las-
civious* surge towards the body of another woman."[22]

Such desires may have complicated consequences for the act of reading. Because of the dearth of explicit lesbian images in the history of literature, the lesbian reader is forced to rely on her ingenuity. As Jean
Kennard wryly notes, "if as lesbian readers we can only appreciate literature that reflects our own experience, we are likely to be very limited
in our reading pleasure."[23] Thus erotic engagement may be sparked by
analogy rather than identity, by suggestive echoes, fragments, and
traces in a literary work. A text may plausibly lend itself to a reading in
terms of same-sex desire, even if such desire is not explicitly named.
For example, as the heterosexual plot recedes into the background, a
heroine's intimate moments with other women become more interesting and worthy of attention. Flickering traces of female-female eroticism may be found in many texts that are not in any obvious sense
"about" lesbians.

As well as being hyperalert to the nuances of relations between
women in literature, lesbian readers may also engage in complicated
acts of cross-identification. For example, some critics have talked about
allying themselves with male rather than female characters when reading a conventional love story. In a culture which provides very few images of lesbian desire, reading in this way is one way of imaginatively
experiencing an erotic connection to another woman. Descriptions of
the sexual power and beauty of women's bodies through a man's eyes
may also have a powerful impact on other women. Thus the vagaries of

desire may cut across and complicate a politics of gender identification.[24]

Such conflicts have made it difficult to invoke the female reader as a self-evident concept. Once we acknowledge the dramatic differences among women, what happens to a feminist theory of reading? One possible route is to splice the concept of woman into ever smaller segments, while still holding tight to the idea that readers relate to a text in terms of a shared identity. This path has been followed by some scholars who want to replace a general model of the female reader with a more specific definition of a black female reader or a lesbian reader. Such critics still stress the compelling need to find one's experiences reflected in a work of literature, while expanding experience to include not only gender but also race and sexuality. Identity is not discarded but fine-tuned.

Where, however, does the process of defining the reader's identity come to an end? There is a long list of social factors—gender, race, class, age, nationality, religion, able-bodiedness—that help shape the kind of people we become. Yet the more exhaustively we specify these social influences, the harder it becomes to use them as a reliable basis for predicting literary taste. It is one thing to argue that what people read and how they read is shaped by their life experiences. But it is quite another to assume that readers only value works that reflect those experiences back to them. This is to reduce aesthetic pleasure to a very limited role in the shoring up of social identity. It is to shrink the many functions and facets of reading down to the single fact of self-recognition. And it is to assume that individuals cannot enjoy, empathize, or learn from works of art that explore worlds different from their own.

This is not the path that feminist criticism should follow. It is not compelling either as a description of how women do read or as a vision of how they should read. I am reminded of the eloquent essays by female writers that pay tribute to the books that have inspired them. bell hooks talks about her love of Emily Dickinson and Rainer Maria Rilke as well as Audre Lorde and Toni Morrison. Jeanette Winterson is a devotee of T. S. Eliot. Angela Carter writes with passion about Colette, Grace Paley, and Katherine Mansfield, but also about Edmund White, Edgar Allan Poe, and D. H. Lawrence. Kathy Acker pays tribute to Georges Bataille, William Burroughs, and the Marquis de Sade. Doris

Lessing's favorite writers include Gogol, Stendhal, and Dostoyevsky. Germaine Greer is a fan of Dickens. Buchi Emecheta praises John Updike as well as Gloria Naylor. And Alice Walker's powerful homage to Flannery O'Connor sent me back to reread O'Connor's short stories.[25]

These are just a few instances of women reading across divisions of race, gender, or sexuality. While most of these writers agree that their personal histories have left a mark on how they read, none of them conclude that works springing from other circumstances must be alien, inaccessible, or out of bounds. Some express their delight at the growing recognition of literature by women and people of color, but they do not assume that this writing is only relevant to readers from the same milieu. Indeed, the everyday practice of millions of readers provides countless instances of passionate engagement across divisions of gender, race, and sexuality. Yet feminist criticism has often been reluctant to talk about this fact except in a negative light. We need more capacious models of reading that can explore the pleasures as well as the risks of transgressing boundaries and entering imaginatively into worlds that are different from our own.

Conversely, the fact that an author and reader belong to the same demographic group does not tell us very much. If we knew that the work of a white, middle-class, female writer would automatically appeal to white, middle-class, female readers, for example, the job of being a publisher would be far easier and more lucrative than it is now. Of course, what people choose to read is partially shaped by their level of education, their race, and their gender. But a host of other factors also come into play, including the reader's idiosyncratic tastes (she enjoys hard-boiled crime but not whodunits, Anne Tyler but not Margaret Atwood) and the fit between these tastes and the skills and inclinations of a particular writer. Jean-Paul Sartre once famously observed that Valéry was a petit-bourgeois individual, but that not every petit-bourgeois individual was Valéry. Sartre's remark is still a useful warning against trying to reduce complex and often unpredictable flows of influence to cookie-cutter social schemas.

When women enjoy reading literature by other women, furthermore, this pleasure is not always best explained in terms of a language of recognition and shared identity. For example, the two most compelling books I have read recently were both written by women, yet the most common ways of talking about women's writing do not begin to explain why I found these books so memorable. I opened Jamaica Kincaid's *Autobiography of My Mother* with little knowledge of the author's work but was immediately mesmerized by the bleak cadences of its opening lines: "My mother died at the moment I was born, and so for my whole life there was nothing standing between myself and eternity; at my back was always a bleak, black, wind."[26] The lyricism of Kincaid's prose draws the reader in yet keeps her at arm's length, refuses reciprocity, insists defiantly on the solitude of the speaking subject. The book is an exercise in superbly modulated rage that is all the more chilling for being honed to such stylistic perfection. Kincaid's furious and beautiful sentences circle around relentlessly in elegant and mesmerizing loops.

Because of her exploration of existential pain in bare, luminous prose, Kincaid has been compared to Albert Camus (in fact the vituperative Austrian writer Thomas Bernhard strikes me as a more plausible parallel). Unlike Camus, however, Kincaid does not shirk from plumbing the political meanings of race. The everyday humiliations and privations of an impoverished creole woman are a central theme of her book, recorded in merciless and heartrending detail. Yet Kincaid's portrayal of her tormented heroine Xuela deftly intertwines the social with the metaphysical, the political with the existential, refusing to reduce psychic complexity to the banality of a case study. Her novel is an achingly powerful and uncompromising exploration of psychic extremity and primal loss, haunted by the rarely invoked but always present specter of the absent mother as a potent symbol of the metaphysical void.

The second book that has stayed in my mind was Anne Fadiman's *The Spirit Catches You and You Fall Down*, which I picked up casually during a lunch break at an academic conference. For the rest of the weekend I was oblivious to everything that was going on around me, impatiently turning the pages under the desk while pretending to listen to the papers being delivered on the podium. Fadiman's book is a work of nonfiction written like a novel, a profoundly moving and disturbing story of a clash of belief systems and its tragic consequences. It tells the story of Lia Lee, the much-loved child of members of the Hmong tribe of Laos who have settled in southern California. To her proud and doting parents, Lia's dramatic seizures are a sign of her special links to the spirit world. To the doctors treating her at the Merced Community Hospital, they are symptoms of a severe but treatable form of epilepsy. Fadiman's rendering of the disastrous misunderstandings between Lia's impoverished parents and the harried emergency doctors trying to do their best in the face of what they see as parental ignorance and incalcitrance is a suspense-filled masterpiece, a dispassionate yet deeply compassionate confrontation with the irreconcilable nature of certain cultural differences.[27]

If I think about why I found these books so extraordinary, the reasons have little to do with the pleasures of recognition. In different ways, they both jolted me, disturbed me, and caused me to see things in a new light. In each case, I identified with the main characters in the sense of being immersed temporarily but powerfully in their perspective on the world. But this experience did not involve a belief that we shared a common identity (whatever that might mean), or that our lives were ultimately the same. Here I find myself at odds with some common views about how people read. Politically minded critics sometimes argue that any act of identifying is dangerous: that a reader must annihilate otherness by assimilating it to his or her own sense of self. Furthermore, it is often taken for granted that being absorbed in a novel or a film is incompatible with having a critical perspective. Involvement does away with any hope of skepticism or detachment. "Identification," writes Anne Friedberg, "can only be made through recognition, and all recognition is itself an implicit confirmation of the ideology of the *status quo.*"[28]

What actually happens when we are drawn into a text is surely more messy and contradictory than this view suggests. A reader's absorption in a fictional world can easily coexist with an ongoing and often intense awareness of the difference of that world. Involvement and distance are not necessarily opposed but may fold into each other repeatedly as we read. Indeed, some of the most powerful experiences of reading surely involve an ongoing movement between differing registers of thought and feeling. Readers have a sense of being drawn in by the seductive pull of a work of fiction, but without losing sight of its strangeness and distance from their own life.

Furthermore, reading is not an all-or-nothing affair, where I must either resist a text fiercely and adamantly or else find myself nodding in agreement with every word. There is a lot of give and take involved in the act of interpretation; periods of intense enthrallment may be followed by moments of refusal or only grudging assent. Readers are often seduced by what they read; but they may also refuse to be seduced or decide not to go all the way with the work in question. Or they may find a particular work appealing for reasons which have nothing to do with its apparent aims and intentions (as in "campy" readings of serious novels or films). Within cultural studies, which has paid a great deal of attention to these questions, the name given to the messy and unpredictable interaction between reader and work is *negotiation*.[29]

I would add that the connections between the crest and fall of the reader's involvement and the social identities of readers and authors are by no means clear-cut. For example, the fact that Fadiman and Kincaid are women has no doubt shaped their writing, making them more attuned to the many rich and haphazard details of female lives. Yet the theme of estrangement and miscommunication that winds through their works does not encourage a consoling belief in the redemptive power of female solidarity. Similarly, the racial and cultural background of these two authors may help to shape what they care about and how they write about it. But can we blithely conclude that a shared universe binds together a reader and author of the same race while excluding those of a different background?

This is to assume that the primary role of literary works is to sort readers into insiders and outsiders, the privileged and the excluded. Yet the otherness and strangeness of a piece of writing can be a virtue rather than a fault, a way of being forced, at least temporarily, out of well-worn grooves of thought and perception. As Wolfgang Iser puts it, to read is to think alien thoughts.[30] And sometimes, that strangeness is willful and intentional; it is painstakingly fashioned in the laborious craft of writing and rewriting rather than flowing naturally from the author's race or sex.

"As readers," writes Minrose Gwin, "we may often find ourselves visitors in a different land, perhaps a strange land; we learn its dimensions as we travel through, not by any maps we have constructed prior to reading."[31] Gwin's *The Woman in the Red Dress* is a richly illuminating and many-sided expansion of this insight. Reflecting on her engagement with works by Toni Morrison, Dorothy Allison, Harriet Jacobs, and others, Gwin uses the motif of space travel to describe reading as a form of dislocation, an opening of perspective, a shifting of identity. Fully cognizant of the complexities of the hermeneutic circle, Gwin describes reading as a mutual encounter, in which the reader travels the text but the text simultaneously travels the reader. Agreeing with Georges Poulet that reading involves a displacing and scrambling of the self, she draws out the many consequences of this insight in terms of its gender and racial politics. Gwin's powerful and important book adds to a growing body of feminist work on reading that is moving beyond the dichotomies of outside versus inside, resistance versus identification, politics versus pleasure.

Rethinking Reading

I want at this point to pull together the various threads of my argument. I began by pointing out that Emma Bovary's femaleness affects what and how she reads and that her example invites us to think about the connections between gender and reading. I went on to discuss some early feminist theories and to suggest that they fall short in their attempts to develop a general theory of the female reader. How, then, can we bring these two insights together? How can we put gender in the picture without making sweeping assumptions about how women read or how they should read?

Feminist critics have poured much of their energy into defining the ways in which female readers differ from male ones. This is an unsurprising response to the scholarly neglect of women's point of view. Looking back through the history of literary criticism, one can find countless examples of writing that patronizes or ignores women and that takes it for granted that the universal reader is male. To read as a woman in such a context was to have a sense of eavesdropping on a private conversation. Such cavalier assumptions that all readers are the same have become less common. It now seems clear that a woman may respond differently from a man when she is invited to sympathize with an author's complaints about the foolishness, inconstancy, or treachery of the female sex. It now seems plausible that a woman who identifies with a male character is not doing the same thing as a man identifying with that same character. Without building walls around gender, we can

hazard the modest thesis that men and women sometimes read with different priorities and different concerns.

Again, no one will dispute the fact that certain kinds of fiction appeal to readers of a specific sex. Publishers' surveys reveal, to no one's great surprise, that those who buy romance novels are women. The phrase "chick flicks" recognizes that a certain kind of Hollywood film is targeted at one sex (though, significantly, we have no male equivalent of this mildly disparaging term). The stories that Emma Bovary loved to read, stories of "romantic love in far-away places," still speak to the needs and desires of large numbers of women, while causing many men to shake their heads in condescension or puzzlement. One of the tasks of feminist criticism has been to take seriously books that are aimed at female readers. Such books have often been seen as less significant, less valuable, less geared to the universal because of their concern with romantic love, female friendship, domestic life, or other "trivial" themes. As Virginia Woolf pointed out long ago, the fact that stories of battle and heroism have been seen as having universal resonance, while stories of drawing-rooms and domestic life have not, speaks volumes about the perspectives that have shaped the history of literary criticism.[32]

There is a big difference, however, between recognizing that gender is an influence on how people read and advocating a gender-segregated theory of reading. By this, I mean a belief that male and female readers inhabit separate worlds and that women are only enriched by reading the works of other women. In fact, while some scholars have espoused such a view, the overall practice of feminist criticism does not provide much support for it. On my bookshelf, recent recoveries of out-of-print women writers stand alongside feminist defenses of Shakespeare and Milton. Discussions of Virginia Woolf are matched by sympathetic readings of Henry James and Marcel Proust. This eclecticism of taste can also be found in more popular forms of reading. Women may be the exclusive readers of romance novels, for example, but they are also prolific and enthusiastic readers of many other genres.

Why, then, should anyone assume that only literary works by and about women are of interest to female readers? This is to constrain rather than enlarge women's capacities, to fence them off in a separate sphere and to define their access to art in terms of their sex. Defending what she calls the "strange prismatic worlds" of art, Jeanette Winterson writes, "I do not want to read only books by women, only books by Queers, I want all that there is, so long as it is genuine and it seems to me that to choose our reading matter according to the sex and/or sexuality of the writer is a dismal way to read."[33] In fact, female readers are probably more "bi-textual" than male readers. That is to say, they are more attuned to the cues and conventions of different plots and more accustomed to reading through the eyes of both female and male characters. A recent British survey found that women are more willing to read novels by male authors than men are to read the works of women. Rather than women giving up their bi-textuality, men surely need to increase theirs.[34]

Some feminist scholars share my discomfort at being hemmed in by a constraining vision of what it means to be a female reader. The growing interest in images of transvestism and cross-dressing is a sure sign that attitudes toward aesthetic experience are changing. Such metaphors convey the idea that readers may take on many different personae in the act of reading. Rather than reinforcing an essential difference between male and female lives, reading is a more labile and fluid activity. Fantasy often involves an experience of identifying across gender; the fictional worlds created by novels and television, poetry and film, allow readers to align themselves with lives and perspectives different from their own. To identify in this way can be pleasurable rather than constraining. It offers a temporary release from the tyranny of the status quo, allowing individuals to imagine alternative ways of being in the world. These involvements are often temporary and mobile, shifting from one place to another in the course of reading. There is no simple, one-to-one match between the reader's social self and the imaginary personae she or he may assume. Identifications, in Diana Fuss's words, spill over and exceed the boundaries of identity.[35]

The field of queer theory, in particular, has inspired some memorable acts of self-description by those whose patterns of attachment and affiliation do not fall along tidy, predictable lines. Male readers and viewers can identify with women; women can experience an imaginative connection to the masculine that is felt as exhilarating rather than alienating. Eve Sedgwick, for example, has explored her intense identification with gay men, scrutinizing the complicated affinities that underlie her scholarly interest in reading and writing about male homo-sexuality. Wayne Koestenbaum dissects his long obsession with opera divas in an extended meditation on the echoes and connections between homosexuality, femininity, and opera. And British critic Alison Hen-negan, describing her history as a lesbian reader, talks about her adoles-cent fascination with classical Greek culture, war poetry, and other forms of writing devoted to intense bonds between men. More impor-tant to her than the difference of gender was a sense of powerful affin-ity with individuals drawn to members of their own sex.[36]

This interest in cross-gender identification is not, of course, com-pletely new. Carolyn Heilbrun, for example, was an early advocate of transvestism, urging female readers to draw on the riches of tradition-ally male plots. Given the constraints that have shaped women's litera-ture, Heilbrun argued in 1979 that women should turn to men's writing for bolder and more inspiring visions of desire and action. Fem-inist film critics have also long puzzled over the ambiguities of identifi-cation, exploring the ways in which women may shift between male and female points of view.[37]

The question of what this all means politically, however, remains open. Does such imaginary involvement have any tangible effects? Does identifying with others bring a particular pay-off? In the tradi-tional humanist view of art, experiencing different lives through the medium of literature is supposed to make the reader a more sensitive and socially responsible person. By seeing through the eyes of others who are unlike ourselves, by feeling their pain and experiencing their joys, we come to recognize our common humanity. In a recent version of this argument, Martha Nussbaum claims that by reading about and empathizing with the experiences of differing social groups, we are in-spired to seek a more just society.[38]

Feminist scholars have often been suspicious of this view, preferring to stress gender inequality rather than shared humanity. In the gloomi-est version of this scenario, any form of cross-gender identification is a zero-sum game in which women always lose. Women who identify with a male viewpoint must suffer a wrenching alienation from their own identity. Conversely, men who align themselves with a female per-spective are automatically suspect. Male authors who adopt the per-spective of female characters or male critics writing about women's texts are appropriating femaleness for their own dubious ends. Only women can tell the truth about women.

More recently, the pendulum has swung back and some feminist critics now view the traffic across gender boundaries in a positive light. Indeed, identifying with a different sex is now often seen as having a transgressive edge. The man who dreams of being Greta Garbo, the woman who imagines that she is Stephen Dedalus, are powerful reminders of the shakiness and fragility of our "natural" sense of gender. The realm of aesthetic experience—meaning not just high culture, but the full spectrum of imaginative art, including popular film and television—allows us to escape temporarily the stern and persistent social injunction to "be" a man or a woman. It allows us to explore alternative and imaginary selves. Rather than being cemented to characters who share their biological bodies and social identities, readers and viewers may identify in unpredictable and often unsettling ways.

Which of these arguments is the most persuasive? All of them strike me as containing a grain of truth, yet each seems insufficient as the last word on the politics of reading. On balance, my sympathies lie with a feminism that seeks to expand rather than restrict the range of aesthetic experience. Yet it is also true that empathizing with imaginary others is not always as benevolent a process as the humanist critic makes out. Elaine Showalter and Ann duCille have written witty and caustic essays on this subject; Showalter questions the motives of male scholars who want to muscle in on feminism to prove they can do it better, while duCille points to the patronizing views that are often displayed in white feminist commentary on black women's writing. Yet both scholars are also careful to distance themselves from the territorial claims of identity politics and to stress that they do not see literature as the exclusive property of those readers who share the author's gender or race.[39]

Much of the writing on how readers identify is speculative, based on little more than the critic's own experience. However, the few studies that actually compare male and female responses to similar texts suggest that the relationship between how readers read and their sex is not particularly straightforward. Gender is one important axis of meaning around which men and women organize the way they read, but it is not the one that always predominates.

One of the most comprehensive studies is Kim Chabot Davis's survey of patterns of viewing and reading among three different mixed-sex groups.[40] Her meticulous map of the flows and detours of identification turns many common assumptions on their heads. Women, she suggests, can be active and desiring viewers whose responses to gender cues are often complicated and unpredictable. They do not, for example, automatically ally themselves with female characters on the screen, partly because their own sense of gender varies so widely. Conversely, male viewers may identify with rather than objectify female characters, or they may choose to align themselves with "feminine" rather than "masculine" male figures.

Davis finds equally complicated patterns of racial and ethnic affiliation when looking at how viewers responded to *Northern Exposure*, a television series that explicitly embraces a multiculturalist ideology. Many viewers, she observes, spoke of identifying with their social "others" rather than with those characters that most closely matched their own social selves. Such responses are not necessarily typical, given the liberal leanings of this specific show. Yet this qualification merely underscores Davis's point, which is that attitudes, affinities, and political leanings are more important in predicting how viewers identify than the mere fact of belonging to a particular sex or race.

As well as discovering examples of viewers connecting across group differences, Davis also came across strong conflicts of opinion even within groups of apparently similar women. For example, when she canvassed responses to Jane Campion's film *The Piano* in a university community, it became clear that different kinds of scholarly training had an important impact on how women responded. Students and professors with a background in the social sciences often expressed a dislike for the film, claiming that it presented a romantic view of women's oppression. By contrast, viewers with literary interests tended to read the film rather differently and often saw Campion's heroine as an erotically powerful and subversive figure. Such strong disagreements even within a small sampling of feminists suggest that the fact of gender may be less important than the way in which a reader has learned to think or talk about gender.

Similarly, when feminist scholars in the 1980s championed the cause of "reading as a woman," what they often really meant was "reading as a feminist critic." This, of course, is a learned technique, not something that flows naturally from the fact of being female. In *Reading the Romance*, her groundbreaking study of a group of readers of romance fiction, Janice Radway points out that feminist scholars and the typical romance reader do not form part of the same interpretative community.[41] That is to say, they do not read in the same way and with the same goals in mind. To point this out is not to deny that the romance plot has a powerful hold on many women's psychic and social lives. Furthermore, it is perfectly possible to be a feminist and a fan of romance fiction (I have had many such students in my classes).

Still, analyzing romance novels from an academic viewpoint is clearly a very different activity from reading for pleasure. The feminist scholar who earns her living by analyzing texts is not doing the same thing as the female reader who picks up a book in the hope of finding several hours of enjoyable distraction. Indeed, this latter figure is perhaps the most powerful argument against seeing literature simply as a tool of patriarchal subjugation. Those women who turn to novels for a precious respite from stressful and exhausting lives clearly find a pleasure and consolation in aesthetic experience that they do not encounter elsewhere.

It is with this question of pleasure that I want to end. I mentioned in my introduction that conservative scholars love to accuse feminist critics of being zealous puritans hostile to any form of aesthetic enjoyment. There are clearly some strands of feminism that lend themselves to such a charge, but as a summary of the current state of feminist criticism, it falls seriously short. Indeed, it is highly ironic that feminists now stand accused of destroying pleasure in reading. As we have already seen, there is a long-standing tradition of male-authored scholarship that is deeply suspicious of the language of emotion, identification, and enjoyment.

In fact, feminist scholars are now drafting thoughtful and thought-provoking reflections on the pleasure of reading. They are also demurring from the usual ways that scholars have talked about aesthetic pleasure, that is, as a purely disinterested and disembodied experience. They are more inclined to ponder the emotional, even the erotic, undercurrents of how we respond to books or films. The joy of reading, they insist, is not only cerebral but also engages the passions and the senses.

Many of these ideas first came to fruition in studies of popular culture. Taking to heart the thorny question of the difference between academic and nonacademic forms of reading, feminist scholars began to look carefully at the texts enjoyed by ordinary women. Rather than complaining that women's magazines or romance novels were insidious forms of brainwashing, they began to ask why such genres were appealing and what points of purchase they offered for women's needs and desires. Already in the early eighties, Ien Ang suggested that the "structures of feeling" inspired by a television drama such as *Dallas* did not line up neatly with a particular politics. To act as if works of popular culture could simply be labeled as progressive or regressive was, in Ang's view, a short-sighted response. The pleasures of fantasy do not lend themselves to this kind of means-end calculation; an enjoyment of certain kinds of aesthetic experience does not automatically translate into a particular political viewpoint.[42]

We now have a large and important body of work on female pleasure. Much of this work has concerned itself with the pleasure of the "other woman," that is, the ordinary, nonacademic reader. Increasingly, however, female critics and writers are bringing these ideas closer to home and are crafting personal descriptions of their own pleasure in reading. Rather than continuing to uphold the ideal of the detached scholar, they are happy to admit that their own practice of reading engages the emotions as much as the intellect. And it is not only trashy fiction that can inspire a sense of intense identification and passionate absorption: one can be turned on by *Jane Eyre* as well as by Judith Krantz.

We have, in effect, gone full circle, back to the figure of Emma Bovary absorbed in the magical world of romantic novels. After spending much time and effort distancing themselves from this image of the female reader, some feminist critics have begun to question the wisdom of such a response. Why should they simply echo the conventional separation between intellect and feeling? Were there alternative ways of thinking about reading that did not require such absolute distinctions? Emma Bovary, for many reasons, is not the quintessential or archetypal female reader, yet she is one resonant symbol of the emotional and often erotic pull of reading. Whether rightly or wrongly, it is women above all who are associated with this kind of response. Perhaps feminist scholars now need to make room for pleasure in their theories rather than repudiating it or pretending that it did not exist.

In a thoughtful essay entitled *How Reading Changed My Life*, Anna Quindlen tackles some of these themes. Commenting on her own early passion for the novels of John Galsworthy and the frosty reception with which this passion was met by her professors, she urges a more capacious understanding of the pleasures of reading. The teaching of literature, she suggests, has often been fueled by intellectual snobbery and an impoverished conception of how people should read. "Reading has as many functions as the human body," argues Quindlen, "and not all of them are cerebral."[43] Passionate involvement, the desire for escape, the absorption of the plots and characters of fiction into one's very soul—these are essential aspects of reading for many people, yet they have long been dismissed as naive, even as embarrassing, by those who teach and write about literature. Still, it is not clear that scholars have completely purged themselves of such pleasures, nor is it clear that they should.

Like Quindlen, I find that I read differently and for different reasons: skeptically and with abandonment, resisting yet identifying, in search of various kinds of pleasure and instruction. Sometimes these conflicting needs and desires are fulfilled in the same book and sometimes they are not. When I was a graduate student, one of my professors warned me that after I had learned to read with a critical eye, I would never again be able to lose myself in a work of fiction. His prediction has not come true. My professional training as a literary scholar does not prevent me from being transported, even overcome, by some of the books I read. Recent accounts, mainly by women but also in some illuminating instances by men, confirm that such an experience is far from unique.[44]

Traditionally, studying literature meant acquiring the skills necessary to decode the complex language and forms of canonical works. More recently, as we have seen, this view has been challenged by scholars who speak of resistance and solidarity and see literary works as helping or holding back oppressed groups. Yet the emotional absorption and visceral pleasure of reading remain unaccounted for in both of these frameworks. Formalists and political critics are often united in their mistrust of the unpredictable vagaries of feeling. In a thoughtful exploration of these issues, Janice Radway talks at length about the "tactile, sensuous, profoundly emotional experience of being captured by a book." Contemporary scholarly language, she suggests, is very impoverished when it comes to describing that "peculiar act of transubstantiation whereby 'I' become something other than what I have been and inhabit thoughts other than those I have been able to conceive before."[45]

Radway is not, of course, suggesting that critics give up analyzing books in order to talk about their feelings. It is hard to imagine anything more unappealing than such an exercise in academic narcissism. Rather, the best feminist work on reading interweaves the scholarly and the personal, the critical and the confessional, using each to illuminate the other. The role of emotion and pleasure in aesthetic experience is a question for thoughtful investigation, not simply an excuse to emote or an alibi for anti-intellectual sentiments.

I believe, finally, that much feminist criticism now allows for a genuinely capacious understanding of aesthetic experience. Rigid divisions between good and bad ways of reading have given way to much more supple and nuanced descriptions of what is going on when we pore over the pages of a book or gaze transfixed at a screen. To quote Gwin once more: "That the imaginative process of reading is, and indeed must be, richly pleasurable—that it is an aesthetic process at its very core—does not deprive it of social consequence. That it can be consequential in the social realm does not rob it of its beauty and power to give us immense pleasure."[46] Increasingly, scholars are interweaving political analysis with a keen interest in the power of pleasure, fantasy, and imagination. Feminist scholarship, while keeping a firm grip on critical analysis, has clearly overcome its fear of feeling. In this respect, it is far ahead of most other forms of contemporary criticism.

2

AUTHORS

The writer is born of our fantasies.

LYNN SHARON SCHWARTZ

N the 1970s and 1980s, literary critics began to take up arms against the idea of authorship. Before long, the "death of the author" was a phrase on almost everyone's lips; first associated with French intellectuals such as Michel Foucault and Roland Barthes, it soon found many eager disciples in American universities. No longer would anyone be foolish enough to try to pin down what a work really meant by appealing to the thoughts, desires, or circumstances of the person who had written it. Invoking the author was a way of repressing the richness and exuberance of writing by confining it in the straitjacket of a single, original, true meaning. To debunk the author was to debunk authority and to demote the godlike presence behind the text to the status of a historical footnote. The death of the author meant the liberation of the reader.[1]

Feminist scholars, however, often saw things differently. In large part, this was because many of them were busy retrieving the works of lost women writers as well as rereading such well-known authors as Jane Austen and Emily Dickinson, whose work, they insisted, had been persistently misread. Critics speculated about the ambitions, desires, and fantasies swirling through the minds of female writers and wondered how the distinctive contours of women's lives might inform their creative output. Some scholars invoked the idea of a distinctive female literary tradition that yoked women together in a chain of influence stretching across time. They listed the many hurdles and obstacles faced by women who wanted to write: economic dependency, lack of time and space, the relentless intrusion of everyday life in the form of squalling infants or testy husbands, the disparagement faced by women who chose to remain single or childless to devote themselves more fully to their writing.

No less important than such material constraints were the prevailing myths and visions of authorship. The Promethean hero, the Oedipal rebel, the Bohemian artist, the visionary sage are all indisputably male figures. There are no like visions of creative power available to women. To be labeled an authoress is to lose rather than gain authority, to be branded as dainty, trivial, and feminine—a painter of delicate miniatures rather than broad, sweeping canvasses. Women have not been readily granted the numinous powers of world-making and self-fashioning. Their work has often been seen as derivative and secondary, minor rather than universal, authorized by others rather than self-authorizing. Thus authorship was vigorously defended as an indispensable part of the feminist toolkit, a way of tracking the historical injustices faced by women writers and of moving toward more adequate and inclusive forms of scholarship.

Critics, in other words, have often clashed on the merits of recourse to the author. Feminists who noted this conflict of opinion were often not content to stop there. It is no coincidence, they claimed, that at the very moment women were gaining prominence in the academy, male scholars began to disparage all talk of authorship as passé. Threatened by the dramatic upsurge of interest in writing by women, these scholars were trying to sabotage feminist criticism by discrediting one of its guiding concepts.

Admittedly, the breezy dismissal of the author could be infuriating to critics who were beginning to grapple with the question of female creativity. In response to Foucault's "What matter who's speaking?" they replied that it mattered a great deal. When Barthes spoke of debunking the Author-God, they pointed out that being confused with God was not a common problem for female writers. Yet most of those who proclaimed the death of the author were, I suspect, indifferent rather than openly hostile to feminist criticism. Obsessed with their own Oedipal relationship to male myths of authorship, with debunking

Shakespeare or bringing down Racine, they did not pause to think that not all authors carried the same metaphysical weight.

In fact, some feminists also chose to side with Barthes and Foucault. An often cited debate in the early eighties between Nancy Miller and Peggy Kamuf hinged on precisely this issue. Miller insisted that it always matters whether a work is produced by a man or a woman; Kamuf felt that feminists should actively question the norms of gender rather than help to shore up rigid distinctions between male and female authors.[2] At the same time, Toril Moi was also questioning some feminist approaches to women's texts, arguing that they were trying to ascribe a single, fixed essence to women, female writers, and women's writing. "If we are to undo this patriarchal practice of *authority*," wrote Moi, "we must take one further step and proclaim with Roland Barthes the death of the author."[3]

The truth of authorship or the death of the author? It is surely misleading to pose the question in such starkly antithetical terms; as I will show toward the end of the chapter, there is a third feminist approach to authorship that is steadily gaining ground. But I want first to look at some images of the woman writer that have had a powerful impact on feminist criticism. While these images have been widely used to interpret texts, they themselves cry out for interpretation, for a close reading of their symbolic meanings and encoded beliefs.

I use the term *allegories of authorship* in order to highlight their aesthetic dimension; they are not empirical descriptions of female authors so much as potent, densely packed metaphors. An allegory says one thing and means another; it deploys an image in order to convey a larger moral, political, or philosophical message. Thus feminist scholars, depending on their political or theoretical proclivities, have crafted very different images of female authorship. My goal is to take some of the most influential feminist allegories of the last twenty years and put them under the microscope. What do these figures of the female author tell us about trends in feminist criticism? And how do they guide the questions that feminist scholars ask about literary texts?

Authorship and Authority

I remain largely unpersuaded by what is often seen as an axiom of contemporary literary theory: the conviction that the self is nothing more than an ephemeral and unstable illusion fashioned from an endless weave of words. This belief in the absolute power of language to determine reality will soon, I suspect, come to seem like an eccentric interlude in the history of modern thought. Few people would deny that human selves are formed by the ebb and flow of taken-for-granted beliefs and attitudes as well as the unremitting pressure of material realities; our lives are scripted in large part by forces that remain beyond our ken. Yet this embeddedness is not antithetical to our subjectivity but the very basis of it. We can think of the self as an embodied perspective anchored in space and time; it is a nodal point at which infinite influences converge to create a unique combination of traits.

Clearly, attitudes to personhood fluctuate wildly across cultures: the modern yearning for self-actualization is a historical novelty, not a universal norm. But we can recognize this variability without endorsing the tendentious claim that the self is a bourgeois illusion. The value of Barthes's and Foucault's ideas, I believe, lies not in any general assault on the concept of the self but in the specific questions they raise about authorship. For example: under what conditions does the creator of a text become an author? A moment's reflection makes it clear that the terms are not synonymous. In medieval times, many of those who labored over what are now seen as great works of art remained unknown. The identity of the artist was simply not seen as having anything to do with the meaning and purpose of what had been created. The personhood of the creator was subordinate to the supreme glory of the creation. Authorship was anonymous.

This belief still flourishes today in rather different circumstances. The folk art and tribal art displayed in Western museums is often authorless; it is a common experience to see a vase or a sculpture attributed to a nameless person ("tribesman, Congo, 1940"). This practice, of course, speaks volumes about the politics of museum display. Non-Western art is often read not as the creation of a unique intelligence but as the symbolic expression of a collective or a folk. The lack of a signature serves as a guarantee of the work's "authenticity" and its links to native traditions. Its meaning is not dependent on its author.[4]

There are many other instances of texts without authors. Foucault mentions that most scientists, with obvious exceptions like Newton and Einstein, are not seen as authors. That is to say, while they may arrive at groundbreaking discoveries, the results of their experiments are also in a sense anonymous. Once proven and written up, these results can be repeated by anyone with the right equipment and are not tied to the psyche of a creator. Mass-market fiction is another striking example of the shifting valence of authorship. Here, the writer's name is often less important than the drawing power of the genre: romance, mystery, thriller. And when publishers do trumpet a new book by Stephen King or Danielle Steel, these names function like a genre, a guarantee that the reader is buying a familiar and reliable product. This is not, of course, how the names of great writers are supposed to operate. Here the author's signature radiates an aura; it is a sign of a unique and incomparable body of work, not just a reliable brand name.

What these examples suggest is that the author is not a neutral label or a self-evident idea. An author is not just a writer; "author" is a term used to designate a certain kind of person who writes a certain kind of work. Authors come before us as charismatic creators or intimate confidantes, figures haloed with glowing, highly charged, intensities of meaning. For example, some popular ways of talking about authorship often make it sound as if a book were an extension of the writer's soul, an intimate outpouring of the writer's inner self. We are encouraged to read autobiographically, to imagine an intense, symbiotic connection between author and work.

This way of thinking is often so deeply ingrained that it seems natural. When we turn the pages of a book, we may imagine an individual behind the words: sympathetic or judgmental, warm or distant, someone who is friend, enemy, or coconspirator. We find ourselves nodding with agreement at what we think that person is saying, or looking askance at their opinions and judgments. This impulse to visualize the author in our mind's eye is encouraged by the current vogue for memoirs, autobiographies, confessions, and other acts of soul-baring and self-exposure. The division between writing and the world becomes ever more indistinct; the authorial persona and the real-life individual seem to merge into one.

Yet authors are skilled in the art of deception and concealment, in putting on masks and performing in elaborate disguise. This is the case even, or perhaps especially, when they claim to be giving accurate testimony, to be telling us the truth as it really happened. When we read a book and create in our mind an image of its author, we are working backward from sketchy and unreliable evidence. We fashion an imaginary figure out of shards and scraps of language, but that figure is a mirage, not a reliable guide to a real historical person. Observing the adoring readers and fans who flock to meet their favorite authors at readings and book signings, Lynn Schwarz suggests that this meeting often ends in disappointment. To see the writer in person is to be brought—often painfully—down to earth.[5]

With these ideas in mind, we can look at Barthes's and Foucault's essays on authorship and separate out two distinct propositions. The first claim is that discussions of authorship are politically conservative and shore up the status quo. To do away with the author is to overthrow his or her authority to legislate meaning. Hence the call to "kill" the author in an act of Oedipal revolt. This idea is developed much more aggressively in Barthes than Foucault. It is Barthes, after all, who proclaims the death of the author, whereas Foucault is more interested in figuring out how the name of the author functions. It is Barthes who proclaims, "once the Author is removed, the claim to decipher a text becomes quite futile."[6] The author, he insists, is always a stand-in for God, a fake idol, a pseudo oracle. The craven worship of the author must give way to a revolutionary criticism that refuses to pursue the hidden truth of the author's intention and that glories in the abyss of endless and uncontrollable meaning. Theology gives way to antitheology.

Yet most feminist critics would not agree that all interest in authorship is politically suspect. When we think about how often female authors have been disparaged, trivialized, or ignored, this case seems hard to sustain. Of course, any critic who sees the author's gender as the alpha and omega of literary meaning does veer dangerously close to criticism as theology. But we can think of gender as one important layer in a work rather than as a magical key that will deliver the ultimate truth and clear up all ambiguity. Neither does talk about authors require us to believe that we can fully recover the author's real intentions and that these intentions decree once and for all what a work must mean. Given the many different ways we have of referring to authors, there is, I would argue, no particular politics that clings to the idea of authorship.[7]

The second part of what we can call "the death of the author thesis" is that looking to an author to explain the truth of a work of art is a historical and cultural bias, not a natural and immutable response. It is only one possible way of thinking about how texts work. An author is not a solid and unshakable presence that precedes a work of art and guarantees its meaning, but a figure created by a particular way of reading. In this way of reading, writes Barthes, "the *explanation* of a work is always sought in the man or woman who produced it, as if it were always in the end, through the more or less transparent allegory of the fiction, the voice of a single person, the *author* 'confiding' in us."[8] The author does not simply create a text; rather a text—or more precisely a particular way of reading a text—creates an author.

To make this point is not to deny that real authors exist or that they are sentient, intelligent individuals who intentionally craft their work in certain ways. Rather, it is to recognize that a novel or a poem is a zone of unstable, oscillating, and often clashing interpretations. Moving into historical and cultural arenas far removed from their starting point, such works will always proliferate meanings that reach far beyond anything that their creators may have imagined. These mutating meanings may in turn beget wildly differing visions of the persona behind the text. While appealing to the author may give us a sense of security, a solid foothold for interpretation, the ground beneath our feet is likely to crumble and give way at any moment.

This second claim strikes me as more telling and persuasive. The author is "dead" in the sense that the work's presence is predicated on his or her absence. The text is a trace, an enigmatic mark left for others to decipher. When we try to fashion a likeness of the author out of these textual remains, we are involved in a project of imagining rather than truth-telling. The author is, as Foucault argues, a projection, a figure who is heavily invested with the reader's fantasies, dreams, and desires. Of course, we can try to rein in our fantasies about a writer by consulting external sources such as biographies. Still, it is obvious that such sources are by no means free of projections and myths about authorship. Think, for example, of the wildly varied accounts of Sylvia Plath as a feminist martyr or a self-destructive hysteric.

Some feminist critics have sought to make a polemical distinction between their own political convictions and the more esoteric, abstract concerns of other forms of criticism. Feminism, they insist, concerns itself with the real, material lives of women. Yet things are hardly this straightforward, especially when critics turn to literary works for evidence about female experience. They hope to glimpse traces of psychic or social truths about women's lives that remain invisible in the public record. Yet when books talk, their utterances are often sibylline and enigmatic. Their surfaces may reflect back the reader's image rather than opening a window onto the self behind the text.

Rather than a sturdy presence behind the text that guarantees its real-world politics, in other words, the author is often a projection. She can easily become a receptacle for the reader's fantasies and desires. Surveying some popular allegories of female authorship thus tells us a great deal about differing perspectives in feminist criticism. Each allegory brings with it a new body of literary works to be read, interpreted, and pored over. These works are scrutinized for hidden clues about what it means to be a woman writer; they are weighed down with exemplary meaning and symbolic authority. Certain works are read over and over again because they strike a chord with large groups of critics. And yet what readers find in such works is also shaped by their own dreams, hopes, and fears. Feminist critics do not just rediscover or reclaim the female author; in a certain sense they create her.

Madwomen in Attics

Scenes of enclosure and entrapment. An intense, suffocating sense of hopelessness and frustration. Victorian women confined in tight-laced corsets, airless rooms, and the strictures and structures of language itself. Victim-heroines who seem docile and acquiescent, drained of all desire. Anxiety and dis-ease. Agoraphobia, hysteria, and anorexia as eloquent expressions of women's suffering and a muted protest against that suffering. The home as prison and tomb. Women reduced and diminished in stature, under the constant watch of their male wardens. The texts of literature and culture as an inescapable prison, trapping women within the forbidding walls of a male-defined world. Submerged expressions of resistance and refusal. Madness as a metaphor of female anger and revolt.

These motifs cluster around one early and influential discourse on female authorship. Two works of literature, in particular, define this vision: Charlotte Brontë's *Jane Eyre* and Charlotte Perkins Gilman's story "The Yellow Wallpaper." These two texts of nineteenth-century

English and American fiction have become feminist monuments, works that are widely taught and endlessly reinterpreted. In the 1970s and 1980s, *Jane Eyre* and "The Yellow Wallpaper" were often hailed as works that cast light on an entire female literary tradition. They were eloquent allegories of the travails of female authorship, crystallizing the peculiar anguish of being a woman writer in a patriarchal culture.

Sandra Gilbert and Susan Gubar's *The Madwoman in the Attic* was the founding text of this critical method. Gilbert and Gubar's ambitious book proclaimed a new feminist poetics that would expose and defy the phallic myths of literary history. The madwoman in the attic was a powerful allegory, yoking together spatial imagery, psychological diagnosis, and linguistic analysis. Like any good metaphor, it created new ways of seeing, casting familiar works of literature in a startling yet compelling light. The drooling, deranged figure of Rochester's first wife, Bertha Mason, was no longer a bit-player in Brontë's novel, a creaky stereotype of the lunatic borrowed from old Gothic novels. Rather, she was the key to a feminist understanding of *Jane Eyre* and indeed to an entire tradition of women's writing. Bertha Mason was not Jane's foe so much as her dark double and her other half, the deflected expression of her anxiety and rage. She was an eloquent reminder of the terrible consequences of warping and repressing women's desires. It was, wrote Gilbert and Gubar, "as if the very process of writing had itself liberated a madwoman, a crazy and angry woman, from a silence in which neither she nor her author [could] continue to acquiesce."[9]

The demure heroines of Victorian literature, it turned out, were less docile than they seemed; behind every angel in the house lurked a female demon, a monster of maniacal rage. The livid-faced creature who crawled on all fours, ripped apart a wedding veil, and burned down her husband's home was a powerful emblem of female protest, of a seething unconscious in revolt against the constraints of patriarchal culture. While in the drawing-room Victorian ladies poured tea and engaged in decorous conversation, unspeakable things were going on upstairs in the attic.

Feminist readings of "The Yellow Wallpaper" echoed this view of madness as a defiant response to the impossible constraints placed on women's lives. In Gilman's story we witness the mental deterioration of a woman diagnosed with mild hysteria and obligated to take a rest cure by her physician husband. Confined to her room and forbidden to engage in intellectual activity, she begins to see a woman creeping about behind the strange, disturbing pattern of the wallpaper. Finally, she imagines both of them tearing down the wallpaper to emerge triumphantly into freedom. The growing derangement of the heroine, as expressed in her hallucinatory visions and increasingly incoherent prose, was translated into the inchoate voice of female protest. Women's madness, critics agreed, was a logical response to the irrationality of patriarchal rule. "In her mad-sane way," concludes Elaine Hedges, Gilman's protagonist "has seen the situation of women for what it is. . . . Madness is her only freedom."[10]

But the madwoman is not just everywoman but also, more importantly, the woman writer. For Gilbert and Gubar, she reflects that part of the author's self that is in silent yet seething revolt against the patriarchal chains that bind her. The madwoman, they write, "is usually in some sense the *author's* double, an image of her own anxiety and rage."[11] In this way, *The Madwoman in the Attic* recasts Victorian women authors as protofeminists, unconsciously rebelling against their own confinement. With a stroke of the pen, Victorian literature was cast in a new light. A literary tradition often associated with antimacassars and overstuffed sofas, stifling decorum and fusty gentility, was suddenly awash with subversive energies, seething desires, and feminine rage.

Through this bold act of rereading, Gilbert and Gubar laid the foundations for their feminist literary history. In the opening pages of their book, they take on Harold Bloom's influential theory of poetic creation, conceived as a tormented act of Oedipal struggle to throw off the influence of mighty precursors. Such a framework, Gilbert and Gubar claim, simply does not hold true for female writers. Bereft of confidence and lacking authority, they do not seek to defy and overcome their literary foremothers. Rather, they look for encouragement and inspiring example, seeking for female precursors who have successfully defied patriarchal prohibitions.

In fact, Gilbert and Gubar's view of the essential dynamic of female creativity may tell us more about the political exigencies of a certain historical moment. By depicting Victorian writers as seething rebels rather than moral guardians, as maimed victims of patriarchy rather than prim and censorious foremothers, they created precursors very much after their own heart. Their description of Victorian women struggling against a repressive society to find their true selves often made these women sound remarkably like American feminists of the 1970s.

Of course, in the case of "The Yellow Wallpaper" in particular, imagining a feminist consciousness behind the text was hardly a stretch. Gilman was a prominent speaker and writer actively engaged in the struggle for women's rights. Yet at the time of its first publication "The Yellow Wallpaper" was read as a horror story, a Poe-like tale of a respectable woman's descent into madness. Not until the 1970s did critics begin to read it as an allegory of the female condition. The meaning of Gilman's story was dramatically transformed. A spine-chilling story of delirium and the supernatural turned into a parable of the social conditions that can drive all women insane. "The Yellow Wallpaper" became legible in a new way, as an autobiographical account not just of Gilman's own rest cure but of the psychic and social condition of the female author. What had once been strange and uncanny now became a "feminist document."[12]

The attic rooms that house Brontë's and Gilman's madwomen are resonant symbolic spaces. These rooms stand for the constraints placed on female mobility and freedom; they are graphic reminders of the places off limits to women who are consigned to the margins of culture and the periphery of the father's house. The madwoman locked up in the attic was both an echo and a grotesque parody of the Victorian middle-class woman fettered by femininity and trapped in the suffocating confines of the drawing room. The home was a patriarchal fortress, a house of torment that disabled and often destroyed its female captives. "Almost all nineteenth-century women," write Gilbert and Gubar, "were in some sense imprisoned in men's houses."[13] The words of other critics are equally adamant. To be female in the nineteenth century was to be assigned to the status of "domestic slave," to belong to an "entire class of defeated, or even destroyed women."[14]

Female confinement is, of course, symbolic as well as literal. Imprisoned in male houses, women are also locked inside the forbidding edifice of a masculine culture. Images of enclosure carry particular resonances for the female author; they remind her of her own crushing sense of paralysis in the face of an alien and alienating tradition. The world of literature and culture is a resoundingly patriarchal world, offering women only false echoes and distorted reflections of their real selves. Rattling the bars of her cage, the Victorian writer cannot break free of male-defined literary conventions to imagine an autonomous female reality. But she is able nonetheless to fashion secret messages and surreptitiously subvert male truths. The figure of the madwoman is one such cipher, a hidden message or palimpsest that lies beneath the reassuring veneer of Victorian literary conventions.

"The Yellow Wallpaper" is a particularly inviting terrain for meditations on the straits of the woman writer. Gilbert and Gubar, for example, refer to a "paradigmatic tale which (like *Jane Eyre*) seems to tell *the* story that all literary women would tell if they could speak their 'speechless woe.'" Annette Kolodny speaks of the story as a "fictive rendering of the dilemma of the woman writer."[15] Gilman's story is told in first-person form, as the heroine records in her journal the stages of her gradual decline into madness. She must do so in secret, for her husband, seemingly solicitous of her health, has forbidden her to work. The very act of writing is thus intimately linked to stealth, subterfuge, and the defiance of male authority. The broader symbolism of such a scenario is easily retrieved. Men seek to control women's words, to bar them from writing their own reality. They literally cannot understand what women are trying to say, dismissing their words as comical, foolish, or insane. Yet in the act of writing, the narrator defies this patriarchal sentence and exposes the arrogance and obtuseness of male authority. In an act of covert triumph, she becomes the author of her own text.

From these readings of *Jane Eyre* and "The Yellow Wallpaper" we can get a good sense of how some early feminist critics viewed the female author. First of all, they agree that women have been sentenced to live in a pervasively masculine world. The artifacts of language and literature, history and culture have all been fashioned by men in order to enforce male interests and secure men's power over women. To be female, then, is to experience a condition of exile. It is to be stranded in a state of existential homelessness. Women's literal and symbolic homes are patriarchal institutions designed to keep them in a state of tutelage. Women are ineluctably marked as lesser beings, demoted to the status of children, prisoners, invalids, domestic chattel.

The grim, ubiquitous reality of male domination silences other voices, preventing any expression of women's distinctive experience as women. It ruthlessly frustrates their aspirations toward an autonomous, self-defined identity. This failure has traumatic consequences. The contradictions of patriarchal culture are writ large on women's bodies, expressed in psychic and physical symptoms. Madness is a logical response to the impossible condition of being female; female disease echoes and exposes the pathology of a male-authored culture.

The deep-rooted alienation of the female psyche in turn leaves its marks in women's writing, which provides a key to the truth of female experience. At first glance, this writing may appear to condone and even to endorse traditional views about men and women. But read correctly, it will yield compelling evidence of the author's struggle to find a real self behind the "copy selves" of patriarchal culture. The true meaning of women's writing lies beneath the surface, in covert messages and submerged clues. Because this meaning is socially unacceptable and even subversive, it is buried deep within the text. The feminist critic is involved in a project of excavation, burrowing through the layers of language to uncover muffled traces of female identity and desire. She is able to retrieve these subterranean messages because of her kinship with the female author. Her own experience as a woman renders her an ideal reader of women's texts, allowing her to decipher the covert marks of the female psyche.

This kind of reading is by now very familiar; in fact, in the popular imagination, it is often seen as more or less synonymous with what feminists do. It is also, I've found, the default setting of many undergraduates who express any interest in feminist ideas. Among feminist scholars, however, the once irresistible metaphor of the madwoman has lost its luster. Giving the lie to Gilbert and Gubar's view of intense sympathy and affiliation among women writers, feminist critics have vigorously contested the metaphor of the madwoman as the key to female authorship.

Let me briefly list some of these objections, which span the realms of both aesthetics and politics. One popular target was the claim that the madwoman in the attic was the symbol of everywoman under patriarchy. Thinking about the many differences between women and the impact of race and class on the fate of the Victorian heroine soon made it clear that such a thesis did not stand up. For example, describing

Bertha Mason as Jane Eyre's repressed self and "dark" double meant turning a blind eye to the colonial themes of the text. Rochester's wife is, after all, a creole woman brought over to England from the West Indies, not just a facet of Jane's psyche. This monstrous figure of colonial otherness must perish, remarks Gayatri Spivak, "so that Jane Eyre can become the feminist individualist heroine of British fiction."[16] Seeing Brontë's novel as an allegory of universal womanhood became much less plausible once feminist critics began to consider its very different treatment of women of different races.

Women's lives in the nineteenth century were also divided by the realities of class. For example, middle-class women were restricted by their economic dependency on fathers and husbands as well as the rigid social and behavioral norms of their milieu. Yet they could also exercise a certain moral authority and cultural influence in domestic, and sometimes in public, life. The ruling ideologies of Victorian life were by no means purely masculine, nor were women of the period as constrained and helpless as Gilbert and Gubar made out. Thus we now have a large body of feminist work that looks closely at middle-class women's power and their involvement in various forms of moral regulation and social surveillance, including their earnest attempts to educate but also to discipline and control women of the working class.[17]

Some feminist scholars were also wary of the madwoman as an example of a feminist monomyth. They were troubled by what they saw as a flattening out of literary ambiguity, a zealous desire to impose a single framework and a false coherence onto a many-voiced and many-sided history of women's writing. Mary Jacobus suggested that reading "The Yellow Wallpaper" as a document of nineteenth-century sexual politics meant turning a blind eye to its disturbing and uncanny powers as a work of Gothic fiction. Susan Lanser, in an important argument that yoked together aesthetic and political critique, claimed that the allegory of the madwoman had exhausted itself. In their relentless pursuit of a single truth of women's lives and women's writing, she argued, feminist critics had overlooked many of the subtleties of the texts they were analyzing. Using literature as a mirror for their own sense of self, they were oblivious to the many other meanings that literary works might hold.[18]

Rather than rehearsing the details of these disputes, however, I want to turn to two more allegories of female authorship. All such allegories are unstable: they are not factual descriptions but imaginative leaps, bold attempts to conjure into being a visionary parable of female creativity. When they are successful, such images can be richly suggestive, illuminating a body of work with a burst of light that makes everything fall into place. Yet this revelatory power often wanes with the passing of time. How could I ever have thought *that*? a critic may wonder, looking back at what seems in retrospect like a lackluster set of ideas. The canon of feminist criticism is not just a history of changing politics but a revealing record of the rise and fall of metaphors.

Masquerading Women

A short story by Colette illustrates my next allegory of authorship remarkably well. "The Hidden Woman" is told from the viewpoint of a doctor who is attending a masquerade ball. His respectable wife has declined the invitation to accompany him with a delicate shudder of disgust. "Oh, no! Can you see me in a crowd, all those hands . . . What can I do? It's not that I'm a prude, it's . . . it makes my skin crawl."[19]

Gazing idly around him at opulent expanses of bared flesh and costumed couples locked in amorous embrace, the doctor glimpses a masked Pierrot in tunic and pantaloons who has the same cough, the same gestures as his wife. Could it really be Irene? Did she lie to him about wanting to attend the ball? Because he too has engaged in subterfuge (he is supposed to be at the sickbed of a patient), he dare not confront her. And can this Pierrot, with its free and uninhibited movements, really be his respectable wife? Is she there to meet someone? Distraught, he decides to watch and pursue her, sure that she is at the ball for the purposes of a sexual assignation. "She's here for someone, with someone. In less than an hour I'll know everything" (236).

The female Pierrot slips easily and nonchalantly through the crowd, like a knife blade slipping into its sheath, as the bewildered doctor stumbles awkwardly after her, tripping over the skirts of his domino costume. She allows herself to be imprisoned by anonymous arms and surrenders to multiple embraces. She yields, laughing, to the weight of an almost naked wrestler, dances silently with a warrior clad in iron only to abandon him once the music comes to an end. After pausing calmly to observe what is going on around her, she amuses herself by placing her hands on the throat of a nervous Dutch girl. Bumping into a handsome young man, she leans over and kisses his panting, half-open mouth.

By this point, the husband has given up hope. "Dismayed, he no longer feared, he no longer hoped for betrayal" (237). He realizes that there is no assignation, that his wife does not know any of the people that she is embracing. The story ends with the following words:

> He was sure that she was not waiting or looking for anyone, that the lips she held beneath her own like a crushed grape, she would abandon, leave again the next minute, then wander about again, gather up some other passer-by, forget him, until she felt tired and it was time to go back home, tasting only the monstrous pleasure of being alone, free, honest, in her native brutality, of being the one who is unknown, forever solitary and without shame, whom a little mask and a hermetic costume had restored to her irremediable solitude and her immodest innocence. (237–38)

Colette's story comes together around a series of eloquent silences, absences, and blank spaces. Most obviously, it is not told from a woman's point of view; it reveals nothing of Irene's motives, feelings, or thoughts. This refusal to divulge her secrets is, of course, the point of the narrative: the woman of the title remains hidden. The author purposefully refrains from entering her mind. All that we know about her we learn from the perspective of her husband; yet he, jealous, confused, and clearly at sea, is not a voice to be trusted. The male view of women is undermined, yet we are offered no alternative. Woman remains an enigma; she resists interpretation.

The masquerade ball is a place set apart from the humdrum routines of everyday life. From the opening lines of the story the stage is set for promiscuous pleasures, chaotic confusion, and a dreamlike dissolution of boundaries. The exhilarating freedom of the mask allows the rules of gender and sexuality to be turned upside down. Irene is robed in pantaloons and wears a lacy beard; prowling, autonomous, and free, she slices through the crowd like a knife or an eel. Her husband is hobbled, womanlike, by his anxiety and insecurity and his domino skirts. Gender confusion brings sexual ambiguity in its wake; when Irene dressed as a man flits from a man's to a woman's embrace, what exactly are we witnessing? The lines between same-sex and heterosexual desire, be-

tween the normal and the perverse, are exploded by the free-floating
eroticism of the masquerade.

Clearly, it is the anomalous space of carnival that sanctions this
erotic license and gender play. After the excesses of the ball, respectable
citizens return once again to their mundane, everyday routines. Yet the
distinctions between carnival and everyday life are less evident than
they seem. Masquerade, Colette's story suggests, is not just something
that happens at balls and parties. The everyday life of a doctor's wife is
also a disguise, an elaborate performance of genteel, middle-class femininity. Should we conclude, with the husband, that this performance
has been a sham all along, that the liberating anonymity of the mask allows woman's true nature to finally reveal itself? Or does Colette's
story undermine the very idea of female nature, blurring the lines between real and fake, everyday life and masquerade?

One argument in support of the latter view is that Colette's story relentlessly chips away at the husband's viewpoint. He stands for what
poststructuralist critics like to call logocentrism, the belief in a final, definitive truth. The story is propelled forward by his burning desire to
know. He hopes to expose his wife's adultery, if only because this discovery will provide a tangible, understandable motive for her actions.
His desire for certainty is treated with irony in the story, yet it is an uncomfortable irony that implicates the reader rather than allowing her
to feel superior. For the doctor's desire is also our own; we too are im-
pelled to read on, eager to discover the truth, our curiosity provoked by
an intriguing narrative puzzle. Why is Irene at the ball? What is she
looking for? What are her thoughts and feelings? Like her husband, we
are anxious for the mystery to be cleared up. Feminist critics, as we have
seen, often have a particular stake in trying to sound out the depths of
the female psyche. But Colette toys with her readers, refusing to satisfy
our desire to know. She parades before us a dazzling array of surfaces,
images, and masks, but offers no final resolution. Instead of the truth of
woman, we are left only with woman-as-sign.

In her influential manifesto "The Laugh of the Medusa," first published in English in 1976, Hélène Cixous cites Colette as one of the rare
practitioners of feminine writing. Cixous, like some other well-known
"French feminists," is not interested in solving the question of female
identity. The American obsession with discovering the self and using

literature as therapy is often a target of Parisian disdain. Men have persistently sought to pin down woman, to say what she is and should be. To be female is to be a saintly and self-sacrificing mother, a seductive Siren, a monstrous Medusa. It is to be frozen into a deathlike state, as a passive reflection of male desire. A revolutionary feminine writing, claims Cixous, must explode identity rather than reflect it, subvert coherence and the desire for truth, liberate an inexhaustible flood of writing. "If woman has always functioned 'within' the discourse of man . . . it is time for her to dislocate this 'within,' to explode it, turn it around, and seize it; to make it hers, containing it, taking it in her own mouth, biting that tongue with her very own teeth to invent for herself a language to get inside of."[20]

Taken together, Colette's story and Cixous's manifesto point to an alternative vision of female authorship that luxuriates in poetic language and reveals a sensual fascination with the forms, sounds, and textures of words. Writing is a shifting, dazzling, seductive veil rather than a window into the female soul. It is not a record of selfhood so much as a graphic reminder of the fragile, mutable, and uncertain nature of identity. Here, writing speaks of desire and eros rather than truth; it is utopian rather than realistic, visionary rather than pragmatic, shamelessly flouting the rules of reason and common sense. "Writing is precisely *the very possibility of change*, the space that can serve as a springboard for subversive thought, the precursory movement of a transformation of social and cultural structures."[21] A feminine writing, according to Cixous, draws on the resources of poetic language to explode identity into endless fragments, contradictions, ambiguities. It does not express femaleness but permanently calls it into question. This writing, like Colette's story, cannot be pinned down; its slippery surface repels interpretation and refuses to deliver up tidy nuggets of meaning for the reader's consumption.

The shimmering richness of feminine writing is also open to the pleasures of bisexuality. Cixous imagines a fruitful interplay of masculine and feminine as highly charged differences jostling against each other that are not canceled out in a bland androgyny. Whereas men cling to their "glorious phallic monosexuality," Cixous writes, women are far more willing to embrace sexual ambiguity.[22] This theme is, of course, central to Colette's story; Irene smoothly crosses the boundaries of sex and gender, whereas the doctor, grounded in the world of science and rational knowledge, is "not good at playacting," out of his depth in the polymorphous perversity of the masquerade. We see Cixous's idea of bisexuality even more clearly in Colette's own writing strategy, her decision to masquerade as a man by adopting a male viewpoint.

This female mimicry of a male perspective reads not as a concession of defeat, a sign of women's entrapment in a male world, but as a sly unraveling of male authority. Imitation, in other words, can be ironic rather than subservient. Indeed, some writers believe that women are uniquely gifted at this kind of subversive mimicry. Trained in the rules of femininity, accustomed to "putting on a face," to presenting themselves for the gaze of others, they know full well that gender is a product of art rather than nature.[23] Women, in this light, are artful and self-conscious, highly adept at role-playing and performance. And this in turn links them to the realm of art and poesis, now redefined as a place of masquerade and metaphor, of endlessly shifting and mutating meanings. Rather than being a bastion of male power, literary works can subvert that power, playing fast and loose with our common-sense notions of gender. Authorship allows women to inhabit different identities, to perform multiple selves, to view the world from both male and female perspectives. No longer confined to the attic, the female writer emerges in stylish new garb as artful trickster and sublime parodist.

This view of authorship as a kind of sexy masquerade received a boost in the last ten years, thanks to the advent of queer theory and the remarkable popularity of Judith Butler's work. Butler's dense and difficult meditations have often been compressed into the catchy and portable slogan of "gender as performance." It soon became a truism of cutting-edge theory that gender was a "regulatory fiction" and that the most subversive thing anyone could do was to expose the fragility of that fiction. Butlerites have been fond of asserting that our notions of male and female are groundless, that is to say, not anchored in any psychological or biological reality. Gender, they claimed, is nothing but language; it is all surface, no depth. Parody was the perfect way of exposing the artificiality of gender, revealing sexual nature to be highly unnatural.

Butler's often cited example of parody was drag. Rather than being a failed copy of a real man or woman, she argued, the person in drag allows us to realize that gender is skin-deep, a copy without an original. In this scenario, we are all male or female impersonators, straining to approximate a nonexistent ideal. "Drag," writes Butler, "constitutes the mundane way in which genders are appropriated, theatricalized, worn and done; it implies that all gendering is a kind of impersonation and approximation . . . there is no original or primary gender that drag imitates, but *gender is a kind of imitation for which there is no original.*"[24] Drag has, of course, close links to gay subcultures, and Butler's corrosive skepticism toward gender was linked to a relentless questioning of heterosexuality as a code word for the natural, the normal, the real. Dividing human beings into "opposite sexes," seeing maleness and femaleness as the most essential attributes of our humanity, were signs of the largely invisible, taken-for-granted and all-encompassing reach of the heterosexual imperative. Gay men and lesbians were always at odds with gender, aware of their failure to fit the standard scripts of male and female behavior.

The point was not, however, to celebrate an alternative gay or lesbian identity; it was certainly not to argue, as some feminists had done, that the lesbian was the quintessential woman-identified woman. In Butler's view, affirming identity always led to the policing of identities and attempts to regulate and control the richly varied spectrum of human behaviors and desires. The aim of queer theory was to work against the grain of categories and classes, to unravel the distinctions between male and female, gay and straight. What seemed like distinct and exclusive modes of being, queer theorists argued, were inextricably entangled and mutually dependent. The chaotic mix of fantasies, identifications, and desires constantly surged over tidy borders and boundaries. Polymorphous perversity threatened the stability of identity.

With this allegory of authorship as masquerade came a dazzling new array of literary exemplars. Modernist and postmodernist fiction, rather than the Victorian novel, were now mined for the new truth of gender—the truth that there is no truth, that femininity is a fragile fiction, that gender is nothing but travesty, surface, and performance. Art was prized in good Nietzschean fashion because it knows what other forms of writing seek to repress: that language is a mirage, an endless chain of metaphors that lead only to other metaphors and that cannot tell us anything about an ultimate reality. The works most favored by feminist critics were those that wove a playful and self-conscious art-fulness into a probing exploration of the ontology of gender and sexuality.

For example, Virginia Woolf's gender-bending novel *Orlando*, which had once inspired lukewarm responses from feminists, now became a cult text. Drawing parallels between the subversion of gender and the artfulness of fiction, Mary Jacobus wrote: "The masquerade—Orlando's transvestite progress through the literary ages—is that of writing, where fictive and multiple selves are the only self, the only truth, the writer knows."[25] The writer was now reimagined as a kind of drag artist, endlessly trying on different genders, behaviors, and personalities.

Among contemporary writers, the works of British novelists Jeanette Winterson and Angela Carter were an ideal pairing for this kind of analysis; indeed, they often foreshadowed the ideas of their critics with remarkable prescience. Informed by feminist ideas, infused with a postmodern sense of the textuality of everything, such works of fiction reveled and gloried in the artifice of gender. Carter's *Nights at the Circus,* for example, is a effervescent celebration of the female performer, embodied in the massive and resplendent figure of Fevvers, the Victorian circus performer and winged *aérialiste*. At one point, a character in the novel reflects on "the freedom that lies behind the mask, within dissimulation, the freedom to juggle with being, and, indeed, with the language which is vital to our being."[26] Here was a perfect summary of the power and pleasures of performance.

Winterson's *Written on the Body*, in particular, was a heaven-sent gift for feminists influenced by queer theory. This novel is a highly self-conscious rendition of a love story, told with the clear-sighted knowledge that romantic love has become a cliché and originality an impossible dream. It is replete with elaborate literary conceits, knowing winks to the reader, bravura exercises in various rhetorical styles. What gives the book its distinctive hook is that we never find out the gender of the narrator. He/she is in love with the exquisitely beautiful, married, and dying Louise, but we never know for sure whether we are reading a heterosexual or a lesbian romance. At certain moments, the narrator's acts of sexual braggadocio point to a male Lothario; at other times, lesbian and feminist in-jokes makes it hard not see the narrator as female. This relentless seesawing invites readers to reflect on their own assumptions, to think about how they view men and women, straight couples and lesbians. *Written on the Body* is disconcerting because it shows how steadfastly we cling to the fiction of gender (how impossible it is to imagine a genderless narrator), yet it refuses to offer us a stable foothold for interpretation.[27]

What is most valuable about the feminist allegory of authorship as masquerade is that it leaves room for the "artness" of art and the skill of those who make it. Rather than reading all works by women as autobiography or therapy, it sees the writer as a shape-shifter, an artful creator of multiple selves. It pries apart the author and the text and insists that literature is not a slavish mirror of identity. Writing can reach beyond the dull facticity of the given; language can be worked against the grain in ways that are seductive, playful, irreverent, often unsettling. The elusiveness of words can call into question readers' attachments to knowable selves and coherent realities.

These attachments include feminism's own desire for tidy schemas, for consoling narratives of male villainy and female virtue. The meanings of gender are always more messy, ambiguous, and contradictory than this particular story will allow. Indeed, for those who favor an aesthetics of the mask, any claim to truth is a source of suspicion. Many-sidedness triumphs over singularity, poetic playfulness over preaching, psychic fluidity over identity. The author disappears behind her creations, leaving behind only her evocative yet enigmatic textual traces.

The best feminist work in this critical vein can be dazzling in its verbal dexterity and aesthetic sophistication. In less gifted hands, however, the allegory of masquerade can lapse into a relentless recycling of the same few clichés. Text X or Y enacts a radical destabilization of female identity, reveals gender as a cultural construction and an illusory performance, leads to a subversion of exclusionary normativity, deconstructs the oppressive binaries of bourgeois humanism. . . . We are faced with the paradox of what we might call the routinizing of transgression, as the idiom of rupture and subversion becomes daily grist for the academic mill, routine fodder for the graduate seminar, a means of accreditation for the aspiring assistant professor.

I am struck, too, by a certain unworldliness in some feminist readings of modernist or postmodernist literature, as aesthetic criteria are transposed without further ado into the realm of politics. One critic, for example, hails Jeanette Winterson's work as the model for a "feminist praxis that avoids the exclusionary normativity of proceeding from an assumed coherence of the category woman."[28] Experimental writing is raised to such dizzying heights for refusing to define, clarify, prioritize, or think in twos—all viewed as grievous intellectual sins in the wake of poststructuralism. The ambiguity and open-endedness of the literary text thus comes to epitomize the most subversive form of gender politics.

I suspect that no outsider could fail to be struck by the solipsism of such arguments, their inflation of the writer's—and the critic's—importance as experts on feminist praxis. Social change is about much more than parody and sexy subterfuge; endless reflection on the indeterminacy of meaning is likely to bring about paralysis rather than political action. By blurring crucial distinctions of purpose and context, the contemporary mantra of linguistic subversion often fails to do full justice to the demands of either politics or art. The metaphor of the masquerade is meant to challenge oppressive notion of a single, true, female identity; but this playful vision of constantly shifting surfaces can easily rigidify into a new form of intellectual and political orthodoxy.

Home Girls

"Home girls," claims Alvina Quintana, is "a universal trope for women of color in the United States."[29] As well as gracing the title of Quintana's own book on Chicana writers, the phrase brings to mind a well-known anthology edited by Barbara Smith. Discussing how she came to coin its title, Smith writes:

> One day, while doing something else entirely, and playing with words in my head, "home girls" came to me. The girls from the neighborhood and from the block, the girls we grew up with . . . critics of feminism pretend that just because some of us speak out about sexual politics *at home,* within the Black community, we must have sprung miraculously from somewhere else. But we are not strangers and never have been.[30]

"Home girls," here, is a forceful response to the charge that black women who speak out against sexism are traitors to their own communities. Rather, the women in Smith's book insist on a distinctive heritage of black feminism rooted in African American culture and history.

The pressure of politics affects the clarifying power of metaphor. That the madwoman in the attic fails dismally as an allegory of the black female author has everything to do with differing social realities. African American women were not seen as delicate, helpless creatures in need of protection; they were not fettered by the constraining norms of genteel femininity or imprisoned and sentenced to inactivity in the middle-class home. Inevitably, the images of paralyzing anxiety and isolation that define Gilbert and Gubar's portrayal of female authorship carries absolutely no resonance with black feminist critics.

Instead, we see an emphatic and abiding concern with maternal lineage: strong generational links between mothers and daughters are a recurring theme in both fiction and criticism. Whether symbolic or literal, these mothers often radiate a powerful and commanding presence. Critics often speak of a sense of confidence on the part of black women writers that stems from this maternal example. "Certainly there is a connection," writes Mary Helen Washington, "between the black woman writer's sense of herself as part of a link in generations of women, and her decision to write."[31]

The metaphor of "home girls" crystallizes this very different vision of the female author. It sees home and its offshoots, such as tradition, community, and maternal presence, as a source of solace and inspiration. Home is not a desolate patriarchal prison, nor the sign of an oppressive identity that must be endlessly unraveled through movement and masquerade. Home is open to resignification, pressured to yield different, more fruitful visions of female power and creativity. "It was undoubtedly at home," writes Barbara Smith, "that I learned the rudiments of black feminism."[32]

Against the solitary and singular madwoman, furthermore, home girls is a noun cast in the plural, invoking a vision of women at ease with other women. "Girl" can be a term of disparagement or even insult, but among friends, it bespeaks warmth, familiarity, a sense of being at home with others. As a phrase from colloquial black speech, moreover, "home girls" conveys a sense of directness and immediacy, invoking a circle of readers familiar with its use. Against the abstractness of femininity-as-sign, it speaks to the everyday, concrete, and familiar: women as sisters, mothers, friends, lovers, neighbors.

And yet metaphor and politics cannot be neatly disentangled. Settling on an appropriate image of creativity is not just a question of pointing to the solid and tangible "thereness" of black women's reality. The grittiness of politics is inseparable from the endless flux of interpretation. Like the other allegories in this chapter, figures of black female authorship are contested; the symbolism of home, tradition, and maternal lineage has been modified, questioned, and challenged in the rapidly expanding discourse on black women authors.

One striking feature of this discourse is the often close relations between writers and critics. The explosion of black women's writing in the last thirty years has occurred roughly in tandem with the development of black feminist criticism, and the boundaries between creative and critical work are often crossed. Some of the most influential statements of black feminist criticism—Alice Walker's "In Search of Our Mothers' Gardens," Toni Morrison's "Rootedness: The Ancestor as Foundation"—have been drafted by well-known novelists. Writers as well as critics have created influential allegories of the black female author.

How, then, does the theme of home connect to the question of black female creativity, and in particular literary creativity? Smith's *Home Girls*, to take one example, was published by the Kitchen Table/Women of Color Press. In this linking of the kitchen to the printing press, the domestic to the public, we see a bold refusal of certain familiar dichotomies. Thus the home is often invoked as an essential source and wellspring of black women's writing. Paule Marshall, for example, talks of listening to her mother and her mother's friends as they gathered together around the kitchen table after an exhausting day's work. She speaks of "the insight, irony, wit and their own special force which they brought to everything they discussed; above all, their poet's skill with words. They had taken a language imposed upon them, and infused it with their own incisive rhythms and syntax . . . They were, in other words, practicing art of a high order."[33]

Here we see a very different vision of both home and art. Home is not, as a generation of white, middle-class feminists would have it, a space of female desolation and silent despair: rather, it is where black women gather together for welcome communion and respite from exhausting labor. It is a refuge and sanctuary rather than a prison. "Home," writes Smith, "has always meant a lot to people who are ostracized as racial outsiders in the public sphere."[34] Rather than a zone of solitary confinement, it is a welcoming space where friends, family, and neighbors gather together and where generations meet. And it is above all at home that tongues run free, that wit sparkles and the imagination soars in the endless telling and retelling of stories.

The stories exchanged between women, and above all, the power of the mother's voice, are an often invoked model for the black female writer. Alice Walker notes that "many of the stories that I write, that we all write, are my mother's stories."[35] Mary Helen Washington speaks of black female writers "assuming the voices of their mothers" and "signing their mother's name."[36] Marshall pays tribute to the eloquence of the stories overheard in her mother's kitchen, declaring "I grew up among poets."[37] In this allegory of authorship, then, women speak to other women in an intergenerational chain of cultural transmission. The mother is the source of language; she puts the words into one's mouth. The word does not come from the father, bearing the mark of patriarchal law. Rather, language is the mother tongue; it springs from the mouths of women. Hence to be "at home" is to be securely housed in language rather than alienated from it. It is to be conscious of a rich and sustaining oral tradition, of the power of language wielded with skill and dexterity by women.

To recognize the artistic impulses that express themselves in everyday life is thus to bring to light a tradition of black female creativity. The history of black women is not just a story of absence from the canons and pantheons of high culture but also of an achieved presence in the arts of the everyday. This is, of course, the theme of "In Search of Our Mothers' Gardens," which evokes the pain of generations of black women unable to become artists, "who died with their real gifts stifled within them." But Alice Walker also describes the astonishing achievement of beauty in the midst of cramped and impoverished circumstances. The lush magnificence of her mother's garden reveals a masterful grasp of color, design, and form; in the patterns of an ancient quilt, Walker sees the sign of "an artist who left her mark in the only materials she could afford, and in the only medium her position in society allowed her to use."[38]

Walker's essay is a powerful expression of indebtedness and affiliation. The daughters who become writers, who seize hold of the new opportunities unavailable to their mothers, remain deeply obligated to the power of maternal example. So, too, Walker suggests, their writing continues to draw on the creative energies and traditions of everyday life. Art is not something cut off from the world, the province of a small and educated elite. Rather, black feminist critics often question the division between "high" and "low," insisting on black literature's closeness to the expressive beauty and power of popular forms. Aesthetics, argues bell hooks, has been an integral element of black everyday life, a necessity for survival. She writes: "art was necessary to bring delight, pleasure and beauty into lives that were hard, that were materially deprived. It mediated the harsh conditions of poverty and servitude. Art was also a way to escape one's plight."[39]

One way of exploring the aesthetics of everyday life is by drawing attention to the power and beauty of ordinary language. "Perhaps the proper measure of a writer's talent," writes Paule Marshall, is a "skill in rendering everyday speech," as well as an "ability to tap, to exploit, the beauty, poetry and wisdom it often contains."[40] Rather than seeing literature as requiring a deliberate distortion or defamiliarization of everyday speech, the black woman writer often looks to the language of hearth and home for inspiration. Yet here it is not a question of choosing the quotidian over the poetic, but rather of challenging such a dichotomy by highlighting the hidden poetry of everyday life. Marshall, for example, lists the rich rhetorical devices that shaped the women's talk she used to overhear in the kitchen.

> They had taken the standard English language . . . and transformed it into an idiom, an instrument that more adequately described them—changing around the syntax and imposing their own rhythm and accent so that the sentences were more pleasing to their ears. They added the few African sounds and words that had survived. . . . And to make it more vivid, more in keeping with their expressive quality, they brought to bear a raft of metaphors, parables, Biblical quotations, sayings and the like.[41]

A great deal has been written on how black women's literature strives to emulate the grain and texture of the spoken word. Susan Willis, for example, talks about the importance of anecdote as a structuring device, echoing the informal patterns of everyday speech; black women's writing strives, she suggests, to reproduce a traditional, communal, and noncommodified relationship to language.[42] To tell stories is, of course, not just to transmit knowledge or information; it is also to express a particular form of kinship between speaker and listener. Toni Morrison evokes this idea when she writes of the emotional power of black art, its ability to create "an affective and participatory relationship between the artist or speaker and the audience."[43] A novel, she suggests, should buttonhole its readers and move them powerfully like the oratory of a preacher; it should inspire them to feel, to change, and to cry.

In this allegory of writing, then, the author is imagined as fully present in her speech. Her voice is not that of a madwoman locked up in a patriarchal fortress nor is she a fleeting, enigmatic trace masked by ambiguous and self-subverting layers of language. Instead, she is firmly anchored within a language, a culture, and a powerful maternal history. The titles of discussions of black women's writing in the 1980s often highlighted this theme, stressing key words such as heritage, community, rootedness, matrilineage, tradition. Yet, as some scholars recognized, the treatment of such themes in the fiction of black women was by no means straightforward. Rather than simply celebrating tradition, they also explored its many tensions and ambiguities.

These themes of separation and connection, of home and away, are beautifully explored in Alice Walker's "Everyday Use," a superbly constructed story that has much to say about the complexities of home and tradition. It considers and contrasts the fate of two sisters. Dee is stylish, confident, ambitious, ashamed of her rural origins and desperate to escape her poverty-stricken background by going to college. Maggie is the timid, awkward daughter who stays home, fearful and envious of her bolder sister. In the story, narrated from the mother's viewpoint, we witness Dee's triumphant return home from college to visit her sister and mother. She is almost unrecognizable, dressed in a dashiki, wearing an Afro and equipped with a new African name and a Muslim boyfriend. Black nationalism is now the rage on college campuses and Dee is suddenly eager to affirm and celebrate her racial heritage.

This emerging culture of black pride also causes Dee to see her old home with new eyes. The humble shack that was once a source of shame now seems quaint and delightful; like a tourist, she snaps pictures of the place she couldn't wait to leave. She eagerly snatches up handmade artifacts to take and display on her coffee table. She now delights in the folkloric charm of her origins. But when Dee tries to pick up some handmade quilts (quilts that she had earlier disdained for being old-fashioned), her mother balks.

> "The truth is," I said, "I promised to give these quilts to Maggie, for when she marries John Thomas."
>
> She gasped like a bee had stung her.
>
> "Maggie can't appreciate these quilts!" she said. "She'd probably be backward enough to put them to everyday use."[44]

In snatching the quilts out of Dee's hands and returning them to Maggie, the mother makes a judgment, a judgment that the story as a whole seems to endorse. Maggie has learned to quilt from Grandma Dee and Big Dee; she knows about the people and the stories behind the ordinary things that surround her. She deserves the quilts, precisely because she will put them to everyday use. Dee, by contrast, is not immersed in tradition but views it from outside. She relates to her past through modish, secondhand ideas about blackness that she has picked up at college. She turns useful everyday things into works of art and objects of display, wrenching them out of their immediate, lived context. To aestheticize something in this way, Walker's story seems to suggest, is to rob it of its soul.

Readings of Walker's story have tended to support this view. Houston Baker and Charlotte Pierce-Baker, in particular, read Walker's story in starkly antithetical terms. "The stylish daughter's entire life has been one of 'framed' experience," they write; "she has always sought a fashionable 'aesthetic' distance from southern expediencies." They go on to dismiss Dee as a sellout and a fake, her phony Afrocentrism a creation of Western media and fashion systems rather than an authentic indigenous history. Instead, Baker and Pierce-Baker praise the rural folk tradition that is embodied in the "earth-rooted and quotidian" sister Maggie. The message is clear, they claim. "Not 'art,' then, but use or function is the signal in Walker's fiction of sacred creation."[45] The realness of black culture, they suggest, stems from its rootedness in everyday life.

What Baker and Pierce-Baker fail to notice, however, is that in expressing such sentiments they are talking very much like Dee. That is to say, they are framing a form of life, reading black culture as a symbol of the authentic, indigenous, homespun. In fact, what is so interesting about Walker's story is that it places the reader in a difficult position. She cannot side with Dee, whose take on the world is shown to be superficial and self-satisfied. But if she concludes that the uneducated and inarticulate Maggie must therefore stand for a more genuine form of black identity, she falls into the trap of reiterating Dee's own brand of romantic nostalgia. The older daughter, after all, does not idealize just Africa, but also her own rural origins; the distance afforded by a college education bestows a retrospective patina of quaintness onto the grinding reality of childhood poverty. Thus romantic visions of folk culture, Walker's story makes clear, do not come from those who actually inhabit that culture. To enthuse about quilts, oral traditions, and rural life as symbols of organic community is to do so, by default, from a position of distance. The growing emphasis on authentic racial heritage, suggests Valerie Smith, is not unrelated to black anxieties about becoming middle class.[46]

In fact, both the author and most potential readers of this story are much closer to Dee than they are to Maggie. Walker's own story clearly transcends the taken-for-grantedness of everyday use. It is taught in seminars and writing classes, subject to scrutiny, weighted with exemplary and symbolic meaning. Both author and reader are implicated in the very artfulness that the story seems to call into question. "Everyday Use" thus casts an ironic light on its own reception, underscoring the ways in which attitudes to black women's culture—whether stories or quilts—are shaped by the politics of class and education. So, too, Alice Walker's own success as a writer is largely due to the very influences that her story places in a critical light: the growing interest in black identity and culture in universities, the media, and similar institutions.

Mary Helen Washington is one of the few critics to note this paradox, and hence to recognize the anxiety and ambivalence of "Everyday Use." "Like Dee," she writes, "Walker leaves the community, appropriating the oral tradition in order to turn it into a written artifact, which will no longer be available for 'everyday use' by its originators. Everywhere in the story the fears and self-doubt of the woman artist are revealed."[47] The daughter's return to the mother is treated here with a robust skepticism, as the daughter who flaunts her roots turns out to be indifferent and insensitive to her own kin. Mothers and daughters distanced by class and education do not always speak the same language; the insistence on generational continuity may conceal harsher realities of separation and estrangement. To want to return home, after all, is to reveal that one has already left; any original unity has been definitively ruptured. Tradition, as Deborah McDowell remind us, is a multivalent word; it may speak of invention, movement, and re-creation rather than simply of sameness and stasis.[48]

In fact, some critics have forcefully criticized the idea of a single black female tradition and challenged the desire to anchor black women's writing in an idealized folk idiom. Such an idea, according to Hortense Spillers, Hazel Carby, Ann duCille, and Valerie Smith, denies the essential modernity of black women's writing as well as its many borrowings from other genres, cultures, and traditions. It downplays the literary and often highly self-conscious elements of black women's art. And it may result in the creation of narrow and prescriptive canons, where authors such as Zora Neale Hurston and Alice Walker are sanctified while other writers whose work does not comfortably fit into the mold of authentic southern rural blackness are dismissed or ignored.[49]

Other critics have sought to replace "roots" with "routes," to espouse a very different language of mobility, travel, and migration. Carole Boyce Davies, for example, conceives of black women's writing as a series of boundary crossings, a way of unsettling ethnic and spatial divisions. Carving out a more expansive definition of such writing that includes the work of Caribbean and African as well as African American women, Boyce Davies argues that home is not a safe place but rather a fraught place for women of color excluded from the dominant myths of race and nation. Her vision of the black woman writer as a "migratory subject" lays stress on hybridity and fracture rather than wholeness and authenticity; this writer is restless and often unhoused, caught between competing cultural traditions and imperatives rather than firmly rooted in any one.[50]

Davies draws on the work of Gloria Anzaldúa, one of the founding figures of Chicana feminism. Anzaldúa constantly invokes a sense of fluidity and fragmentation, describing the woman of color as a border crosser living in multiple worlds. The *mestiza,* she writes, is plagued by psychic restlessness; she straddles cultures, is forced to confront contradiction, to accept and even rejoice in ambiguity. She is multilingual, speaking in many tongues in order to articulate her sense of multiple allegiances and ambiguous, often contradictory, forms of inheritance. And in direct contrast to the image of the "home girl," punning off her own lesbian sexuality, Anzaldúa writes of her own "home-ophobia: fear of going home."[51] Clearly, not all women of color are equally eager to celebrate home as a universal symbol of female creativity.

Writing Women and "The Woman Writer"

By this point, the reader is surely asking herself: why have these various allegories of authorship carried so much weight in the history of feminism? Why have critics sought so eagerly for an overarching metaphor that can sum up the essence of a body of writing? Clearly, the issue of visibility is key: a striking image is a way of pulling together individual works into a coherent grouping, of highlighting distinctive traits that connect disparate texts. To identify a tradition is to place a body of writing on the map. But this does not fully explain why these images center on the figure of the author. Feminist allegories of authorship are best understood, I believe, as catering to a widespread hunger for countermyths of creativity. Faced with a tradition that has so often associated authorship with maleness, critics have sought to forge new images of female imaginative power. The force of such images is expressive rather than analytical; they crystallize a notion of the woman writer as the reader wishes her to be.

In other words, allegories of authorship are best read as speculative fictions or myths; they do not tell us anything very reliable about the motives, desires, or situations of actual female authors. This is not to deny that the allegories I've discussed make some sense as a way of highlighting common elements in a cluster of texts. The figure of the madwoman does throw some light on the constellation of *Jane Eyre* and some other Victorian novels; there are, indeed, affinities between Judith Butler's theories and the works of Jeanette Winterson; the metaphor of home resonates powerfully with some examples of black women's fiction. The problems arise when such findings are extended into an all-encompassing theory of authorship. It is here that the critic leaves herself open to the charge of reading with a predetermined agenda. Either she must reject out of hand all those writers who fail to fit her favorite theory, or she must try to cram a disparate body of writing into a very small box.

An obvious and increasingly common alternative is to opt for approaches that are more pluralistic, pragmatic, and piecemeal, that are more cautious about presuming what a woman writer must be. This means being attentive to the rich densities of literary and historical detail, open to the oddities of the special case, willing to leave room for the idiosyncratic, quirky, and ambiguous. And it means resisting any temptation to group literary works around moral poles of virtue versus villainy or political dichotomies of repression versus resistance. As Marianne Noble points out in an interesting feminist study of American sentimental novels: "Female sentimental authors were not simply victims who were silenced or forced to function as mouthpieces for patriarchal ideology, nor simply virtuous crusaders for truth and justice. . . . They had selfish desires, violent fantasies, contradictory ambitions, and competing identifications."[52]

In fact, there have always been scholars interested in female authors but skeptical about grand theories of female authorship. In the mid-1980s Judith Newton and Deborah Rosenfelt voiced their dissatisfaction with popular ways of talking about women's writing, complaining about a tendency to pit male domination against female powerlessness and virtue, to present women as both totally dominated and essentially good. They called for a more tough-minded feminism that would be willing to see women as both victims and agents, to address the many divisions of experience, ideology, and politics between women, and to replace a monolithic model of male power with a more nuanced account of how maleness is formed under intense ideological and social pressures, such that men of differing classes, races, and sexualities have very different access to power and privilege.

This multidimensional model of history and politics demands a different kind of literary method. Newton and Rosenfelt express their misgivings at attempts to read literary works as more or less transparent renditions of the female psyche, pointing out that all such works are enmeshed in complex webs of images, stories, myths, and beliefs that far exceed the boundaries of identity. And they also warn against the tendency to assume that women's writing is liberating or subversive;

not only do such arguments give too much credit to the power of language to change the world, but they pay scant attention to the ways in which literary meanings can change over time and in relation to different audiences and groups of readers. A materialist-feminist perspective, they conclude, offers a more complex, less tragic view of history. It

> encourages us to hold in our minds the both-ands of experience: that women at different moments in history have been both oppressed and oppressive, submissive and subversive, victim and agent, allies and enemies both of men and one another. Such an analysis prompts us to grasp at once the power of ideas, language and literature; their importance as a focus of ideological struggle; and their simultaneous embeddedness in and difference from the material conditions of our lives.[53]

One good example of such a method at work is Mary Poovey's *Uneven Developments: The Ideological Work of Gender in Mid-Victorian England*, published in 1988. Poovey sets out to explain how Victorians understood the distinction between men and women, what these terms meant in literature and in everyday life. Trawling through an extensive sampling of historical materials—parliamentary debates, medical lectures, periodicals—Poovey links readings of Victorian novels to a comprehensive rendering of their cultural milieu. She shows that the ideology of separate spheres (men venturing in the hurly-burly of public life, women guarding hearth and home) was influential but also shaky and unstable, that it was open to very different interpretations, and that men and women, including some Victorian feminists, could draw on such ideas to defend and further their own interests. Wary of generalizing and alert to the dangers of projecting present-day values onto women of the past, Poovey presents an admirably nuanced and multifaceted picture of the workings of gender in Victorian England.[54]

Newton and Rosenfelt also urged feminist critics to give up their search for a separate female literary tradition and to pay much more attention to the many forms of influence, borrowing, and interconnection between male and female writers. Until recently, the discourse of authorship has been primarily a discourse about female authors. As I've already noted, some feminist critics have always been interested in literature by men, but they tended to focus on the work itself rather than

the persona behind it. The variables and complexities of male authorship were rarely given serious attention.

This, too, is changing, partly because of a growing interest in the
subject of masculinity. As the study of women expands to consider
broader questions of gender, scholars are questioning the caricatures
and stereotypes of maleness that appeared in some early feminist work.
For example, in an important book that urges a conceptual overhaul of
the feminist project, Susan Stanford Friedman points out the problems
of pitting female writers against what she calls "a unitary foil" of male
authorship. While feminists have trumpeted differences between
women, they have paid much less attention to differences between
men. There is a need, she writes, to "think about women writers in relation to a fluid matrix instead of a fixed binary of male/female or mas-
culine/feminine. In so doing, the justification for focusing on women
loses its cogency. Instead, the interactional, relational, and situational
constituents of identity for both male and female writers should be
read together."[55] In a brief but dazzlingly suggestive sketch, Friedman
shows how such an approach can change our understanding of the history and politics of modernism, deftly tracing out the weblike matrix of
multiple affinities and differences between Joyce, Woolf, Lawrence, and
Rhys.

Rather than either killing the author or reading literary works as allegories of female authorship, feminist critics are now most likely to
opt for what Cheryl Walker calls a "third position." This view, she
writes, "does not naively assert that the author is an originating genius,
creating aesthetic objects outside of history, but does not diminish the
importance of difference and agency in the responses of women writers
to historical formations."[56] We can recognize that female authors have
themselves been authored—that is to say, shaped by a multiplicity of
social and cultural forces that exceed their grasp—without thereby
denying their ability to act and to create. Similarly, we can factor the
author into our readings of literary works without reducing literature
to autobiography or assuming that such links determine the meaning
of the work once and for all. Authorship is one strand in the weave of
the text rather than a magic key to unlocking its mysteries. The trick, as
Elaine Showalter puts it, is to avoid "over-feminization," the belief that
everything in women's writing can be explained by gender, as well as

"under-feminization," the complete neglect of signs of gender in women's texts.[57]

Writers themselves have often reacted angrily to acts of "over-feminization." In a book on several well-known American women poets, for example, Betsy Erkkila zeroes in on examples of conflict and dissent among these poets, questioning idealistic visions of sisterhood and calling attention to "acts of violence and violation that women have practiced among and against each other."[58] One theme that crops up in her work is the strenuous resistance of several of her subjects to being labeled a "female poet" or a "woman writer." Elizabeth Bishop, for example, was notorious for refusing to allow her work to be published in women-only anthologies and her antipathy to any kind of literary segregation.

One common feminist response was to shrug off such views as evidence of antifeminism or a retrograde attachment to art for art's sake. Authors, of course, are not the final experts on their own work, but if feminist critics wish to engage in dialogue with women writers rather than simply using them as foils for their own theories, they need to attend to their views. For example, such well-known writers as Margaret Atwood, Jeanette Winterson, and Joyce Carole Oates have often objected to being labeled as women writers and to what they perceive as feminist misreadings of their work. This response is surely a sign that they have found feminist perspectives too constraining, unable to accommodate their own desires to experiment with viewpoint, character, or form. To be classified as a woman writer is often to be pigeonholed as an authority on women's things, as only able to write about certain kinds of female experience. It is hardly surprising that writers would chafe at such a limiting of their artistic and intellectual aspirations.

Toril Moi has recently tackled this question at some length. She writes:

> Ever since feminism became part of public life, some women writers and painters (and so on) have felt that feminism is an ideology that locks women up in their particularized subjectivity. Opposing such versions of feminism, they have refused to be called "women writers" and "women painters." Feminists have usually agreed that there is something antifeminist about such a refusal to call oneself a woman, often responding by

accusing such women of being male-identified and sadly lacking in solidarity with their sex. But the fact is that women are right to refuse attempts to make their subjectivity out to be coextensive with their femininity.[59]

As Moi points out, this refusal does not mean, or should not mean, denying that one has a gender (or race or sexuality) in the misplaced hope of achieving a disembodied, impossible, "view from nowhere." Rather, it is a question of recognizing that one is a woman, but that is not all one is; that one's self—and one's art—is shaped but not fully termined by one's femaleness. Women writers have often suffered from being reduced to their sex; it is hardly surprising when they bridle at feminist readings of their work as coextensive with their gender.

Authors, of course, have a natural tendency to think of their own work as different and unique. Critics, by contrast, are often interested in the bigger picture; moving beyond the author's explanations and intentions, they look for patterns, conventions, and clusters of themes that span multiple works and can tell us something revealing about a certain sensibility, worldview, or historical moment. There is nothing wrong with reading in this way or with searching for signs of commonality in writing by women. Yet scholars must also be willing to admit the limits of their sample, the partiality of their explanations, the power of the counterexample, the texts that disprove the rule. Allegories of authorship can inspire and energize; they allow critics to rally around a powerful metaphor and to impose some provisional coherence onto a shifting sea of writing. But when such allegories turn into hard-and-fast assertions about how women do write or how women should write, their problems outweigh their potential usefulness. As feminist critics are coming to recognize, to prescribe what it means to be a female author is to do a disservice to the rich and unending variety of real female authors.

3

PLOTS

*Can the female self be
expressed through plot or
must it be conceived in
resistance to plot?*
GILLIAN BEER

FICTION means plot. From perfunctory potboilers to modernist masterpieces, novels rely on the bare bones of storytelling, on connections made across time, on one thing following another. Avant-garde writers have often flirted with the idea of plotless prose; surrealists, for example, hit on the idea of putting together piles of unbound pages that could be reshuffled at the whim of individual readers. Yet such experiments have proven to be little more than curiosities; the desire for narrative shows few signs of abating. Rather, old stories continue to beget new stories in endless chains of revision and repetition. Plot is an indispensable handle, a way of getting a grip on a large and nebulous mass of words. Because it holds a work together in so many ways, it is hard to know whether plot is a matter of form or content. The story supplies the structure of a work of fiction, its shape-giving skeleton, but it also gives us the heart and much of the meat of what we read.

Plots are ubiquitous not just in literature but in life. We are all raconteurs, our minds awash with anecdote and example. In the ebb and flow of daily talk, in coffee shops and kitchens, bars and bedrooms, we connect with others by trading stories (did you hear what happened to me yesterday?). But we may also be tempted to think of our life path as conforming to a larger pattern. The children absorbed in schoolyard games of playing pretend will grow into adults who still imagine their lives according to the rhythm of plot. Am I ambitious? Looking for love? Eager to discover my true self? All these desires come equipped with ready-made plotlines that can be snipped and shaped to fit my needs. Such scripts are magical and seductive, endowing the fleeting shadows of our lives with solidity and meaning. They weld fragments into wholes, sew scraps of fabric into larger pieces of cloth. Stories, writes Carolyn Steedman, are interpretative devices, powerful tools for making sense of our world and ourselves.[1]

It is hardly surprising, then, that feminist critics care so deeply about plot. To ask what stories are available for women is to pose a question relevant not just to literature but to life. Everyone knows that feminists scoff at Sleeping Beauty and Cinderella, that they complain about stories that turn women into trophies, freezing them into a state of passivity, waiting to be saved by a man. Let us do away with the old stories! was an early cry of feminism. Let us get rid of the sleeping princesses, evil stepmothers, seductive sirens, wicked witches, women frozen in glass coffins. Not to mention the blatant fiction of "they got married and lived happily ever after." For the world to change, new stories were necessary.

Except, of course, that stories do not vanish so obligingly at the wave of a wand. Many of the old plot patterns persist, often with surprising stubbornness and tenacity. We recognize this persistence by calling them myths. A myth, simply put, is a story that everyone knows. Myths are time capsules, stories that endure over centuries and that travel across cultural boundaries. "A myth," writes A. S. Byatt, "derives force from its endless repeatability."[2] Nowadays, some feminist scholars are willing to take myth more seriously. They are less likely to decry old stories as fraudulent falsehoods, to counterpose patriarchal myth against female reality. Many traditional plots, after all, appeal to women as well as to men. As Wendy Doniger points out, myths survive because they are polysemic, teeming with multiple meanings. What appear to be simple and straightforward tales can acquire very different resonances across periods and cultures. Myths are shape-shifters; they generate many variants of their basic plotline and often reveal very different faces in their endless retellings.[3]

George Steiner, for example, marvels at the staying power of Greek myths. "Is it so very difficult," he wonders, "to devise new 'stories'?"[4] To survey the history of Western culture is to encounter again and again a scant handful of often told tales. Antigone, Oedipus, Narcissus, Medea, Prometheus: these are the figures who have inspired endless dramas, novels, poems, and works of philosophy. Their stories survive, suggests Steiner, because of their remarkable economy and aesthetic power; they crystallize powerful psychic truths and elemental impulses in simple yet enigmatic form. Our lives differ unimaginably from those of the Greeks, yet we remain their epigones, still beholden to the stories they have bequeathed us.

For Steiner, the modern era is less about inventing new stories than about an ironic relationship to old ones. Ezra Pound's famous injunction to "make it new" remains a bravely tendered hope rather than an achieved reality. Beneath the iconoclastic gestures of modern literature, the bold experiments of language and style, lie the archaic myths of the past like ancient layers of sedimented rock. Modern writers may treat these myths with a certain irony, yet parody is an act of dependency as well as of disavowal. "This is the double bind of the inherited form," writes Franco Moretti; "it is possible neither to do without it, nor really to believe in it."[5] The metaphysical certainties of past eras are no longer part of the air we breathe. Modernity, in Hegel's famous argument, means a world with no more heroes. We lack the conviction for epics, tragedies, great mythic quests, yet our thought is indelibly stamped by the forms of our ancestors. We are latecomers, unable to create new myths and unable to free ourselves from old ones.

It needs only a moment's thought to realize that this sense of belatedness may not be universal. There is, for example, no rich and sustaining tradition of female heroes in Western culture. Often, we find nothing more than the relentless repetition of the same constraining design. "Woman is the Sleeping Beauty, Cinderella, Snow White, she who receives and submits," writes Simone de Beauvoir. "In song and story the young man is seen departing adventurously in search of a woman; he slays the dragon, he battles giants; she is locked in a tower, a palace, a garden, a cave, she is chained to a rock, a captive, sound asleep: she waits."[6] The old stories do not tell of women's action and achievement, creation and triumph. The feminine virtues are patience, submission, selfless love. At best, as in *Medea*, the facade of contented servitude may explode in a vehement outburst of rage and resentment, a furious railing at women's lot. But heroism and femaleness do not happily coincide. The handful of counterexamples that spring to mind—Antigone, Joan of Arc, the Amazons—merely underscore the power of the rule. The male hero embodies the potential of masculinity; the female hero, by contrast, is at odds with her sex.

Women are, of course, central to the history of the novel; yet as we shall see, feminists have argued that their role as heroines rather than heroes, hobbled by the ubiquity of the romance plot, continues to compromise their agency. Such a division of labor, remarks Nancy Miller, grants men the world and women love.[7] How, then, can we speak of female antiheroes when we have so few female heroes? How can women feel that the best stories have already been told when they look back at a tradition so conspicuously lacking in images of female power and authority? The great myths of Western individualism, according to Ian Watt, are the stories of Faust, Don Juan, Don Quixote, and Robinson Crusoe. "It is a striking fact," he observes, "that there is no female in the modern Western pantheon of myth."[8]

We might conclude, then, that women must look forward rather than back; today's women are moving into unknown territory, striving to fashion new stories of action and freedom. Women's relationship to plot is surely a matter of creation rather than deconstruction, of innovation rather than irony. If men's plots are played out, those of women are still in their infancy. Hence the optimistic tone of some feminist accounts of modern literature. "The son of many fathers," write Susan Gilbert and Sandra Gubar, "today's male writer feels hopelessly belated; the daughter of too few mothers, today's female writer feels that she is helping to create a viable tradition which is at last definitively emerging."[9]

And yet, some feminist scholars would respond, can we really draw such an absolute distinction between the perspectives of men and women? Is women's writing enclosed in an impermeable bubble, completely untouched by contemporary currents of irony and belatedness? And can women simply bypass an age-old history of male-authored plots, creating new meanings by fiat and pure force of will? Male and female literary traditions are not sealed off from each other by an insurmountable wall. Writers of both sexes draw on a common pool of motifs, metaphors, story lines, stylistic techniques; they are immersed in the same world, breathing in many shared beliefs and taken-for-granted assumptions. Can women, then, really create new plots for women? Or are they too prisoners of the past, doomed to repeat the same old stories? Can women bend narrative to suit their own desires and purpose? Or is plot a patriarchal trap rather than a path to freedom?

The Prison-House of Plot?

The feminist case against plot is eloquently made by Joanna Russ in an article published in 1972, "What Can a Heroine Do? Or, Why Women Can't Write." With polemical flair, Russ argues that almost all plots in Western literature are reserved for men. The heroic battle; the journey into the wilderness; the triumphant attainment of worldly ambition; the glamorous self-immolation of the doomed poet; these are all stories that require a male protagonist. There are, of course, plenty of women in such stories, but they do not guide or drive the narrative. They are without psychological depth or plausible motivation, existing only in relation to the hero, as dangerous threat or enticing reward. They are fantasies of what men desire or hate or fear: the immaculate virgin, the faithful wife, the bitch goddess. Not one of these images, concludes Russ, "is of the slightest use as myth to the woman writer who wishes to write about a female protagonist."[10]

Russ's key point is that plots are essentially rather than contingently male; we cannot get around the problem simply by placing a female character in a traditional male role. If we try to imagine a female Faust seducing and then abandoning a village boy in her quest for knowledge, or Odyssea returning home to her faithful husband after many years of perilous adventure on the open seas, the result is comical rather than convincing. "Reversing sexual roles in fiction may make good burlesque or good fantasy," concludes Russ, "but it is ludicrous in terms of serious literature. Culture is male. Our literary myths are for heroes, not heroines."[11]

The major plotline available to women is, of course, the love story. "The tone may range from grave to gay, from the tragedy of *Anna Karenina* to the comedy of *Emma*," writes Russ, "but the myth is always the same: innumerable variants on Falling in Love, on courtship, on marriage, on the failure of courtship and marriage. How She Got Married. How She Did Not Get Married (always tragic). How She Fell in Love and Committed Adultery. . . . As far as literature is concerned, heroines are still restricted to one vice, one virtue, and one occupation."[12] Even when other plots gain a foothold in the margins of the text—stories of female education or rebellion or achievement—they are curbed and tamed by the tenacious hold of the romance. A woman's story, it seems, can only end in marriage or death.

If female-centered plots are so impoverished and male-centered plots are unusable, how can women find new ways of writing about women? Russ suggests that a female writer may opt for lyricism: casting off the yoke of chronology and causation in order to explore the rhythms of association and repetition, the dense layering of images, phrases, memories. This is the path followed by Virginia Woolf. Alternatively, she may resort to a form of documentary realism: trying to record the details of women's lives without resorting to plot. Yet such an approach runs the risk of being seen as formless, chaotic, aesthetically uninteresting. Ultimately, Russ is most optimistic about genres such as science fiction, which may allow the writer more scope to create new myths outside traditional gender roles. (Russ's well-known novel *The Female Man* is one attempt to create such a myth.)

Russ's observations have been fleshed out and expanded in several decades of feminist scholarship. In a wide-ranging survey of English and American fiction, Joseph Boone shows how stories of courtship, seduction, and wedlock have shaped the history of the novel. Marriage is the fitting finale of traditional fiction, the means by which personal wish and social need can be symbolically reconciled. For the male hero, however, falling in love is only one part of a many-sided process of learning and self-development. By contrast, writes Boone, "the growth of the female protagonist has come to be seen as synonymous with the action of courtship: until very recently the only female bildungsroman has been a love-plot."[13] Boone's arguments are underscored by Susan Fraiman, who teases out the difficulties residing in the very notion of a female *Bildungsroman*. In the Victorian novel, the heroine finds few mentors; her movement into the world is hedged around with constraint and prohibition; her teacher is usually her husband; affiliation triumphs over ambition. Many other feminist scholars, including Nancy Miller, Rachel Blau du Plessis, Patricia Meyer Spacks, and others, have also shown how, across different periods and national traditions, female action is curbed and contained by the ubiquity of the love plot.[14]

Like all of us, however, Russ is much better at diagnosing the past than at predicting the future. Today, the most striking thing about her essay is how many of its claims no longer hold up. For example, Russ argues that most popular genres are closed to women; thus a heroine, she declares, cannot be a private eye.[15] Sue Grafton, Sara Paretsky, Sandra Scoppetone, Marcia Muller, and many other writers have proved her spectacularly wrong. The female hard-boiled detective, like the female forensic pathologist, is now a staple of best-selling mystery fiction. When we look closely at the works of these crime writers, we see that they confound the tidy dichotomy that Russ sets up between male and female plots. Female authors take over familiar aspects of the hard-boiled genre; the isolated hero, the laconic, deadpan style, the big city milieu, the hero's embroilment in danger and corruption. Yet they also modify or discard other elements: the femme fatale, the casual misogyny, the glorification of violence. Plots, in other words, are more malleable than Russ implies. It is not a matter of dropping a female protagonist into a male story and leaving everything else unchanged, but of adapting and tinkering with the old structure so that it fits the new protagonist. What we have at the end is a form that is the same, yet different, a hybrid of masculine and feminine, the old and the new.

Again, Russ declares (with what now seems like excessive confidence), "It is impossible to write a conventional success story with a heroine." Clearly, she did not anticipate the appearance of the "money, sex, and power novel" featuring a glamorous, ambitious heroine fighting her way to the top of a corporate empire (think Judith Krantz, Jackie Collins, Barbara Taylor Bradford).[16] In these novels, female ambition and entrepreneurial success are euphorically rewarded, not punished. Russ's claim that stories of women engaged in heroic conflict are unimaginable seems equally premature. We are now surrounded by endless images of women warriors, tough girls, females flourishing knives and firing guns, from Sigourney Weaver's Ripley to Xena the Warrior Princess.

Love stories, of course, still generate massive sales. The most recent incarnation of the genre gives us the quirky-ironic voice of a young professional woman in the city dating a series of philandering or unavailable men while becoming ever more obsessed with her biological clock (see *Bridget Jones's Diary, The Girl's Guide to Hunting and Fishing, Animal Husbandry,* and many others). There is also a new variant that is more aptly described as a sex-plot rather than a love-plot: *Sex and the City* is an obvious example. But there are also plenty of other genres vying for women's attention. Think, for example, of the enormous popularity of the novel of female friendship, which ranges in tone from sentimental celebrations of sisterhood to clear-eyed dissections of rivalry and betrayal among women (*Waiting to Exhale, The Robber Bride, Divine Secrets of the Ya-Ya Sisterhood, Two Girls Fat and Thin*). Or the many novels and autobiographies exploring the bonds between mothers and daughters (*The Joy Luck Club, Beloved, Fierce Attachments, What Girls Learn*). Meanwhile, a plotline introduced by Henrik Ibsen and popularized in the early days of the women's movement—the woman who chooses to leave her husband in order to discover who she really is—continues to spawn many new and interesting variants.

These are just some of the most familiar plot patterns in contemporary fiction. There are, of course, many others. One can read about a middle-aged female painter who accepts financial and sexual favors from a wealthy male admirer but remains obsessed with her art rather than with love (Mary Gordon's *Spending*). Or a young woman who goes on a murder spree after taking great relish in torturing and killing the man who raped her (Helen Zahavi's *Dirty Weekend*). Or a female adventurer who treks alone for thousands of miles through the Australian desert (Robyn Davidson's memoir *Tracks*). Or a runaway slave who joins a community of vampires (Jewelle Gomez's *The Gilda Stories*). Or a female hero who undergoes a surreal transformation into a large pig (Marie Darrieussecq's *Pig Tales: A Novel of Lust and Transformation*).

It isn't easy anymore to come up with plotlines that are off-limits to the female sex. Indeed, much of the energy and innovation of contemporary fiction comes from stories written by and about women. Female authors have become a potent force in publishing, generating impressive sales and garnering generous amounts of critical acclaim. For example, Ferdinand Mount, then editor of the *Times Literary Supplement,* recently declared: "The truth is that the modern novels I read

with real, deep pleasure are almost all written by women." Mount contrasts the formal ingenuity and showy but sterile pyrotechnics of the
recent crop of male writers with the more substantial literary achievements of Margaret Atwood, Jane Hamilton, Anita Brookner, Carol
Shields, and Zadie Smith. Lauding the moral sympathy of such novelists, their ability to get inside the skin of their characters, Mount argues
that this sympathy is closely correlated with their adept use of narrative technique:

> Novels must deal in consecutive movements and the effect of people upon
> one another. It is a social and hence, in some measure, a narrative art, be-
> cause what people do or don't do to one another has consequences which
> must be followed through. However cunningly disguised, there is a story
> in there somewhere. To get rid of the consequences and make your text
> free-flowing, arbitrary and timeless is to discard what is most interest-
> ing.[17]

In this view of the current literary scene, women are among the
most accomplished and successful practitioners of narrative rather
than excluded outsiders peering forlornly through the windowpane.
Mount's opinions are not, of course, shared by everyone, yet it seems
obvious that the layout of the literary landscape has changed dramatically in the thirty years since Russ's essay was published. The massive
explosion of women's writing seems to confirm the flexibility of plot,
its openness to new demands and desires.

Yet, strangely enough, feminist pessimism about plot has not disappeared but intensified; many scholars continue to wax eloquent on the
dangerous designs of plot. Indeed, there is a widespread distrust of storytelling among contemporary intellectuals of both sexes. Stories are
deemed suspect because of their excessive tidiness: ambiguity is pa-
pered over, contradictions excluded or resolved, loose ends neatly tied
up. Stories con us into seeing reality as coherent, orderly, sequential,
shaped by individual will and purpose. They are charged with being not
just deceptive but authoritarian, imposing order onto complexity and
flux, forcing phenomena into patterns of predetermined meaning. Plot,
in short, is where social norms assert themselves as literary forms.

Some feminists enlarge on this theme by arguing that plot is phallo-
centric, that it perpetrates a male-defined view of the world. The linear

sequence of storytelling, they insist, cannot come to grips with women's experience. The lives of women disrupt the order of plot; their form is repetitive, diffuse, ambiguous, without closure. According to Ellen Friedman and Miriam Fuchs, traditional narrative is a sign of patriarchal mastery, an attempt to impose a single, fixed, order of meaning; feminine writing, by contrast, is marked by disorder, rupture, disorientation, incoherence, nonlinearity. Because plot is the enemy of feminism, it is experimental writers who are at the vanguard of social change; "subverting closure, logic, and fixed, authoritarian points of view, they undermine patriarchal forms and help fulfill the prophecy of a truly feminine discourse, one practiced by women."[18]

Another plot pessimist is Judith Roof. Surveying the lesbian fiction of the last thirty years, Roof is despondent. "Why is the story always the same?" she wonders. "Why am I rarely happy with any narrative that represents or suggests the presence of lesbian sexuality?"[19] The growing body of literature by and about lesbians is no cause for celebration, according to Roof, because it continues to rely heavily on traditional plot structures. Such structures, she claims, mimic the mind-set of heterosexuality; they set up oppositions that are ultimately resolved through synthesis, they organize events into a purposeful movement toward a final climax. Replacing straight characters with gay ones does nothing to challenge the tyranny of narrative form. Plot, for Roof, is a closed circuit, a heterosexist trap, locking our minds into predictable and predetermined grooves.

Roof, like other plot pessimists, draws on Teresa de Lauretis's influential discussion of gender and narrative. According to de Lauretis, all stories lead back to Oedipus. The Oedipal story is the founding myth of Western culture, the prototype of narrative. It is a tale of a man's move toward self-knowledge, where woman appears only as obstacle or goal. The act of storytelling is anchored in the primary fact of sexual difference, in an age-old opposition between masculine and feminine, active and passive, subject and object, movement and stasis. Linear narrative is synonymous with male desire: the longing to return to the mother and the fateful encounter with paternal law. Thus any active protagonist, regardless of gender, is symbolically male; gender is a matter of narrative form rather than content.[20]

Feminists are not the only ones to argue for a close link between masculinity and plot; in fact, it is a commonplace in recent theories of narrative.[21] But what exactly does it mean to say that narrative is a phallic or Oedipal form? It can simply be an admission that stories of adventure, discovery, and achievement have traditionally been the provenance of men. Hence when women engage in such activity, they will be seen as following in male footsteps. This may be true but it is hardly catastrophic. All of us, feminists included, have to come to terms with the burden of history. No writer creates in a void; all stories are in dialogue with past literary traditions and long-held beliefs. Yet as writing by and about women flourishes and grows ever more varied, this link between being an active protagonist and being a man begins to loosen. We come to see more stories as open to everyone, not just to those of one sex.

Yet some critics want to push their claims much further. Drawing on the evidence of psychoanalysis rather than history, they write as if narrative were intrinsically masculine, forever bound to the male psyche and male desire. The logic of plot, they insist, is a mirror of male sexuality, with its urgent, purposeful drive toward resolution and final climax. And it is men who yearn to control and master the messiness of reality by turning it into a tidily packaged story. Hence women who draw on the resources of plot are being co-opted into masculine ways of thinking. It is not just specific plots that are suspect, in this view, but the very essence of plot, the belief that reality can be ordered into an intelligible, coherent, sequential story. Most feminist critics interested in narrative, writes Margaret Homans, "take it as axiomatic that the structure of narrative itself is gendered and that narrative structure is cognate with social structure."[22]

The critics who engage in this crusade against plot often pride themselves on their progressive credentials, seeing themselves as implacably opposed to all forms of hierarchy and authority. Yet what could be more authoritarian than insisting that every story is really the same old story, that millennia of fables, myths, folktales, epics, novels, dramas, novellas, and short stories are all nothing more than minor variants of one master plot with a single, prescribed meaning and politics? This is, indeed, to paint with a very broad brush, to generalize with a vengeance. It is to tell a remarkably simple story about the aesthetics and politics of storytelling. The argument suffers, furthermore, from a thoroughly circular and self-confirming logic. Once the critic has made up her mind that any linear sequence must be masculine or that any example of an opposition shores up heterosexuality (on what evidence, exactly?), then every text can be found guilty as charged. As soon as it is fed into her critical machinery, it will obediently spit out the expected answer.

If plot has a politics, it is surely more varied, complicated, and unpredictable than this. Even fairy tales have a much more interesting and varied history than one would ever guess from an endless Disney diet of perky, doe-eyed ingenues.[23] Some variants of folk tales reward female ingenuity and bravery; in one version of the story, for example, it is Little Red Riding Hood who kills and eats the wolf. When we arrive at the novel, a motley, hybrid, multivoiced genre, things become even less predictable. It is, of course, true that until recent times women's stories were dominated by the romance plot; yet those who drew on such plots could also question them or present them in an ironic light, smuggling in subversive messages. The viewpoint from which a story is told may tell us as much as the shape of the story itself. "There never was the perfect patriarchal closed circuit," concludes Alison Booth in her discussion of the gender politics of traditional narrative. "Even the tidy concluding marriages in Austen and others begin to fray under current scrutiny."[24]

A plot, in fact, may be a playground as well as a prison-house. Feminist scholar Patricia Yeager pursues this point, arguing that we should celebrate the novel's formal capaciousness rather than mourning its constraints. "We could profit from a catastrophe theory of the novel," she writes, "one that accounts for its appearance of linearity, but notices that novels are marked with caesuras, holes, pauses, shifts onto different ground."[25] When critics accuse storytellers of yoking events into a tightly controlled, teleological sequence ending in an all-too-tidy resolution, one cannot help but wonder what examples they have in mind.

Nowadays, in particular, the long stories that we call novels are often more messy, aleatory, desultory, multiclimactic, hesitant, and circuitous than such a complaint would suggest. They have a plot in the sense that they allow a sequence of events to unfold over time, but there is often no triumphant climax, no complacent "aha!" of final enlightenment. And even in Victorian novels that conclude with a marriage, a moral and a punctilious tying up of every last loose end, there is no reason to assume that all the meaning is to be found in the final formulaic flourish and none in the baggy and unwieldy middle. Writers in the past as well as the present have often found ways to modify, customize, or meddle with the constraints of narrative.

Nor, finally, can we simply assume that any example of a marriage plot is bad news for women. The ubiquity of this plot during much of the long history of the novel may pose a problem for feminist scholars; yet it is hard to make the case that every work of fiction that moves toward marriage is imposing a male-defined worldview on unsuspecting female readers. In fact, as some critics have pointed out, a genre such as the romance novel reveals much more about women's fantasies than about men's; it does not simply reflect current gender roles but imaginatively reworks and reshapes them in the light of its readers' desires. Hence the persistent motif of the romantic hero who is callous yet caring, magnetically masculine yet impossibly nurturing. The romance, in Janice Radway's terms, serves a compensatory function; in offering a fantasy of unconditional love, of being the object of a man's eager attention and anxious solicitude, it caters to needs and desires that are often inculcated in women and yet that may remain unfulfilled in their everyday lives.[26]

Ann duCille also reminds us that stories of love and marriage may have an especially rich and powerful resonance for those long denied the right to marry. In an illuminating analysis of diverse examples of African American women's fiction, she offers an implicit rebuke to those who would offer sweeping indictments of the marriage plot: "While modern minds are inclined to view marriage as an oppressive, self-limiting institution, for nineteenth-century African Americans, recently released from slavery and its dramatic disruption of marital and family life, marriage rites were a long-denied basic human right— signs of liberation and entitlement to both democracy and desire."[27] Here again, the politics of race undermine global attempts at feminist interpretation, demanding a nuanced and careful reading of the changing politics of the marriage plot.

Thus the social import of narrative may shift dramatically across time and place. Stories are more supple than some scholars have recognized; preoccupied with the repetition of certain formal markers, they

fail to consider how the meaning of such markers is affected by changing content and context. So, too, it is a mistake for feminist critics to assume that the only viable options for women writers are negative ones:
subverting, fragmenting, disrupting, or undermining existing plots.
Just as important are acts of creative revision: embellishing, rearrang-
ing, modifying, supplementing, expanding.

In fact, critics are right to note the persistence of many traditional
plot patterns. The vast upsurge of women's writing in the 1970s and
1980s sometimes led women to think that they were throwing off the
shackles of tradition, creating completely new stories, telling the un-
varnished truth of women's lives. While such a view may have been
comforting, it was also largely mistaken. In fact, popular feminist fiction drew heavily on older forms such as the *Bildungsroman* and the
confessional novel, chopping and changing them to fit the needs of contemporary women. All writing, of necessity, depends on past writing.
Change in literature, as in life, usually happens in piecemeal fashion,
with people tinkering, adapting, and gluing new parts onto old. Those
who insist that a truly liberating women's writing must be radically
new and without precedent, that women must be born again in order to
be saved, are doomed to disappointment.

Why this demand for either/or? Narrative strikes me as a precious
resource in literature and in life; I find it hard to see why some critics
would want to disparage such a resource or be so quick to dismiss
women's revisions and reworkings of traditional stories. I agree with
Susan Stanford Friedman's defense of narrative and women's hunger
for narrative, her view that plots are polyvocal and do not carry an in-
trinsic and inevitable patriarchal script.[28] I am persuaded by Wendy
Doniger when she talks about the malleability of myths, their changing
meanings and openness to repeated retelling. Many stories, Doniger
points out, have been used to argue for diametrically opposed morals,
political theories, or social codes: there is no single ideology frozen in a
plotline that dictates its meaning and use.[29]

I also agree with Maria Pia Lara when she argues that storytelling
has been a vital means of carving out a feminist presence in the public
sphere. Narrative, observes Lara, is a mode of self-fashioning; it allows
us to reimagine and redescribe the lives of women in a way that carries
aesthetic, moral, and political force.[30] Of course, much recent fiction by

women is not feminist in any strict ideological sense, nor should its value be assessed in such a light. But it exists, by default, in the aftermath of the women's movement, which has created endless eddies and currents that flow in often surprising and unexpected directions.

Libertines and Loners: The Lesbian Picaresque

In recent years a new form of lesbian fiction has appeared on the literary scene, a heady blend of cynicism and sex, urban sleaze and everyday anomie. Its location is usually the gritty environs of the American inner city: New York, San Francisco, Boston. The narrator writes in the first person, in the everyday language and vernacular rhythms of the street. Her tone is deadpan; her persona is ironic, detached, even jaundiced. She sees herself as an exile, stranded on the outskirts of human society, a stranger among strangers. Straying from one lover to the next, she is eager to connect, yet instinctively shies away from the treacherous glue of intimacy. Her gaze is wary and weary, bleached free of sentiment, the epitome of urban cool. She writes about seedy bars and bad sex, about getting drunk and the ignominy of going home with an unattractive stranger to avoid spending the night alone. She wastes no time agonizing over her sexuality; her world is filled with women who desire women. But the existence of other lesbians is no panacea or safe haven. There is no escape, it seems, from loneliness, melancholy, stalled relationships, self-laceration, and the other diseases of modern life.

Jane DeLynn's *Don Juan in the Village* and Michelle Tea's *Valencia* are particularly good examples of this new genre; other writers such as Sarah Schulman and Eileen Myles take up many of the same motifs.[31] In spite of their verbal panache, edgy tone, and sharp eye for detail, these novels have not made as much of a splash as they deserve. Some critics reach, rather desperately, for the catch-all concept of postmodernism to explain the newness of this writing, its difference from what is often seen as lesbian literature. What few people seem to have noticed is that we are seeing the resurgence of a very old plot pattern, newly updated and refurbished for the present: the picaresque.[32]

We can sum up the essence of the picaresque by saying that it has a hero who goes everywhere and a plot that goes nowhere. This hero is an outsider by birth or circumstance, a homeless orphan thrust into empty space. He is footloose and constantly on the move, roaming across endless vistas in pursuit of some uncertain goal. The picaresque is a story of adventure and happenstance, an admixture of surprising events, unexpected encounters, and strangers met by the wayside. It is made up of self-contained episodes, strung together casually in a loose chain that follows no particular logic. The plot is disjointed, random, spiraling from one incident to the next without progress or purpose. By the end, the hero has learned nothing; the quintessential naïf, he is eternally hopeful yet always crestfallen at how things turn out.

A popular genre in seventeenth- and eighteenth-century Europe, the picaresque has turned out to be a perfect match for contemporary Americans obsessed with the romance of the road and the glamour of the outlaw. Jack Kerouac is an obvious prototype, but there are numerous other examples of the modern American picaresque, from *Blue Highways* to *Housekeeping,* from *A Confederacy of Dunces* to *Even Cowgirls Get the Blues.*[33] Nor is it at all surprising that such a form would appeal to lesbian writers. The figure of the eternal outsider speaks to women who find themselves defined as outcasts, perverts, a menace to society. Like the picaro, the protagonist of the new lesbian fiction is dislocated; she has no history, no past, no sense of embeddedness in a tradition. She lives in the now, fully immersed in the burning immediacy of the present. Seemingly without mother or father, she pays little heed to the ties of family and generation. She exists in space rather than time, defining herself through the restless rhythms of constant movement. She is a drifter, a wanderer, restless and unhoused, isolated and unencumbered, propelled forward by a recurring rhythm of anticipation and disappointment.

The territory of this new lesbian hero may be the locales and neighborhoods of the inner city, or a broader, more expansive terrain. In *Don Juan in the Village,* for example, individual chapters bear such titles as "Puerto Rico," "Iowa," "Ibiza," "Key West," "Morocco." Wherever she goes, the narrator is a tourist and a voyeur; she tells stories of embarrassing misunderstandings, disastrous sexual encounters, a recurring failure to understand local codes. In Puerto Rico, she is politely ostracized when she wears gold pants to a gay bar; in Verona, the prostitutes laugh at her when she takes out her wallet; in Morocco, she misreads a gesture of hospitality as a sexual invitation, waiting in vain for her hostesses to join her in the bedroom. Misanthropic and paranoid, ironic and judgmental, caught "in the immense vanity of . . . self-love and self-hate" (*DJ* 240), Don Juan is immured in the prison of her own tormenting self-consciousness, unable to experience fully the reality of others. When she finally returns to the New York bar scene, she is still a stranger, watching the goings on around her with melancholic detachment and mild curiosity, "as I would have the natives of New Guinea or a married couple in Passaic, New Jersey" (*DJ* 239).

Don Juan, according to George Steiner, is the only myth that is uniquely modern in recognizing the absolute demands of erotic desire.[34] Like Don Juan, the hero of the new lesbian picaresque slides from one sexual partner to the next. She lives in a world of bar pickups, desultory couplings, lovers that often seem faceless and interchangeable. The initial exchange of looks, the tantalizing flirtation in the bar, promises more than the final encounter can ever deliver. Her true love is always the woman she has not yet met or the girlfriend she has just lost. The plot is built around a series of anticlimaxes: the hero ends up going home with someone she doesn't desire or has lackluster sex with someone she does desire or falls obsessively in love with someone who doesn't desire her.

Lesbian writing was once reticent about what women did in bed, veiling nitty-gritty details in hazy allusions and romantic images drawn from nature. The new lesbian picaresque, by contrast, does not mince words. It owes an obvious debt to the "sex wars" of the eighties, when arguments erupted about women's right to sexual freedom and experimentation in the light of the antisex and antipornography stance of some sections of the women's movement. The debates around lesbian sexuality were often especially protracted and angry. Were lesbian relationships inherently different from heterosexual ones, as some lesbian-feminists insisted? Did female lovers treat each other with respect and reciprocity, seek intimacy rather than sexual objectification, decouple sex and power? Or were such views thoroughly oppressive and moralistic, as other lesbians argued, continuing a long history of policing and controlling female desire? By rushing to condemn so many forms of sex as "male" or "male-identified," did feminists close off options rather than opening them up, threatening to excommunicate all those women whose erotic yearnings and fantasies did not neatly line up with standards of political correctness?

The lesbian picaresque takes an unambiguously prosex stance: the protagonist is open and unembarrassed about her lust for other women. Her descriptions of sexual encounters are often graphic but intentionally unromantic, pitilessly dwelling on moments of awkwardness, clumsy embraces, fumbled orgasms, and the momentary excitement of sex with strangers. Anonymity and unavailability heighten desire; familiarity erodes it. Contrasting the behavior of gay men and lesbians, Don Juan wonders why women so often feel the need to dredge up a romantic justification for "that utterly simple desire to explore the wet insides of another's body" (*DJ* 236–37). The narrator of *Valencia* is equally blunt and unapologetic about her desire for sex without ties. The chapters of her book are littered with ex-girlfriends and one-night stands she is anxious to avoid. At one point, in desperation, she places an advertisement in the gay personals: "Don't Want a Girlfriend . . . Just a Hard Sleazy Fuck" (*V* 127).

A famous part of the sex wars was an angry and protracted dispute about the gender politics of sadomasochism. While some lesbians passionately defended the pleasures of role-playing and acting out S/M scenarios, others denounced such practices as the worst possible symptoms of a retrograde patriarchal sexuality. Here the issue is no longer up for debate; it is simply taken for granted that sexual thrills are linked to the dance of conquest and submission, the experience of humiliation and pain. Eros and violence are inextricably intertwined for women as well as men. Tea's heroine describes the scary yet addictive excitement of a sexual encounter in which she is teased with a knife, conveying the sense of reference points destroyed and boundaries lost. At another point she writes: "I wanted to be whipped into numbness by a stranger. I wanted to be slapped around until I left my body, slid into an altered state of consciousness" (*V* 129). Similarly, DeLynn's Don Juan finds a momentary respite from agonizing self-consciousness in the mind-altering yet strangely soothing rituals of sadomasochistic sex. At another point, she dwells on the experience of being fondled at a party by a woman she finds repellent; her sense of disgust only fuels her excitement. Characters have difficulty distinguishing pleasure and pain, lust and disgust: sex takes them to a place where categories are blurred, boundaries confused, and the sense of self shattered.

The new lesbian writing draws on male literary influences boldly

and without apology. One obvious source is the French tradition of literary bohemianism: the charismatic figure of the glamorous, doomed,
delinquent poet that stretches from Baudelaire to Jean Genet. There is
the same *nostalgie de la boue,* the same mystique of marginality; the
protagonist feels a powerful affinity with junkies, beggars, the urban
poor, and all those who fall outside the sacred circle of middle-class re-
spectability. Rather than denying the link between homosexuality and
deviance, she brandishes it defiantly as a badge of honor. Sexual transgression offers the promise of transcendence, a testing of the limits of
being, an annihilation of the self in extremity and ecstasy; when Don
Juan speaks of her longing for the "calm purity of utter degradation,"
we hear the echoes of Baudelaire as he plunges into the abyss. The new
lesbian hero is the latest figure to slip on the mantle of Baudelaire's flaneur. She too wanders aimlessly through the streets of the city, curious
but detached, briefly locking glances and then moving on. She shares
the flaneur's ineffable hopes, his insatiable yearnings, his fascination
with the eroticism of the brief encounter and the endless urban pan-
orama of myriad selves. "DeLynn's flaneur," writes Sally Munt, "wears
the melancholy of the disappointed desire, searching the labyrinthine
city for a vast, unfulfilled promise."[35]

Yet there are also other echoes, other tones in this new lesbian writing, reminiscent of Philip Marlowe, Jack Kerouac, Henry Miller. The
narrator's voice owes much to the tones and rhythms of hard-boiled
crime fiction and film noir. The style is slick, polished, self-mocking: an
often pitch-perfect rendition of a tough-guy American vernacular. Like
the private eye, the protagonist is an antihero who mocks ideals and
sneers at sentiment, yet who still feeds a romantic flame under a hard-
bitten exterior. This influence comes to the fore in Sarah Schulman's
After Delores, which is built around the familiar trappings of urban
crime fiction: guns, violence, an unexplained murder, a down-at-heel
protagonist. In another Schulman novel, *Girls, Visions, and Everything,* the narrator turns eagerly to the writing of the Beats for inspiration and solace. Kerouac speaks to her own feelings of being an outlaw,
her desire to keep moving, her scorn for middle-class smugness. "The
trick," she decided, "was to identify with Jack Kerouac instead of with
the women he fucks along the way. . . . Everyone else just sits around,
but Jack *does* it. No grass grows under his feet" (*G* 17).

Just as important as the precursors to whom a writer pays homage are the texts that she writes against. The new lesbian fiction takes aim at a familiar formula: the coming-out novel. A staple genre of the 1970s and 1980s, the coming-out novel traces the heroine's quest for identity as she moves toward a growing acceptance of her sexuality. It usually ends in a blissfully suspended moment of romantic love *à deux*, or with the heroine finding a new home in the lesbian community. The tone is educational, earnest, and optimistic, painting a glowing picture of lesbian love as an oasis of affinity, reciprocity, and mutual respect. Critics often treat the coming-out novel with a certain ambivalence. Bonnie Zimmerman, for example, is eager to defend the value of what she describes as an inspiring myth of sexual emancipation. Given a long history of seeing lesbians as pathological deviants or tragic victims, the novelty of a happy lesbian protagonist has an obvious and powerful appeal. Yet she also points to some of the problems of the genre: an often sanctimonious and preaching tone; clumsy writing; a patent discomfort with ambiguity and innovative form.[36]

The lesbian picaresque, by contrast, is a much more playful and self-conscious genre, openly in love with the beauty and power of words. There are moments when language pours forth in a molten flow of shimmering energy and excitement. Tea's prose, in particular, is fast-paced, breathless, exuberant, exulting in the joy of being alive and a young lesbian living in San Francisco. Yet this often lyrical delight in form goes along with a harsh puncturing of romantic, soft-focus visions of lesbian community. The reader's face is shoved in the gutter, forced to confront the disorders of modern life: urban poverty, squalor, the grime of the street. Everyone drinks too much; drugs are everywhere; work is a distracting and burdensome chore, to be avoided whenever possible. In *After Delores* the narrator is a working-class waitress; in *Valencia* she drifts from a dead-end job in a courier company to a brief stint as a prostitute to acting in a lesbian porn film. There is no *Bildung* here, no education of the protagonist or the reader, only sardonic, street savvy reportage of life at the edge, of bad girls set loose in the city in search of drugs and sex.

It is hard to miss the ebullient glee with which these novels kick over the pedestal of female virtue. The lesbian picaresque takes delight in debunking the belief that love between women is wholesome, egalitarian, and largely asexual. It underscores the urgent and unpredictable rhythms of sexual arousal, the kinship of love and cruelty, the enigma of attraction. Desire overflows the boundaries of moral prescription, playing havoc with attempts to hyphenate feminism with lesbianism, to reconcile politics with sexual preference. Above all, it is a genre deeply at odds with those forms of feminism that see "male-identified" as the ultimate insult and celebrate the lesbian as the quintessential woman-identified woman. Instead, the lesbian picaresque greedily grabs hold of male freedoms and pleasures and pays tribute to the heady attractions of masculine style. Gay men, too, are valued kinfolk and allies; the lesbian outlaw has more in common with queer men than straight women. "I would wonder," reflects Don Juan, "if I were . . . a man in a woman's body, perhaps a redneck man in a woman's body or maybe something even worse; a man who liked to fuck men in a woman's body; that is, a man in a woman's body who fucked women because this was the closest a man who was a woman could come to being a homosexual" (DJ 237).

Here we are clearly a long way from a gender politics that pits women against men, portraying the sexes as alien and antagonistic species. What happens, wonders queer theorist Judith Halberstam, "when boy rebellion is located not in the testosterone induced pout of the hooligan but in the sneer of the tomboy?"[37] What does it mean for a girl or a woman to be assertively and even aggressively masculine? The response of many feminists to such a spectacle mirrors the discomfort of society at large. Halberstam, by contrast, wants to take seriously the many forms and styles of male identification among women. Masculinity, she suggests, is much too interesting to be left to one sex. For feminists to argue that certain ways of being and doing are off-limits merely because they are masculine is to collude in the narrowing and shrinking of female worlds.

Applying such an argument to theories of plot would allow feminist critics to think in more expansive ways about women's use of classical male narrative. The allure of the hero, the outlaw, the rebel, is hardly limited to one gender; there are women as well as men who want to be James Dean. Yet we are used to the spectacle of male drifters, rebels, and outlaws; we shrug our shoulders when men are raucous, sullen, asocial. The woman who displays such traits is an outlaw twice over, estranged not just from society but from her sex. Similarly, few people flinch at the sex scenes of contemporary fiction; graphic, hard-core descriptions of who-did-what-to-whom are routine, rarely worthy of comment. Yet it is still rare to see sex between women portrayed in the same matter-of-fact manner. Sarah Schulman laments the fact that mainstream publishers still shy away from explicit lesbian content; the books I've discussed, almost all published by small presses, seem to bear out her claims. Rather than being a sign of capitulation to social norms, women's borrowing of traditionally masculine story lines clearly still has the power to shock.

In a useful recent book on lesbian narrative, Marilyn Farwell surveys some standard approaches to plot. Feminists are right, she suggests, to point out that a story is not just a neutral device for conveying content. Plot patterns carry a great deal of cultural baggage and much of this baggage is linked to gender. Form itself is a kind of content. Yet Farwell believes that feminists have often exaggerated the power of that form, portraying women as helpless victims of the tyranny of plot, struggling helplessly to free themselves from the meshes of age-old stories. In fact, she argues, narrative is more elastic than this account would suggest, more malleable, more open to new modulations of meaning and purpose.

My own discussion would seem to bear out Farwell's ideas. As we have seen, putting female characters into traditionally male plots does make a difference. Texts stretch and change to accommodate the changed gender dynamic, unfolding new and unexpected layers of meanings. Drawing on a familiar plotline, the lesbian picaresque re-imagines it in bold and often startling ways. Assailing received ideas and long-standing taboos, it writes visceral new scripts of sexuality and the self, of identity and desire. Infused with an array of energetic, mocking, often subversive female heroes, the same old story, it turns out, is never quite the same.[38]

Mother-Daughter Plots

What do the stories of mothers and daughters look like? Can we point to a shared form or a common design? How can a writer hope to capture the often elusive rhythms of rapprochement and withdrawal, the fond embraces and wounding words, the pull toward intimacy and the equally powerful desire for distance? I spoke earlier of a recent spate of novels, autobiographies, and memoirs that take as their subject the bond between mothers and daughters. Chinese American authors are at the forefront of this trend. The spectacular success of Maxine Hong Kingston's *The Woman Warrior* helped to inspire a slew of other stories about Chinese families told by American-born daughters, including Amy Tan's *The Joy Luck Club* and *The Kitchen God's Wife,* Fae Myenne Ng's *Bone* and Mei Ng's *Eating Chinese Food Naked.*[39]

The history of Western literature is silent, writes Adrienne Rich, on the subject of mothers and daughters. "The loss of the daughter to the mother, the mother to the daughter, is the essential female tragedy. We acknowledge Lear (father-daughter split), Hamlet (son and mother), and Oedipus (son and mother) as great embodiments of the human tragedy; but there is no presently enduring recognition of mother-daughter passion and rapture."[40] The love between mothers and daughters is the great unwritten story: unwritten in part because it diminishes men's importance by relegating them to the sidelines. Rich admits that the mother-daughter bond may give rise to the deepest mutuality and the most painful estrangement. It is an intense yet uneasy affinity braided out of many conflicting emotions: guilt, love, recognition, hatred, rage.

How little we hear in literature, says Rich, about the viewpoint of mothers. To be a mother, it seems, is to be written about rather than to write. Motherhood is our most sacred symbol; it conjures up nostalgic, fuzzy-edged memories of a long-lost time when one was bathed in the bliss of constant love, security, and attentiveness. The mother is the source, the origin, the home that we must all leave in order to become fully fledged human beings. Looming over the landscape of childhood like a massive, all-powerful idol, she is nevertheless oddly invisible. Her body is a blank screen for the flickering, shifting projections of the child: the radiant Madonna; the suffocating, overanxious protector; the mother of nightmare who neglects or hurts her children. But no one asks about her dreams, her desires, her yearnings: no one sees that part of her soul that is not encompassed by the relentless demands of her progeny. "What fabrications they are, mothers . . . We deny them an existence of their own, we make them up to suit ourselves—our own hungers, our own wishes, our own deficiencies."[41]

Feminists, too, have often spurned or ignored the mother. Struggling against the power of an age-old decree that sees childbearing as female destiny, many women were anxious to define themselves as not-mothers. Breaking free of the straitjacket of gender norms meant refusing to identify with the woman who stood for everything one wanted to escape. The story of feminism was often a story of movement away from the mother, of a defiant search for autonomy and independence. Feminists, suggests Marianne Hirsch, have often adopted the viewpoint of the daughter; they have been reluctant to identify with the mother, to listen to her voice, to tell her story.[42]

And yet this is also a contrary impulse within feminism, an intense desire to reclaim motherhood as the symbolic heart of a woman-centered culture. Scholars often invoke Nancy Chodorow's idea that affiliation with the mother lies at the heart of female selfhood. Whereas sons can only express a masculine identity by separating from their mother and defining themselves against her, daughters develop a sense of self-in-relation that is based on continuity with the mother. Female identity, in this account, does not require a dramatic break or separation from the point of origin. The story of female self-development does not follow a purposeful path away from the mother, but constantly circles back to her in an avowal of affiliation and indebtedness. Some feminist critics paint a glowing picture of mother-daughter love as an intimate and deeply symbiotic bond free of conflict and struggles for power. The mother-daughter plot, then, is hailed as a compelling alternative to a history of male-defined narrative.

Recent writing by Chinese American women gives us a useful laboratory in which to test some of these ideas. Here, observing the delicate dance between mothers and daughters is not just a way of delving into the psychic dramas of family life but also a means of reflecting on the import of history and tradition. Culture is passed down through the bodies of mothers; it is by enduring the searing fires of this primary bond that the daughter learns what it means to be Chinese. The mother is the primary link to the myths, beliefs, and values of past generations; she is the key to the vast, unknowable time that precedes the daughter's own. The maternal body is not outside of history but the very means by which history is transmitted. And yet, as we shall see, this history is fraught and contentious, ambiguous and uncertain. There is no haven in the mother's embrace, no safe shelter from conflict and confusion.

The Woman Warrior has been endlessly analyzed by literary scholars, in part because it is a work that reflects so intently and self-consciously on the act of storytelling. A story composed out of many other stories, it is a hodge-podge of Chinese myths, ancestral tales, historical episodes, uncertain memories, and vignettes of modern American life. Fact intermingles with fiction, experience is interspersed with epic, the present bleeds persistently into the past. The narrator begins by repeating a story passed on by her mother: a nameless, never-mentioned aunt in rural China who kills herself after giving birth to an illegitimate child. Out of the bare bones of this story, Kingston weaves different versions of her aunt's life, invents alternative scenarios, speculates about the nature of her desires and dreams. This first section lays out the key motifs of *The Woman Warrior*: storytelling as an act that binds together mother and daughter; the incomplete, fragmentary, and often mysterious nature of the mother's stories; the creative response of the daughter who will revise and retell these same stories.

The narrative scheme of *The Woman Warrior* is elaborately composed, braiding together the words of mothers and daughters, reclaiming, moving away from, and then finally returning to maternal inheritance. We hear about the mythic hero Fa Mu Lan, taken from her parents and trained to become a warrior woman in the wilderness. We discover snippets of the mother's biography; Brave Orchid, an exhausted and overworked laundress in San Francisco, was once a Chinese "new woman," a scientist-doctor and respected shaman. These shards of history and myth are juxtaposed against the daughter's own memories of growing up Chinese American, of the tug of conflicting affiliations, moments of searing shame and self-hatred, outbursts of fury at her mother's power. The overall movement of *The Woman Warrior* takes the reader in a forward direction, from the mother to the daughter, from the past to the present; yet this movement is constantly interrupted by repetitions, echoes, alter egos, uncanny parallels across stretches of historical time.

Beginning her book with tales from Chinese history and myth, Kingston returns in the final pages to the same source, recounting the life of Ts'ai Yen, the Chinese poet who sang to her barbarian captors. This concluding story, which connects Ts'ai Yen's haunting song to Kingston's own grandmother and her all-consuming love of theater, speaks of the transfixing, often painful, power of art. "Here is a story my mother told me . . ." writes Kingston, "the beginning is hers, the ending, mine" (WW 206). If there is progression here, then it is a progression that unfolds into a return, as the daughter comes to recognize and embrace the power of maternal legacy.

Storytelling is a vital part of this legacy; selfhood is forged out of tales handed down through the generations, an ambivalent inheritance that is both burden and gift. Blurring the boundaries between autobiography, biography, and myth, Kingston allows us to see that telling her own story means telling not just her mother's story but also the stories of her mother. "Night after night, my mother would talk-story until we fell asleep. I couldn't tell where the stories left off and the dreams began, her voice the voice of the heroines in my sleep" (WW 19). Stories, we come to realize, are multipurpose tools; they may be used to instruct, to console, to entertain, to warn, to inspire. As she grows up, the daughter rails against the peremptory authority of stories that seem intended to cow and control her spirit, to make her properly female and Chinese, to relegate her to the role of "slave girl" and "a maggot in the rice." And yet the adult daughter who writes *The Woman Warrior* has come to see that her cultural inheritance is rich, ambiguous, impossibly complicated: the mother who scolds and punishes is also the mother who passes on tales of female heroism and defiance. Refracted through memory and reinterpreted through hindsight, the meanings of old stories are less obvious than they once appeared.

The mother is a direct link to China, the conduit to a history that her daughter only knows secondhand. Yet she fails miserably at the task of being a native informant. The stories she tells are vague, unreliable, cryptic, confusing. Important points are left unexplained, details change over time. Is her memory failing, or is she intent on concealment and evasion? At one point, the daughter complains to her mother: "I don't want to listen to any more of your stories; they have no logic. They scramble me up. You lie with stories. You won't tell me a story and then say 'This is a true story,' or 'This is just a story.' I can't tell the difference. I don't even know what your real names are. I can't tell what's real and what you make up" (WW 202). And yet the daughter-author has come to realize the futility of her own desire for clear, unambiguous distinctions. The mother's stories cannot shelter her from the harsh winds of uncertainty and confusion. Mimicking her mother's method in her own writing, she now recognizes the irredeemable messiness of tradition: rather than being authentic, natural, self-evident, its messages are cryptic, scrambled, difficult to decipher.

"Chinese Americans," writes Kingston in an oft-quoted passage, "when you try to understand what things in you are Chinese, how do you separate what is peculiar to childhood, to poverty, insanities, one family, your mother who marked your growing with stories, from what is Chinese? What is Chinese tradition and what is the movies?" (*WW* 5–6). Those Chinese American critics who took Kingston to task and scolded her for a lack of fidelity to Chinese tradition did not see that her book is about the impurity of all traditions, the impossibility of deepfreezing a pristine Chinese past. History is in constant flux, always deformed and reformed by the shifting sands of memory, the mishaps of transmission, the perils of translation and mistranslation. Kingston comments in an interview: "We have to do more than record myth . . . that's just ancestor worship. The way I keep the old Chinese myths alive is by telling them in a new way."[43] *The Woman Warrior* embraces tradition without nostalgia even as it reclaims the mother without sentimentality.

Most works of Chinese American fiction do not reflect so intently on the ethics and aesthetics of storytelling. Yet they often grapple with the same problem: how can the daughter learn to see the mother? How can she come to see her mother as separate from herself, with her own history, memories, secret passions, no longer the all-powerful, godlike dispenser of reward and punishment but merely an ordinary yet mysterious human being? How, in other words, does she learn to see the mother as someone other rather than as just a mother? Amy Tan's *Joy Luck Club* is a multivoiced work of fiction that juxtaposes the stories of four mothers and their four daughters. The mothers are close friends who meet every week to eat, talk, and play mahjong in a ritual that has continued over several decades. Their American-born daughters, in their twenties and thirties, are busy with careers, husbands, children. As Wendy Ho points out, "the daughters have a tendency to stereotype their mothers—to freeze them in space and time as old-fashioned, superstitious Chinese ladies from some mythic time."[44] The inevitable narcissism of children who find it hard to acknowledge their parents is here accentuated and deepened by the pressure to assimilate, the anxious eagerness to play down shame-producing signs of ethnic difference. The mother is not just a symbol of femaleness but a painful reminder of foreignness.

The fourteen stories of *The Joy Luck Club* convey but also decenter the perspectives of the daughters by intermingling them with the voices of mothers. The result is a dazzling polytonality, a tessellation of multiple plots into an elaborate and ornate mosaic. Individual stories reveal progress, development, even resolution; yet the delicately balanced architecture of the book also creates multiple echoes, moments of resonance and repetition. The lives of mothers and daughters both mirror and refract each other. We see clear parallels between stories, persistent patterns that repeat themselves over time. Here, for example, is the voice of one mother, An-Mei Hsu:

> I was raised the Chinese way: I was taught to desire nothing, to swallow other people's misery, to eat my own bitterness.
>
> And even though I taught my daughter the opposite, still she came out the same way! Maybe it is because she was born to me and she was born a girl. And I was born to my mother and I was born a girl. All of us are like stairs, one step after another, going up and down but all going the same way. (*JLC* 215)

Such comments call up a tragic vision of women across the generations united by a shared experience of female suffering. Aspects of *The Joy Luck Club* reenact what Caroline Rody calls the romance of daughterly return, portraying a final redemptive union—whether literal or symbolic—with a lost mother.[45] And yet other episodes explore the gulf between mothers and daughters, their failure to make contact across the differences that separate them. The daughter's inability to speak Chinese is only one aspect of a recurring drama of misunderstanding and failed communication. The mother tongue is not the daughter's tongue. "My mother and I never really understood one another," writes King-Mei Woo. "We translated each other's meanings and I seemed to hear less than what was said, while my mother heard more" (*JLC* 37). Scarred by their own painful lives and failed dreams, the mothers pass on hope to their daughters, but also the burden of impossible expectations. Struggling to escape the grip of maternal control, ill at ease with barely understood traditions and half-alien customs, the daughters do not hear or heed their mother's words. Ying-Ying St. Clair writes: "I love my daughter. She and I have shared the same body. There is a part of her mind that is part of mine. But when she was born, she sprang from me like a slippery fish, and has been swimming away ever since. All her life, I have watched her as though from another shore" (JLC 242). In telling the mothers' stories, *The Joy Luck Club* performs an act of reparation, but it is a reparation that does not gloss over the painful schism of mother-daughter difference.

Leslie Bow has recently voiced a scathing critique of *The Joy Luck Club* and similar works of Asian American women's literature. Finding them guilty of the crimes of sentimentality, popularity, and liberal multiculturalism, she complains of their "capitulation to the most easily commodified common denominator of cultural norms."[46] Contemporary novels by Chinese American women sell in such large numbers, according to Bow, because they serve up saccharine, nostalgia-soaked stories of female empowerment and reconciliation that simply shore up the status quo. Bow simply takes it for granted that commercial success is synonymous with selling out (an echo of the hoary old idea that art should remain unsullied by the marketplace), and that any novels that stir up emotions must be deeply suspect (emotions, affect, and sentiment are all negative terms in her argument). But what I really take issue with is Bow's charge of "triumphalism," her claim that popular Asian American women's texts are linked together by a common plot structure: a simplistic story of progress that contrasts old-fashioned, oppressed, Chinese mothers to their enlightened, emancipated, Chinese American daughters.

In fact, as I've tried to show, these works do the opposite, deliberately unsettling the viewpoint of American-born daughters and their confident, impatient sense of their own superiority. By juxtaposing the stories of different generations, *The Woman Warrior* and *The Joy Luck Club* show how the ghosts of the past continue to haunt and shape the present. Acknowledging the continuing power and subterranean resonance of tradition, they call into question the American myth of self-creation, of a future-oriented narrative based on a sloughing off of past selves. These are stories about the blindness of modern daughters who worship at the altar of the new and the up-to-date and who thus fail to see the many threads that bind them inescapably to the past.

At the same time, there is no consolation to be found in the coziness of nostalgia. The mother's history is marked by movement, displacement, transformation. She does not symbolize home, stasis, a nurturing, womblike space; the mothers of Chinese American fiction are women in motion, travelers who have traversed land and sea, cutting ties to friends, home and family, forging new lives under difficult conditions. They are often hardened and embittered by the traumas of migration, by heartrending experiences of hope and loss, of anticipation and disappointment. To their American-born daughters, this history renders them alien, unfathomable, kinfolk yet strangers. Though there may be a final moment of reunion with the mother, this ending does not wipe out a deeply etched history of misunderstanding, estrangement, and pain.

We can thus think of recent works of Chinese American fiction as a response to two popular story lines within feminism. One of these stories calls for a movement away from the mother; it is she who represents female oppression and the horrors of the past, who holds me back, who is everything I do not want to be. By counterposing the voices of mothers and daughters, Kingston and Tan reveal the paucity of this narrative, its self-serving complacency, its blindness to the mother's rich and complex history, which is not just a story of subservience and victimhood. The smug and self-congratulatory plot of progress rides roughshod over the many-sidedness of past women's lives.

Yet Kingston and Tan also write against an influential feminist counterplot of nostalgia for the mother as a symbol of a blissful, female-centered commonality. Rather, the mother-daughter bond is fractured by differing histories and generational misperceptions, by the scars of migration, by differences of education and class. There is no stable sense of security or sameness to be found in the shared bond of gender. Even as the mother is embraced, she remains irreducibly other, familiar yet foreign, a figure that inspires profound ambivalence. Thus plot, it seems, can be both poison and cure; juxtaposing many stories, Kingston and Tan show us that the intense, fraught ties between mothers and daughters cannot be summed up in a single, simple story.

Women in All the Roles: Margaret Atwood

I turn, finally, to a writer whose work is especially attuned to the perils and pleasures of plot. In a dazzling body of writing stretching from *The*

Edible Woman to *The Assassin's Tale,* Margaret Atwood makes fiction out of fictions, spinning novels out of the threads of myths, stories, and fables. Exposing and exploring the scripts that shape women's lives, she often quotes or alludes to such well-known tales as "Bluebeard," "Sleeping Beauty," "Little Red Riding Hood," "The Little Mermaid," "The Robber Bridegroom," and many others. Atwood's rich portrayals of female friendship and rivalry, love affairs gone wrong, women in extremity, painful childhoods and explosive passions are filtered through a sieve of archetypal figures and mythic motifs. The novel, it turns out, is less novel than it seems; like Frankenstein's monster, it is a composite creature, assembled out of whatever scraps and odd fragments its creator happens to have at hand.

Atwood joins a company of distinguished women writers who are fascinated with fairy tales, such as Angela Carter and A. S. Byatt. Like them, she does not quote old stories merely to debunk them as sorry remnants of a primitive and unenlightened past. If there is parody in her work, then it is parody that is fully conscious of its reliance on past traditions. Atwood boldly reworks her materials, ripping apart old fabric, inserting new motifs, creating ironic or comic contrast, twisting or truncating plotlines. Yet her novels also bear witness to the resonance and uncanniness of myth: its power to enchant, seduce, or disturb. For Atwood, stories make up the dream-work of our culture; they are psychic cryptograms that lead back into the murky, twisted coils of our unconscious desires and fears.[47]

Atwood's revision of fairy-tale motifs reflects feminist arguments but also responds to them. Having more female heroes in literature, she insists, also means having more female villains. That is to say, if women want to read about female characters who are active, purposeful, and make things happen, then some of those things will turn out to be inept, mistaken, or malicious. We cannot have female agency without the possibility of female error and cruelty. In one of her speeches, Atwood laments a feminist reluctance to acknowledge this fact, a firmly entrenched belief that any less-than-flattering portrayal of a woman must be inspired by misogyny. "Where have all the Lady Macbeths gone? Gone to Ophelias, every one, leaving the devilish tour-de-force parts to be played by bass-baritones. Or, to put it another way: If all women are well-behaved by nature—or if we aren't allowed to say otherwise for fear of being accused of anti-femaleism—they are deprived of moral choice."[48] "Moral choice" does not, of course, mean absolute freedom, a self-directed destiny unhampered by social circumstance. Indeed, Atwood's work pores in obsessive detail over the molding of femininity, showing how girls of a certain era, snowed under by parental prohibitions, bedtime stories, girdles, department store catalogs, peer pressure, and the pitiless rules of children's games, gradually metamorphose into women. Yet, as sociologists argue and as novelists have long known, it is a mistake to see individual choice as opposed to social structure; our actions are made possible by the very conditions that also limit and constrain us. To see women only as blameless victims, hapless pawns pushed around the chessboard by the hand of patriarchy, is to diminish them in literature as in life.

In fact, feminist responses to Atwood's fiction are mixed. For example, Gayle Greene delivers a scathing attack on *Cat's Eye*, Atwood's 1978 novel about the rhythms and rituals of friendship among preadolescent girls. *Cat's Eye*, she declares, is a "disturbing tale of female cruelty": "this is a tale not of human evil . . . but of female evil, from which males are generally absent and exempt, in which there is so much fear and loathing of the female . . . a misogyny so pronounced and so unprocessed that it is impossible to say whether it is Elaine's, society's or Atwood's." Greene faults Atwood for her pessimistic view of women and for failing to serve up a clear-cut feminist message; *Cat's Eye*, she complains, in "its severance of personal from political and its unprocessed misogyny," is a "novel of its time."[49]

Yet not all feminists are so quick to measure Atwood against a given standard in order to find her wanting; others admire her fiction precisely for its bracing skepticism toward political orthodoxies. Jean Wyatt, for example, suggests that Atwood's fiction is so powerful because it looks into the abyss, confronting buried emotions and motives that are often glossed over, ignored, or denied by feminism. In particular, Atwood delves deep into the rage, envy, and hostility that women can feel toward other women. Feminism, argues Wyatt, has often continued a tradition of seeing women as more moral, pure, empathic, and self-sacrificing than men; this vision comes at great cost in its denial of emotional ambivalence. Women are expected to feel only empathy and sisterhood toward other women; any less attractive emotions are simply explained away as a result of patriarchal conditioning. This sleight-of-hand appears to affirm women but in fact lessens them by rendering them less than fully human. Atwood, by contrast, "restores women's ability to play all the roles, including those of the powerful and the evil."[50]

Wyatt is referring here to *The Robber Bride*, Atwood's multiperspectival portrait of female friendship, rivalry, and betrayal. The novel is set in Toronto in the early nineties and told from the viewpoint of three different women: Tony, a military historian; Charis, a New Ager; and Roz, a successful business woman. They are linked together by their common friendship with Zenia, a glamorous and charismatic figure with a mysterious past. Zenia befriends each of them in turn, fabricating very different versions of her identity and her origins. Having wormed her way into their confidence and their lives, she seduces each of their husbands and lovers and symbolically consumes them. Apparently killed in a bomb explosion in Beirut, Zenia unexpectedly turns up in a fashionable Toronto restaurant several years later. Her return from the dead forces the three women to face their own past and to confront buried feelings of envy, hatred, and rage. Each of them fantasizes about murdering Zenia, yet the cause of her actual, final death, like the details of her life, is left unexplained. "As for the truth about her, it lies out of reach, because—according to the records at any rate—she was never even born."[51]

In Atwood's novel, Zenia is simultaneously real and fantastic, a messenger from another world. She is a double for each of the characters, uncannily reflecting their own deeply repressed desires. Zenia is both other and same, the stranger within the self. By tracing out the painful childhood and traumatic experiences of each of her main characters, Atwood paves the way for their receptivity to Zenia, their eagerness to befriend her. They come to hate Zenia yet also want to be her; she is both their ideal and the incarnation of what they most hate and fear. She is a whirling vortex of insatiable desire, an uncanny shape-shifter, a symbol of lawlessness and transgression. She stands for rapacious, shameless sexuality; all-consuming, atavistic greed; narcissistic fantasies of power over others and sadistic delight in their destruction. Her presence disturbs and disorients the three protagonists, forcing them to face painful memories and discomfiting emotions.

Zenia, of course, has a history. She is an archetype, a fiction composed of other fictions, a recurring figure of story and myth. The novel couples her with Jezebel, the vampire, the great Whore of Babylon. Yet she is also linked to a male hero in a double movement of imitation and inversion. The Grimm fairy tale "The Robber Bridegroom" tells of a girl betrothed to a rich and mysterious stranger who secretly visits him at his home, only to discover that he has a habit of dismembering and devouring young women. This story makes its appearance in an episode when Roz is thinking back to the time when her twin daughters were very young. Not only did they adore violent fairy tales and beg to hear the most gory and gruesome details, but they would also insist that all the parts be played by women. In Roz's retelling, the robber bridegroom was thus reborn as the robber bride.

> *The Robber Bride,* thinks Roz. Well, why not? Let the grooms take it in the neck for once. The Robber Bride, lurking in her mansion in the dark forest, preying upon the innocent, enticing youths to their doom in her evil cauldron. Like Zenia . . .
>
> Roz is crying again. What she's mourning is her own good will. She tried so hard, she tried so hard to be kind and nurturing, to do the best thing. But Tony and the twins were right: no matter what you do, somebody always gets boiled. (*RB* 292–93)

The figure of Zenia, then, draws on both male and female precursors; she is a reminder that destructiveness and rage are not limited to one sex. She stands for demonic female impulses that are twice repressed: by conventional codes of feminine behavior and by feminist taboos about feelings of anger and envy toward other women. The imagery of violence and war permeates every crevice of Atwood's novel; medieval battles, world wars, the battle between the sexes, the casual cruelty of parents toward children, the enmity between women. All the protagonists have been scarred by violence, yet they are not always willing to face up to their own destructive impulses. The relentless accrual of military metaphors highlights their capacity for cruelty, hatred, and vengefulness. "The personal is not political, thinks Tony: the personal is military. War is what happens when language fails" (*RB* 39).

Nor can Zenia's seductive and dangerous sexuality be dismissed as merely a male fantasy. As Atwood shows, the femme fatale is a richly resonant symbol. Deadly and sexy, predatory and powerful, she is a dream image that appeals to women as well as men. She is the woman who, in Sylvia Plath's words, "eats men like air." "The Zenias of this world . . . haven't let themselves be moulded into male fantasies, they've done it themselves. They've slipped sideways into dreams; the dreams of women too, because women are fantasies for other women, just as they are for men. But fantasies of a different kind" (*RB* 388). In *The Robber Bride*, as in the fairy tales that Roz retells to her daughters, women play all the roles: successful scholars, negligent mothers, abused children, wealthy entrepreneurs, discarded wives, scheming seductresses.

Zenia, moreover, is not just a symbol of the demonic but also the novelist's double. She talks her way into other women's lives by spinning stories, telling tales, serving up the details they want to hear. She is not just a fictional creation but a creator of fictions, inventing differing versions of her past for different ears: a child prostitute in Paris, the daughter of a Romanian gypsy, a Jewish refugee. Like the novelist, Zenia does it with mirrors, conjuring vivid, memorable, almost tangible realities out of thin air. She is a confidence artist, a trickster, seducing her audiences into dropping their guard and giving her their trust. As Atwood explains, "Zenia is, among other things, an illusionist. She tells stories so plausible that each of her listeners believes her; their belief comes in part from the structure of their own inner lives, from their wish and need to be taken in. But isn't this the goal of every novelist— to deceive? Doesn't every novelist play Zenia to every reader's willing dupe?"[52] Zenia's stories, like Atwood's own stories, are not literally true, yet they convey truth of a different kind, uncannily targeting the cover fantasies and hidden desires of those who hear them.

The Robber Bride thus interweaves multiple plots with self-conscious commentary on the act of storytelling. The novel begins and ends with Tony, who as a historian knows full well the traps that lie in wait for those who seek to recount the past. "History is a construct, she tells her students. Any point of entry is possible and all choices are arbitrary" (*RB* 4). The past is murky, formless, inchoate; it is given shape by the hand of the historian, who seizes hold of snippets of facts and marshals them into stories with a beginning and end. Such stories are fragile fictions that are easily unraveled; their authority is suspect. "Tony is daunted by the impossibility of accurate reconstruction" (*RB* 458). The story of Zenia, like any attempt to seize hold of the past, is tentative, insubstantial, "drifting from mouth to mouth and changing as it goes" (*RB* 457).

And yet, this skepticism toward stories is intertwined with ceaseless acts of storytelling and with other, more hopeful perspectives on narrative. Stories can deceive us, but they may also help us to make sense of our own past. They can serve as acts of testimony and witness that record things we need to remember. By recounting at her wedding the story of what she saw at her fiancé's house, the heroine of "The Robber Bridegroom" is saved from the prospect of certain death. The redemption of the protagonists of *The Robber Bride* is less certain, yet telling stories becomes an important way of connecting with others, making sense of the past, stitching together tentative insights about one's own motives and choices.

Tony's own obsession with the past as an academic historian is hailed as an "act of defiance": "these histories may be ragged and threadbare, patched together from worthless leftovers, but to her they are also flags, hoisted with a certain jaunty insolence, waving bravely though inconsequently, glimpsed here and there through the trees, on the mountain roads, among the ruins, on the long march into chaos" (*RB* 458). For Tony, stories are temporary yet indispensable markers: they help her to see, to map the terrain, to remember what has gone before. No story is authoritative, yet some stories are better than others, more adequate to the material they seek to encompass. Above all, storytelling is an act of remembrance, of obligation, of recognizing one's debt to what has gone before. Even as Zenia's ashes are finally dropped into the water, she continues to haunt the present. "The dead return in other forms . . . because we will them to" (*RB* 464). The three women will continue to tell stories about Zenia, to struggle to make sense of their lives, to shape random shards of memory into a provisional and flimsy coherence. To tell a story is to recognize an unbreakable connection to the past and to accept responsibility for making sense of that connection.

The Robber Bride thus tackles many of the same questions that occupy literary scholars in the form of an accessible and widely read novel. Atwood gives us a multilayered meditation on the inescapability of plot, the interweaving of text and life, the role of women in narrative, the status of stories as flimsy illusions and potent truths. The complexities of story and history are even more in evidence in her next work, *Alias Grace*, a stunning reworking of the historical novel that was published in 1995. Based on the story of Grace Marks, a Toronto housemaid accused of murdering her employer in the 1840s, Atwood's text combines conflicting versions of this event into an elaborate patchwork, a spatial design that offers many tantalizing glimpses of the past but never delivers a definitive explanation.[53] To mark the occasion of its publication, the *American Historical Review* printed a public lecture by Atwood on the writing of *Alias Grace* along with several responses by well-known historians. The most striking thing about this exchange, in my view, is how poorly it reflects on the historians.

Lynn Hunt, for example, makes the mistake of condescending toward her subject. Responding to Atwood's sparkling and suggestive comments on history, fiction, and historical fiction, she observes that her evidence darts off in too many directions; Atwood's ideas are deemed to be underdeveloped, rarely taking a precisely defined shape. Donning the mantle of academic expertise, Hunt writes as if the methods of professional historians were the only permissible way of thinking about history, time, and narrative. Even worse, she feels the need to defend and justify Atwood's subject matter, implying that the topics of Canadian fiction may only be of provincial interest and hence unfamiliar to—presumably unprovincial—American readers.[54]

The next respondent, Yale historian Jonathan Spence, takes Atwood rather too much at her word, answering playful metaphor with labored literalism. Responding to her claim that novelists are passionately interested in such universal phenomena as the flossing of teeth, he solemnly weighs up the question of whether flossing is indeed universal, citing the history of dental technology, manufacturing and distributional factors, and other variables. Spence is equally anxious to underscore the differences between historians and novelists and to insist that the historian can "speak with greater authority than others about what might have been and what could not have been."[55] Yet even as they strive to correct and revise Atwood's words by stressing their scholarly credentials, the historians show themselves to be no match for the novelist.

Literary critics, I should emphasize, often do not come off any better in their commentaries on Atwood's work. Any act of interpretation is a fumbling attempt to gain hold of a slippery object that may at any moment slide out of one's grasp. In Atwood's case, one often has the feeling that she is one step ahead of her audience; knowing full well how certain kinds of readers will respond to her work, she enfolds such reactions into the body of her writing. Hence the many gently barbed vignettes of characters who are prone to acts of self-deception and cut-and-dried interpretations of complex realities. Tangling with an Atwood novel, remarks one reviewer, is always a potentially wounding business.[56] While feminists are not the only target of such ironic barbs, Atwood often responds and writes back to feminist ideas in ways that are sympathetic yet critical.

The same is true of all the authors discussed in this chapter, whose work, as I've tried to show, carries out a three-fold act of revision and response. First of all, women writers are plundering myths and stories from literary tradition and the storehouse of culture and rewriting them in novel and unexpected ways. Embracing narrative as an indispensable device, they draw on old plots to fashion new meanings. Second, these authors are writing back to certain strands of feminist thought; while their fiction owes much to feminist ideas about the value and importance of women's lives, they are also chafing against narrow and prescriptive notions of what such lives are supposed to be. Feminism, they suggest, needs to remain open to multiple revisions and rewritings of its own stories. And, finally, their work can be seen as an eloquent rebuttal of some current theories of gender and narrative. Even as some scholars continue to lament the maleness of plot, women writers are mining the energies of narrative to their own ends, writing works that often combine critical acclaim and popular success.

The issue of popularity versus prestige is, of course, at the heart of many discussions of plot. While literary critics often justify their preference for experimental, ironic, literary forms by stressing their socially subversive qualities, it is paradoxically the case that such writing is also more likely to gain respectful attention and scholarly accolades. Plot, by contrast, is often seen as having virtually no value. "In literary fiction," laments one writer, "stories are there on sufferance. Other things are felt to be more important: technique, style, knowingness."[57]

Plot is often seen as a sop to the masses; a sign of competent know-how rather than serious and weighty art. In his provocative "Reader's Manifesto," recently published in the *Atlantic Monthly*, B. R. Myers lashes out at the "growing pretentiousness of American literary prose." Why, he asks, "are writers and critics so contemptuous of the urge to tell an exciting story?" According to Myers there is a gulf between the mass of ordinary readers, with their unquenchable enthusiasm for fast-moving action and page-turning plots, and the literary establishment, which looks down its nose at storytelling and favors ponderous wordplay, heavy-handed irony, and willful obscurity.[58]

And yet the works I've been looking at, it must be said, do not fall on either side of Myers's either/or caricature of the current literary scene. They are neither straightforward examples of genre fiction nor postmodern antinovels clogged down with displays of wordy erudition. These are novels that are accessible and often compellingly readable; yet they also engage in a critical revision of plot patterns. They harness the mysterious power of storytelling; yet the stories they tell are not just the same old stories. Here again, we see the force of both/and, as women writers blend tradition and innovation, pleasure and critical reflection, to forge vital new fictions of female identity.

4

VALUES

*The discourse of value
prevails in every cultural
context one can name.*
JENNIFER WICKE

good starting point for thinking about literature and value is Willy Russell's *Educating Rita,* known to most people through the 1981 film starring Julie Walters and Michael Caine. Rita is a hairdresser dissatisfied with her work, her husband, and her life who plucks up the courage to enroll at the Open University, a British institution that caters to nontraditional students. Her teacher, Frank, is a jaded English professor and former poet who has taken to the bottle. The play revolves around a series of comic and poignant encounters between student and teacher, as Rita struggles valiantly to make sense of the books and ideas she is encountering for the first time. *Educating Rita* asks us to think about the teaching of literature, about who gets to read, and how, and why.

The bouts of verbal sparring between Frank and his eager but nonplussed student tell us pretty much the same thing that the French sociologist Pierre Bourdieu lays out in his panoply of surveys, questionnaires, and statistical charts.[1] That is to say, there is nothing natural about "loving literature." If by literature we mean the standard pantheon of the greats, then most people fall into the category of the baffled, the bored, or the indifferent. Those who value Shakespeare and Shelley, Dickens and Dickinson, have learned to do so. This usually means either growing up in a household where reading and talking about books is taken for granted or taking a lot of literature classes in college.

In other words, aesthetic appreciation is linked to social class and access to education.

Literary critics of a certain cast, however, try to hide this fact. They talk as if appreciating literature were simply a question of taste, sensitivity, and imagination. They seem to believe that any person of undulled mind who encounters a play by Shakespeare or a poem by Wordsworth will thrill to its sublime power. They assume that the value of literature is obvious and unmistakable, emblazoned on the page for all to see. Great books, in this view, transcend the particulars of time and place to speak directly to all humanity.

For Rita, this is so much claptrap. She knows full well that studying literature means learning an alien tongue and a mysterious way of thinking. She senses her own ignorance of the rules, rules that are all the more baffling because they are often left unstated. The most fundamental of these rules is what Bourdieu calls "an aesthetic disposition," that is to say, approaching a work as part of a tradition of art rather than as part of life. Rita flouts this convention on her first visit to Frank's office when she walks up to a Victorian nude print on his wall, inspects it with great interest, and announces, "it's very erotic." Responding to Frank's puzzled look, Rita expands cheerfully: "Y' don't paint pictures like that just so that people can admire the brush strokes, do y'? . . . This was the pornography of its day, wasn't it? It's sort of like *Men Only*, isn't it? But in those days they had to pretend it wasn't erotic, so they made it religious."[2]

Rita's subsequent education as a fledgling student of literature starts off in a flurry of missteps and misapprehensions. In the next scene we find her railing against her first reading assignment, declaring that *Howards End* is "crap." When Frank asks her to justify her comments, she bursts out: "It's crap because the feller who wrote it was a louse. Because halfway through that book I couldn't go on readin' it because he, Mr Bleedin' E. M. Forster says, quote 'We are not concerned with the poor' unquote. That's why it's crap" (*ER* 19). After persuading Rita that such an answer fails to do full justice to Forster, Frank's patience is sorely tried by her next effort. Despairingly, he asks: "Rita, how the hell can you write an essay on E. M. Forster with almost total reference to Harold Robbins?" To which Rita shoots back indignantly: "Don't go on at me. You said; y'said, 'Reference to other authors will impress the examiners'" (ER 24). Frank, returning to this theme: "You seem to be under the impression that all books are literature." Rita: "Aren't they?" Frank: "No." Rita: "Well—well how d' y' tell?" Frank: "I—erm-erm—one's always known really." Rita: "But how d'y' work it out if y' don't know? See that's what I've got to learn, isn't it? I'm dead ignorant y' know" (ER 25).

Frank's lame "one's always known really" speaks of being acculturated into a way of life that is so deeply ingrained as to be invisible. For Frank, it is second nature to talk about paintings as examples of Pre-Raphaelite art rather than as titillating pictures of naked women. It is self-evident that *Howards End* is not the same kind of book as *The Carpetbaggers* and that Forster's indifference to the plight of the poor is not a sufficient reason for dismissing his novels. These things are, as it were, the taken-for-granted assumptions against which the real business of talking about literature goes on.

For some students, of course, they are anything but obvious. But usually they learn to keep their mouths shut and their heads down, and to avoid the gut-wrenching terrors of public humiliation. Rita, by contrast, is unabashed about her ignorance and forthright about her confusion. As the quintessential naïf, the outsider, the person blithely ignorant of what everybody else seems to know, she makes the familiar seem suddenly strange. She allows us to see that what goes without saying is not so obvious after all, and that reading literature is not as natural and spontaneous a process as it may seem. When critics rail against the pernicious influence of literary theory and urge a direct engagement with the work, Rita's response is obviously not what they have in mind. Gerald Graff puts it well in his response to such critics: "the experience of reading a text may *feel* like a pretheoretical, precritical activity," but "that feeling can arise only because the reader has already mastered the contexts and presuppositions necessary for the text's comprehension."[3]

Furthermore, Rita is well aware that those who talk about books the way Frank does are certain kinds of people. They are not randomly distributed among the populace according to gifts of taste, sensitivity, and imagination. And they are certainly not Rita's friends, neighbors, or the members of her family. Rather, they are the same people that buy whole-grain bread, live in large old Victorian houses, and know what kind of wine to take to a dinner party. Like Bourdieu, she makes the connection between taste in literature and taste in food and furniture, clothing and housing. They are all forms of distinction, discreet but unmistakable markers of class, status, and education.

So far, my discussion of *Educating Rita* makes it sound as if Russell's play were on the side of the canon-busters, of those who see the study of great books as nothing more than bourgeois mystification. And yet literature soon becomes a precious lifeline for Rita, a means of survival. It opens up exhilarating new worlds and challenges what she describes as the monotony, conformity, and hopelessness of much of her everyday life. It is a source of hope, energy, and inspiration. When her studies begin to cause a serious rift between her and her husband, Frank suggests that she rethink her commitment to the course. "When art and literature begin to take the place of life itself," he begins, "perhaps it's time to . . ." But Rita bursts out emphatically: "But it's not takin' the place of life, it's providin' me with life itself . . . Comin' here, doin' this, it's given me more life than I've had in years" (*ER* 34). At another point, she tells Frank: "You know what I learn from you, about art an' literature, it feeds me, inside. I can get through the rest of the week if I know I've got comin' here to look forward to" (*ER* 30–31).

Thinking about Rita's response brings to mind Richard Rorty's discussion of the "inspirational value of great works of literature." Rorty argues that contemporary criticism is losing sight of the power of such works, their ability to awe us, amaze us, and inspire us to see the world in a different light. Great literature, he suggests, can radically recontextualize much of what we know. It is about "taking the world by the throat and insisting that there is more to this life than we have ever imagined."[4] Thus young people have often found in the study of literature a precious outlet for romantic enthusiasms and utopian dreams. Yet current trends in cultural studies and political approaches to literature mean that such students are getting short-changed. Contemporary criticism places too much emphasis on demystifying and debunking, Rorty claims, as it prizes knowing sophistication above romance and inspiration. It teaches people how to devalue but not how to value.

Rorty's comments are echoed by others who feel that the study of literature has fallen on hard times. George Levine, like Rorty, writes as if contemporary criticism were synonymous with a whole-hearted embrace of history and sociology and a spurning of aesthetics. "In the current critical scene," laments Levine, "literature is all too often demeaned, the aesthetic experience denigrated or reduced to mystified ideology." While Levine sympathizes with attempts to place works of art in their social context, he clearly feels that the trend has gone too far. Contemporary talk about cultural politics, he suggests, does not help us to understand literature's "peculiar power to move and engage." We do not have to believe in the transcendental, eternal power of the canon to recognize that the aesthetic is a "mode that operates differently from others and contributes in distinctive ways to the possibilities of human fulfillment and connection."[5]

Rorty's and Levine's comments raise two questions that I want to look at in more detail. The first question is about the effect of literary works. Do they inspire or move, teach or disturb, give pleasure or give solace? Or is their main purpose to invite a tranquil state of disinterested contemplation? It is, in other words, a question about the nature of aesthetic experience. The second question is about the goodness or badness of particular works. How do we discriminate between the books we read and on what grounds can we say that some are better than others? This is a question about aesthetic value. These questions are distinct, yet at the same time they are also related. Clearly, what you think counts as aesthetic experience will affect the kinds of works that you find valuable.

Rorty's account of literature is unabashedly romantic. He speaks of shudders of awe and romantic enthusiasm, prophets and demiurges, charisma and genius. His language conjures up an aesthetic of the sublime. Literature, Rorty suggests, offers something akin to religious experience; it is a way of being taken out of yourself into a different world. To be inspired by a work is to be swept off your feet, to fall hopelessly and helplessly in love.

For Rorty, another either/or thinker, this kind of infatuation rules out reflective judgment. "You cannot," he declares, "find inspirational value in a text at the same time that you are viewing it as a product of a mechanism of cultural production." And later, nailing down the point: "Just as you cannot be swept off your feet by another human being at the same time as you recognize him or her as a good specimen of a certain type, so you cannot simultaneously be inspired by a work and be knowing about it."[6] (To which I can only reply, on both counts: I can and I have.) In the Rortyean scheme of things, the value of literature seems to be measured by how much romantic enthusiasm it inspires in the young. As Rorty admits, it means liking Rilke more than Brecht, but also, one would think, Tolkien more than Tolstoy. It is a view of literature that is consistent but strikingly narrow. Championing an emotional surge toward the ineffable as the essence of aesthetic experience, Rorty ignores the many other reasons why people choose to read books.

What about the specific question of aesthetic value? Rorty tackles this issue by distancing himself from what he calls Platonism, that is to say, a view of the canon as embodying universal and eternal values. Rather, says Rorty, "We should cheerfully admit that canons are temporary and touchstones replaceable." The canon "is as changeable as the historical and personal situations of readers." But, he concludes, "this should not lead us to discard the idea of greatness. We should see great works of literature as great because they have inspired many readers, not as having inspired many readers because they are great."[7]

A feminist critic might retort that this phrasing implies an even playing field, where the best works of art rise to the top simply because everyone agrees they are the best. But Rorty's "many readers" is of course a selective group. Until recently, women were close to invisible in most of the institutions that help to shape and cement literary reputation. Greatness was determined by one sex, not two. Furthermore, the language of literary evaluation is replete with gendered meanings; to be associated with woman or the feminine is often to be seen as minor or trivial. It is hard, then, to avoid the conclusion that the cards have been stacked and that aesthetic judgments are mixed up with prejudices and power relations.

Rorty is right, nevertheless, to point out the obvious limits of naysaying and debunking. Those who have chosen to teach literature rather than, say, economics or psychology should be able to offer a cogent rationale for what they are doing. They need to justify the distinctive value of the books they want their students to read. And yet there is also something very one-sided about seeing the aesthetic as a soulful surge toward the sublime that transcends the realm of dry-as-dust social analysis. The value of literature does not have to lie in its opposition to politics.

In the rest of this chapter, I will address the common complaint that feminist critics have banished talk about literary value by looking at three influential fields of feminist criticism: Virginia Woolf, the Gothic novel, and Third World women's writing.[8] I will show that debates over value have by no means disappeared, though they may have become more contentious. There is no longer a gentlemanly consensus about the canon but a clamor of voices and a clash of competing frameworks. And yet value judgments continue to undergird most feminist readings of literary texts; rather than exclusively aesthetic or purely political, these judgments are usually some blend of the two. Literary values may no longer seem eternal and unshakable, but the act of evaluating is, it seems, inescapable.

Feminism and Literary Value: Virginia Woolf

A common accusation leveled at feminist critics is that they have no sense of value. When we look more closely at this complaint, we find that it can mean two different things. The first claim is that feminism encourages readers to debunk and to devalue rather than to appreciate. Feminists have nothing positive to say about literature; they are nay-sayers who spend their time whining, criticizing, and carping. They express their resentment at great works of art by belittling what they cannot appreciate.

The second claim is that feminists do have a system of values but these values are the wrong ones. That is to say, feminist scholars rank books highly simply because they are by women, or because they have been excluded from the canon, or because they convey a politically correct message. Feminist criteria for evaluating works of literature fall short, in other words, because they are political, not literary.

The first argument, I have tried to show in this book, misses the mark. By and large, feminist critics are more interested in looking at works they admire than listing the flaws of those they loathe. Of course, adulation or indictment are hardly the only options; interpretation is often a matter of teasing out the competing voices in a text rather than simply giving it a thumbs-up or a thumbs-down. But certainly those who describe the general tenor of feminist scholarship as one of mean-spirited debunking have got things seriously wrong. One reason feminism has been successful is that it has made more books interesting to more people. It has opened up options rather than closing them off.

This leaves the second complaint: that feminist scholars want to reduce literary value to political value and see no difference between them. This criticism hits closer to home; some feminists do argue that art and politics are one, and that this "one" is ultimately politics. But again, as an account of the day-to-day practice of feminist criticism, it simply will not do. In fact, as I hope to show, most feminist critics routinely engage in acts of aesthetic evaluation. That is to say, they write with enthusiasm about books they admire and back up their claims by appealing to what are recognizably literary criteria.

Of course, feminist critics tend to define the literariness of literature more broadly than Rorty or Bloom. They believe that the aesthetic dimension includes themes as well as forms, social meanings as well as psychic yearning. They are skeptical of the view that aesthetic experience can be completely disinterested, shorn of all reference to the world or stirrings of sensual pleasure. Rather, our response to works of art is messy and impure. We can enjoy much in literature that we would not enjoy in life; art is not a simple mirror or document of the social world. Yet our aesthetic tastes and inclinations cannot be completely severed from our lives and interests as social beings. Feminist critics would agree with Barbara Herrnstein Smith's observation that aesthetic experience is inseparable from memory, context, and meaning, and hence from who we are, where we are, and all that has already happened to us.[9]

Feminist critics are also less likely to think of their likes and dislikes as impartial responses to the inherent qualities of individual works. Terry Eagleton writes: "There is no such thing as a literary work or tradition which is valuable *in itself*. . . . 'Value' is a transitive term: it means whatever is valued by certain people in specific situations, according to particular criteria and in the light of given purposes."[10] Value is created, not given, and it changes over time. This certainly does not mean that we cannot agree to value something "as literature." But it does mean that such a phrase raises more questions than it answers because people will disagree, often quite strongly, about what count as literary criteria. Is the essence of literature to be found in organic unity? Paradox and irony? Ethical enrichment? Radical undecidability? All of these answers have had many supporters over the years.

Even Harold Bloom's own *The Western Canon* pays tribute, however reluctantly, to the influence of feminism on aesthetic judgment.[11] Zora Neale Hurston, listed in the appendix as a canonical writer, is only there because of the strenuous efforts of black feminist critics who rescued her from out-of-print oblivion. And without feminism, Bloom would never have devoted a chapter of his book to Virginia Woolf, even though his avowed intention is to disparage feminist readings of Woolf. For a long time, Woolf was seen as a minor modernist, certainly not in the same league as Kafka, Joyce, or Eliot.

Nowadays, of course, Virginia Woolf is the supreme example of a canonical woman writer. She has become the female Shakespeare, "readily available when one needs a well-known literary figure, a celebrity, to illustrate a point."[12] Not just a great writer, Woolf is now a literary star, whose mournful features stare out at us from postcards and coffee mugs, posters and T-shirts. She has ascended from the teeming crowd of minor authors and also-rans into the pantheon of the greats. Feminist critics, quite simply, have increased Woolf's value.

Like any cultural icon, Woolf exists in many versions. She has attracted hordes of zealous interpreters, all eager to correct the errors of rival readers and to have the final word. These include a number of scholars anxious to save Woolf from the feminists, of whom Harold Bloom is the best known. At one point, Bloom briefly considers the possibility that there may be two Woolfs: a feminist and a distinguished novelist. But in a gesture that we have come to know well by now, Bloom responds by denying her doubleness. Her feminism, it appears, is inconsequential. "Like Pater and like Nietzsche, Woolf is best described as an apocalyptic aesthete for whom human existence and the world are finally justified only as aesthetic phenomena."[13]

How can such a one-sided view claim the high ground of literary sophistication? Bloom's transparent attempt to annex Woolf to his own party does not stand up well against recent feminist criticism. Here, instead of the one-note dogmatism that Bloom derides, we find responses that are much more nuanced than his own. These feminist readings pay careful heed to the ambivalence of Woolf's work: insisting on the logic of both/and, they explore the connections and tensions between art and politics, between Woolf's uncompromising passion for words and her sharp sense of social dynamics and disparities.

We can trace some of the shifts in Woolf criticism by looking at changing responses to her 1927 novel *To the Lighthouse*. For a long time, it was a truism of Woolf scholarship that her work expressed a desire for connection and communion. "Throughout Mrs. Woolf's work," wrote James Naremore in 1973, "the chief problem for her and for her characters is to overcome the space between things, to attain an absolute unity with the world."[14] Critics often fleshed out this idea by tracing patterns of connection and repetition in Woolf's fiction, showing how disparate fragments and snippets of language were woven into a coherent whole. They saw this method as amply justified by Woolf's own aestheticism and the exquisite nature of her prose.

In *To the Lighthouse*, for example, critics were quick to draw parallels between Woolf's practice as a writer and the urge to unify and connect that drives Mrs. Ramsay, the wife and mother at the heart of the novel. For example, back in 1961, Geoffrey Hartman argued that Woolf's works "suppose a mind with an immense, even unlimited, power to see or build continuities." And in an all too common association of the female author with her female protagonist, he continues: "Mrs. Ramsay is the feminine part of the soul . . . with its frightening power for mystical marriage, that refusal to sustain the separateness of things in an overly great anticipation of final unity."[15]

Feminist critics are skeptical, however, about this metaphysical rendition of gender. They point out that Woolf does not just echo Mrs. Ramsay's own desire for unity and connection but also presents it ironically by revealing its painful costs. Discovering further layers of meaning in *To the Lighthouse*, they show it to be a more fraught and complex work than was originally realized. Woolf, it turns out, may be as intent on fragmenting unions as she is on unifying fragments. Here Hartman's vision of the feminine as unifying and connecting reminds us of Mr. Ramsay, who draws comfort from seeing his wife as a beatific symbol of plenitude but who remains oblivious to her thoughts and desires. Woolf's delicate charting of the silent dramas and unspoken undercurrents of marital life is often elegiac, but it is also penetrating and severe. She pinpoints moments of contentment, joy, and even triumph, but she also traces out the many discords, tensions, and painful truths that lie below the surface.

What, then, are we to make of Mrs. Ramsay's gift of linking, uniting, and joining? It is she who smooths the path of social intercourse, who orchestrates the elaborate ritual of meals, who smooths ruffled feathers and soothes the irritated, the awkward, and the malcontent. Looking around the table at her family and guests at dinnertime, Mrs. Ramsay reflects: "the whole of the effort of merging and flowing and creating rested on her."[16] And her further thoughts, borne out by the rest of the book, make it clear that this burden is shaped by the fact of her sex. "Again she felt, as a fact, without hostility, the sterility of men, for if she did not do it nobody would do it" (L 96). We see in Woolf's novel a tribute to the grace and the dignity, but also the arduousness, of a middle-class, middle-aged woman's life. Moving in and out of Mrs. Ramsay's mind, Woolf allows us to glimpse the hidden art and intelligence behind a way of life often dismissed as trivial and feminine.

In a further unifying gesture, we are made to see the links between such traditional female arts and the making of art: the everyday and the transcendent are not opposed but connected. Lily Briscoe, the key figure in the second half of To the Lighthouse, opts for a life very different from Mrs. Ramsay's. She chooses art rather than marriage, engaging in her own struggle to realize her creative vision as a painter. She is, it seems, the new woman rather than the old, unwilling to soothe, charm, and conciliate. Yet in a flash of insight, Lily recognizes the parallels between her own art and Mrs. Ramsay's graceful and creative fashioning of daily life. "Mrs Ramsay making of the moment something permanent (as in another sphere Lily herself tried to make of the moment something permanent)—this was of the nature of a revelation. In the midst of chaos there was shape; this eternal passing and flowing . . . was struck into stability" (L 183).

The mention of permanence speaks directly to the constellation of gender at the heart of To the Lighthouse. It is the men in Woolf's novel who brood about whether their name and their influence will endure. Mr. Ramsay, in particular, is a scholar and philosopher obsessed with the idea of immortality, with the solitary quest for truth and transcendence. Yet Woolf remorselessly exposes the hollowness at the heart of this heroic self-image. She dwells on Mr. Ramsay's voracious and petulant demands on his wife, his childlike dependence on the very female qualities that he often holds up to scorn. In a powerful reversal of traditional values, the male pursuit of transcendence is gently mocked while the seemingly trivial and invisible work of women's everyday lives achieves a delicate and tenuous permanence. Looking around her at the community she has fashioned around the dinner table, Mrs. Ramsay exults in a moment of joyful completion. "Of such moments, she thought, the thing is made that remains for ever after. This would remain" (L 121).

Here, it seems, we have a compelling illustration of a theme that Woolf takes up several times in her essays: "when a woman comes to write a novel, she will find that she is permanently wishing to alter the established values—to make serious what appears insignificant to a man, and trivial what appears to him important."[17] When feminist critics first turned to Woolf, they often praised her for affirming such woman-centered values; her work was hailed as a major cornerstone of an aesthetic grounded in female experience. But in the last fifteen years or so, the tenor of feminist commentary on Woolf has changed. Increasingly, scholars lay stress on what Pamela Caughie describes as "the many ambiguities and equivocations in her writings."[18] What they value in Woolf is her suspicion of fixed positions and orthodoxies, her distrust of partisanship and truth. Rather than affirming femaleness, they suggest, Woolf's fiction is often deeply mistrustful of attempts to fix, define, and delimit what it means to be a woman.

To the Lighthouse, for example, shows that Mrs. Ramsay is not fully seen by others because she is viewed through a haze of sentiment, nostalgia, and idealization. Woolf gestures toward a darkness and discord at the heart of Mrs. Ramsay's life that she never fully faces and that remains hidden to others. She describes the rigorous self-effacement that lies at the core of the traditional feminine role. Mrs. Ramsay is constantly *besieged*: her nascent stirrings of self are relentlessly interrupted by her children, her guests, her husband's need for praise and reassurance. Rather than a stable center of value in the novel, female identity is shown to be a disturbing absence, an existential void. "*To the Lighthouse*," observes Toril Moi, "illustrates the destructive nature of a metaphysical belief in strong, immutably fixed gender identities." As a result, she concludes, Woolf's novel undermines the efforts of those who would see women as essentially different and superior.[19]

From a feminist viewpoint, then, the issues explored in *To the Lighthouse* are neither minor nor inconsequential. Even as Woolf eschews the grand and the heroic, she alerts us to monumental truths about human relations that lie hidden in everyday phrases exchanged between husband and wife. Feminist scholars suggest that there are crucial connections between this vision of a marriage and the formal innovations of her work. "Woolf's manifest modernist styles," writes Margaret Homans, "are not incidental but absolutely crucial to her searching critique of patriarchal institutions."[20] Thus Woolf ruptures the marriage plot that has traditionally exercised such a powerful grip on novels about women. Unlike Mrs. Ramsay, she is not interested in trying to knit men and women together in blissful unions. Instead, she breaks apart sequence and sentence, fractures old forms, searching for new ways of writing women's lives. Joseph Allen Boone writes: "by means of the same narrative devices that violate conventions of fictional realism, Woolf simultaneously dismantles the Victorian marital ideal embodied in the Ramsays' union of complementary opposition."[21]

Thus we find in Woolf's fiction a strenuous struggle to circumvent the familiar feminine script of romance as well as the masculine plot of solitary struggle. Her most memorable heroines are older women, no longer caught up in the intoxicating demands of courtship, embedded in other webs of affiliation, affection, and loyalty. We find many examples of connection without telos, unexpected moments of affinity that cut across the male/female bond. Often, it is the moments of friendship, love, or erotic desire between women that resonate with particular power and intensity.[22] Yet such moments of connection are tentative and fragmentary rather than manifestations of a grand unifying principle. In Woolf's work, masculine knowledge is often linked to the authoritative announcement, the confident pursuit of given truths. In the intentional hesitancy of her own style, we find a refusal of summary and summation, an embracing of contradiction, a suspicion of telos of any kind.

Feminist scholars have written at length about Woolf's language, dissecting the many details of style, tone, and point of view. At the same time, they have dismantled the stereotype of Woolf as a delicate otherworldly aesthete and ethereal prophet of the interior life. They show how Woolf's scrupulous attention to language and form and her delicate tracing of evanescent thoughts and feelings link up to often searing commentary on the relations between women and men. The beauty of her words, they suggest, is inseparable from her struggle to imagine new literary and expressive possibilities for women. Thus Homans speaks of those "who find Woolf's political analysis first and foremost in her writing, in the style and structure of her prose—in the very qualities of beauty and plangency that have convinced other readers that she is above politics."[23] What we find, then, in many feminist accounts of Woolf is a figure who is torn and contradictory, ambivalent and multifaceted, concerned with aesthetics *and* politics. Rather than providing simple answers, Rachel Bowlby argues, "it is precisely in her insistence on the sexual inflection of all questions of historical understanding and literary representation that Woolf is a feminist writer."[24]

This kind of response is a good example of one feminist approach to literary value, an approach that defines many readings of both famous and lesser-known women writers. The critic writes against the grain of traditional interpretations, showing how careful attention to gender can transform our sense of what a work of literature is really about. She brings into focus patterns, themes, and designs that were previously occluded or invisible, showing how the text draws on, yet also rewrites, the meanings of masculine and feminine. At the same time, her commentary also draws on familiar and uncontroversial criteria of literary value. In the case of Woolf, for example, feminist scholars pay tribute to her innovative formal techniques, the allusive and suggestive qualities of her style, and her nuanced and multifaceted forms of characterization. Often such commentaries are couched in the language of poststructuralist or postmodern theory. Yet the underlying claim—that the value of literature lies in its stubborn resistance to paraphrase, fixed truths, and taken-for-granted orthodoxies—is a staple theme of modern criticism that unites a wide range of thinkers from F. R. Leavis to Jean-François Lyotard.

Defending women's writing in terms of its formal innovation, sophistication, and complexity is perhaps the most familiar and well-established form of feminist criticism, a practice that goes on every day in classrooms and lecture halls, at seminars and conferences. It is puzzling, then, that conservative scholars so often accuse feminists of having no interest in questions of literary merit. If there are now more women writers included in a typical survey course, if the library spills over with critical volumes on Woolf and Edith Wharton and Toni Morrison, it is because feminist scholars have made a painstaking case for the importance of such writers *as writers*. In this way, they have influenced what all literary scholars value, not just what feminists value.

In some instances, the shift in perspective has been dramatic. For example, it is hard to imagine that a writer of Edith Wharton's caliber barely used to rate a mention in histories of American literature. As feminist scholars have pointed out, the creation of the American canon was a project driven as much by ideology as by aesthetics: this canon was to be distinctively American, owing little to British or European traditions. Such a stirring vision of national uniqueness was shaped, not surprisingly, by contestable beliefs about what counted as truly American qualities.

Thus the essence of Americanness was often found in stories of solitary males struggling in the wilderness, what Nina Baym calls "melodramas of beset manhood." In such a context, Edith Wharton could be dismissed as a chronicler of drawing-room dramas, a "memorialist of a dying aristocracy."[25] It was only with the rise of feminist criticism that it became possible to read Wharton differently. Here we can see how a rise in literary value correlates with a change in social values. An altered perception of what was worth writing about caused Wharton's work to seem more contemporary and more aesthetically sophisticated than her critics had given her credit for. As a result, her stock has risen. Thanks largely to feminism, more people now think of Wharton as an important writer.

Another Aesthetic: The Gothic Novel

While conservative critics typically ignore this laborious struggle to establish the aesthetic credentials of women writers, it is also true that trying to prove literary greatness is no longer a burning concern for many feminist scholars. One reason is the surprising success of feminist criticism. Many of the early battles have been won. A canon of female authors has been established. It is no longer considered eccentric to write a dissertation on Virginia Woolf or Toni Morrison. Female writers receive much more attention than they used to, not just from feminist critics but from everyone. Certain authors are now in danger of disappearing under the mountain of books, monographs, dissertations, and articles they have inspired. A sense of exhaustion has set in, along with a desire to tackle different kinds of questions.

In fact, some scholars have always been eager to push beyond traditional criteria of literary value. As Lilian S. Robinson points out, feminists "are torn between defending the quality of their discoveries and radically redefining literary quality itself."[26] As newcomers to the academy, they had learned to speak the language of professional criticism. But they soon began to ask searching questions about this language. Where did it come from? What were its assumptions? What did it obscure or occlude? And did feminist critics really want to assent to a peremptory and sweeping distinction between great books and what the Germans unabashedly call *Trivialliteratur*?

Jane Tompkins tackles some of these questions in *Sensational Designs: The Cultural Work of American Fiction, 1790–1860*, an influential account of works of fiction long dismissed as outdated, melodramatic, and even embarrassing. In her concluding chapter, Tompkins addresses the objections of those who concede that works such as *Uncle Tom's Cabin* may be historically important but nevertheless consider them worthless as literature. "For criticism, the objection goes, concerns itself with the specifically *literary* features of American writing. And what distinguishes a work *as literature* is the way it separates itself from transitory issues of the kind I have been discussing." Thus the traditional critic, writes Tompkins, often responds to her interest in sentimental novels with the withering rejoinder: "But are these works really any *good*?"[27]

Such a question, of course, makes a confident appeal to a shared set of aesthetic standards, assuming that such standards are self-evident and indisputable. Tompkins, in response, suggests that talk about literary value tends to be circular and self-confirming:

> The general agreement about which writers are great and which are minor that exists at any particular moment in the culture creates the impression that these judgments are obvious and self-evident. But their obviousness is not a natural fact; it is constantly being produced and maintained by cultural activity: by literary anthologies, by course syllabi, book reviews, magazine articles, book club selections, radio and television programs. . . . The choice between Stedman and Dickinson, Stowe and Hawthorne, is never made in a vacuum, but from within a particular perspective that determines in advance which literary work will seem "good."[28]

Having absorbed certain beliefs about what constitutes good literature, it is not surprising that literary critics are subsequently drawn to works that display similar qualities. Once everyone knows that great writing means irony and understatement rather than emotion and melodrama, solitude and existential angst rather than domesticity and female friendship, then it is a foregone conclusion that Ernest Hemingway is a better writer than Fanny Fern.

Tompkins's point, however, is that established ways of talking about value are not the only ones and that the language of literary evaluation does in fact change over time. I want to take up this idea in my second example of debates over value, the Gothic novel. This genre has recently experienced a sharp rise in literary prestige, due largely, though not exclusively, to feminism. Yet most commentators also agree that Gothic novels are melodramatic, repetitive, implausible, incoherent, and full of clichés. Clearly, then, the aesthetic value of Gothic does not lie in the same qualities that inspire admiration of Woolf. The genre is interesting for different reasons. It is not that critics of the Gothic novel do not talk about aesthetic questions but rather that they highlight different aspects of aesthetic response.

Nowadays, Gothic usually means supermarket reading: paperbacks displaying a lurid cover of a terrified woman fleeing from a dark, looming mansion. The Gothic novel, however, first flourished in England in the late eighteenth and early nineteenth century, when it was one of the most popular forms of fiction. Many writers as well as readers of Gothic were women; Ann Radcliffe, for example, was the best-paid novelist of the eighteenth century.[29] Yet the Gothic novel used to inspire disdainful sniffs from many literary scholars, thanks to its status as a women's genre as well as its continuing mass-market appeal. When the Gothic was not silently passed over in histories of the novel, it was often discounted as a lowly, even debased form. The melodrama and sensationalism of Gothic, critics firmly insisted, had nothing to do with the authentic transcendence of Romanticism.

Its recent change in status is due, in part, to a wave of feminist readings of Gothic fiction. This attention is hardly surprising; not only do many Gothic novels have a female protagonist and adopt a woman's point of view, but they often seem to be obsessed with the murky undercurrents of gender and sexuality. Stranded in an isolated setting, the heroine uncovers an unspeakable secret and is subject to terrible dangers. The emotional intensities of the text swirl around her highly charged encounters with a man who is sinister yet strangely fascinating. In Radcliffe's *The Mysteries of Udolpho*, for example, the heroine is kidnapped by her aunt's new husband, an arrogant and enigmatic Italian nobleman. Held prisoner in Montoni's remote and gloomy castle in the mountains, Emily undergoes various real and imagined terrors. Not only must she confront the calculating cruelty of a man who seeks to subjugate and destroy her, but her spirit is tested by mysterious encounters with what seem to be supernatural forces. Radcliffe's novel blurs romance and terror, fascination and revulsion, in staging an elemental battle of the sexes.

One of the reasons that Gothic is interesting to feminists is that it offers a symbolic expression of female paranoia. Male paranoia, of course, is well catered to; we are all familiar with a long history of deadly women that stretches from the sirens of the Odyssey to the dangerous blondes of film noir. But we have many fewer examples of "hommes fatals," of a male hero portrayed from a female viewpoint as both seductive and dangerous. The Gothic novel, by contrast, gives full rein to female ambivalence toward male sexuality. It treats masculinity as a disturbing mystery. It probes relentlessly into the connections between sex and violence, desire and pain, terror and pleasure. The brooding, enigmatic villain, suggests Patricia Meyer Spacks, is a multivalent symbol of the "paternal sublime," of a father who is seen as remote, fascinating, and all-powerful. "Radcliffean Gothic," she writes, "embodies a specifically *female* view of the family romance: not the competition of fathers and sons, but the dangerous, ambivalent love of daughters for fathers. Mutual attraction governs the relations of fathers and daughters. The relationship, however, also emphasizes women's exclusion from male power."[30]

While it delves into the psychodynamics of erotic and familial relations, the aesthetics of the Gothic clearly has nothing to do with realism as it is normally understood. In fact, the Gothic novel is famous for its stock characters and devices, which, as Eugenia de la Motte remarks, became clichés almost before they became conventions. These devices were already seen as risible and open to parody in 1800, as in the following list: "unnatural parents,—persecuted lovers,—murders,—haunted apartments,—winding sheets, and winding stair-cases,—subterraneous passages,—lamps that are dim and perverse, and that al-

33333333

333

ways go out when they should not,—monasteries,—caves,—monks, tall, thin, and withered, with lank, abstemious cheeks,—dreams,— groans,—and spectres."[31] The Gothic novel moves these devices around in the manner of figures on a chessboard. It has no interest in creating well-rounded, multifaceted characters. There is an archetypal, dream-like quality to the figures that people the Gothic landscape. They are cardboard cutouts or sinister silhouettes rather than three-dimensional individuals. Their language is declamatory, exaggerated, and curiously impersonal; it is closer in spirit to the stylized poses of dramatic ritual than to psychological realism. The recurrence of doubles, mirrors, and split selves make it clear that the Gothic is not about the formation of the self (*Bildung*), but a psychic scattering of the self, a return to a condition of de-individuation and formlessness.

The appeal of Gothic thus has little to do with the modernist cultivation of an exquisite literary sensibility. Its aesthetic is of a different order: extravagant yet enigmatic, it veers toward the visual rather than the verbal, toward elemental drama rather than critical reflection, toward exaggeration rather than nuance. It draws on the condensed associative and emotional power of archetypal symbols—houses, veils, fathers, virgins—coating them with ever more disturbing and densely charged layers of meaning. It organizes these figures into a novelistic architecture whose primary purpose is to generate suspense and anxiety in the reader. In the Gothic hall of mirrors, everything is extreme, distorted, strangely askew. We are invited into a realm of morbidity and madness, the eerie and the weird.

The Gothic novel, writes Coral Ann Howells, is "a shadowy world of ruins and twilit scenery lit up from time to time by lurid flashes of passion and violence."[32] The stability of the external world breaks down as reality is translated into the register of hysteria, paranoia, and madness. The uncertainty and dread of Gothic springs from the sense of a looming, dimly perceived danger that exceeds human grasp. The heroine's susceptible and overactive imagination causes her to imagine terrors where none may exist. Because the reader shares her perspective rather than being distanced from it, we too are placed in a position of ignorance and susceptibility. Confronted with unsettling enigmas strewn throughout the narrative, we are rendered as powerless as the heroine. The voluminous, labyrinthian form of *The Mysteries of Udolpho*, with its embedded secrets and veiled terrors, echoes and repeats the winding corridors, trapdoors, and dead ends of the Gothic castle itself. Enveloped in obscurity, we struggle vainly toward enlightenment.

Freudian thought has an obvious affinity with Gothic fiction, inviting us to read the genre as a symbolic encounter with repressed—or not so repressed—desires. Gothic is, after all, relentlessly fixated on taboo: rape, murder, incest, necrophilia. Feminist critics often see female Gothic as an especially rich source of insight into the psychic dramas of femininity. "Like many women novelists of this period," observes Mary Poovey, "Radcliffe is using the spectral arena of the Gothic castle to dramatize the eruption of psychic material ordinarily controlled by the inhibitions of bourgeois society."[33]

The impulses that the genre brings to light may be unsettling and often uncomfortable. Michelle Massé, for example, argues that the Gothic is an essentially masochistic form, enacting a complex psychic response to female experiences of vulnerability and fear.[34] But Claire Kahane points out that it also allows for an active testing of the boundaries of identity, allowing the heroine a freedom and license that she does not possess in more conventional genres. In the strange and surreal world of the Gothic, the distinctions between life and death, self and other, inside and outside, male and female, are subject to intense confusion and crisis. While Gothic novels are full of dead or absent mothers, Kahane suggests that we can see the castle itself an anxiety-laden symbol of the maternal body, imagined as both womb and tomb.[35] Indeed, this castle is often an overpowering and demonic presence in the genre; seemingly alive and sentient, it swallows up its inhabitants, leaving them to wander helplessly in its dark intestinal pathways.

Yet if Freudian thought seems to shed a great deal of light on the Gothic, this may have less to do with its explanatory power than with a shared pool of motifs, themes, and plotlines. In other words, we can think of psychoanalysis itself as a Gothic genre that dwells on dark secrets, lurking horrors, and the inexplicable eruption of the past into the present. Freud himself notes some of the parallels; his essay on the uncanny makes the point that stories of specters and demons express impulses that we can now explain in psychological terms. Yet Freudian theory does not just replace the language of the supernatural, as his story of science's triumph over superstition would suggest, but also remains indebted to it. Freud's theories, writes Terry Castle, are filled with images of haunting, specters, and possession. Ghosts may have been displaced from the realm of the supernatural into the sphere of psychology, but they have not been laid to rest.[36]

The Gothic challenge to the confident mastery of reason displays itself most clearly in the responses it induces. From its origins, critics of Gothic have stressed its unusual power to disturb and perturb. Ellen Moers speaks of the Gothic targeting the body rather than the soul; it makes the flesh creep and the blood curdle, it makes the nerves thrill and quickens the beating of the heart. Reading Mrs. Radcliffe, observed Walter Scott, was like taking drugs.[37] The Gothic unsettles and troubles its readers by inspiring a sense of fascinated fear. It invites an ambivalent response that oscillates between terror and pleasure, wracking anxiety, and an eagerness to turn the page. Its uncanny aesthetic blurs the division between subject and object that assures a distanced aesthetic response.

Thus the Gothic is a key genre in the retrieval of an alternative history of aesthetic experience. Judged by the standards of modernism, it is an obvious failure, yet there are other literary values than those of irony, ambiguity, and the poetic resonance of the exquisitely crafted sentence. The power of Gothic lies in its unsettling symbols, its nightmarish dislocations, its remarkable attentiveness to the vagaries of emotional and psychic life. Thanks largely to feminism, literary critics are now less likely to assume that sensationalism and emotional extravagance must disqualify a work from serious attention. We are now in the midst of a reevaluation of literary values, not just of Gothic but also of other related genres such as melodrama. Pushed to the margins by earlier trends in modern criticism, these forms are now attracting a great deal of interest.

Aesthetic Value and Political Value

Sooner or later, however, the feminist critic will have to confront some nagging questions. Isn't the goal of feminism, a malcontent might object, to bring about a better world for women? What exactly do quibbles over literary style and sensibility have to do with social change? Isn't art at best an indulgence, at worst a distraction from the pursuit of social justice? And if feminists want to study literature, shouldn't they stick to the question of its usefulness for politics? Why bother with aesthetics at all?

Admittedly, such complaints are less frequent than they used to be. Now that feminist criticism is a well-established literary method, scholars may feel free to dodge questions about the real-world implications of what they do. They may even shrug off such questions as benighted and unsophisticated. Yet the problem of justifying the political payoff of a concern with aesthetics continues to haunt feminist writing. Is feminist criticism just another move in the discourse of criticism, or does it have any relevance beyond the academic world? And what connections are there, if any, between books that strive to change the world and those of interest to scholars of literature? Can political value be squared with aesthetic value?

One place where these issues remain burningly alive and contentious is in the study of women's writing from the Third World. The reasons may seem glaringly obvious. The poverty and material devastation that scar many non-Western societies cry out for urgent remedy. Local feminists are typically involved in grassroots struggles for economic subsistence, basic education, and legal rights for women. Given these compelling priorities, art is often recruited as a direct aid in political struggle. In Africa, for example, many voices have spoken out in passionate support of a literature of commitment, and writers unabashedly wear their politics on their sleeve. The energies of literature are deemed to be collective rather than individual, polemical and didactic rather than allusive and indirect. At its most effective, writing is a goad, a whip, a thorn in the flesh of the powerful. Thus Francophone writer Mariama Bâ comments in an interview: "As women, we must work for our own future, we must overthrow the status quo which harms us, and we must no longer submit to it. Like men, we must use literature as a non-violent but effective weapon."[38] Here, literature is a call to action, a rallying cry, a militant voice of conscience intervening in the public sphere.

Barbara Harlow's *Resistance Literature* is a survey of writing that has sprung from oppositional movements in Africa, Latin America, and the Middle East. Such literature, she suggests, defies Western beliefs about the appropriate role for art. Turning Kantian idealism on its head, it insists that the value of art lies entirely in its social usefulness. Harlow speaks of "the ideologues and theoreticians of the revolution who have articulated a role for literature and poets within the struggle alongside the gun, the pamphlet and the diplomatic delegation." In these words, we see a forceful rejection of any notion of aesthetic autonomy. Art is simply another useful weapon in the struggle against oppression, its value rooted in the practical exigencies of the here and now. At another point, Harlow writes, "The resistance narrative is not only a document, it is also an indictment."[39] Writing serves as a testimony, an act of witnessing, a faithful record of the suffering and exploitation of the powerless.

Many writers and critics thus draw a firm line between the writing of the first and the third world, juxtaposing a sterile notion of art for art's sake against a passionate defense of literature as a force for social change. There is no room, they insist, for the notion of an autonomous art in non-Western societies. In her discussion of Third World women's writing, for example, Carole Boyce Davies is dismissive of any appeal to literary value; aesthetic comparisons and discriminations are, she argues, nothing more than "ideologies of dominance." Here the aesthetic has no independent value and can offer no cognitive insights; it is simply part of the oppressive legacy of patriarchy and colonialism.[40]

The target of the feminist critic, however, is not just Western traditions but also indigenous canons of national literatures that are almost exclusively composed of works by men. Any attempt to invoke an African or black aesthetic, it seems, will always work against the interests of women. For example, Florence Stratton begins her book on African literature by declaring that "canons, rather than reflecting objective judgements of literary merit, are artificial constructs that are imposed by an elite and that operate to reproduce and reinforce existing power relations."[41] She goes on to offer a thorough and wide-ranging analysis of attitudes to gender in African writing by both men and women. But Stratton's distrust of the aesthetic register also leads her to approach fictional works as documents, as more or less accurate representations of women's lives. As Susan Andrade notes, she shows scant interest in the formal properties of the work she discusses or the mediating role of the aesthetic.[42]

Other feminist critics, however, take a very different stance. They warn against overlooking the intricacies of form in order to read literary works as unambiguous documents of identity or oppression. Rather than combating global hierarchies, suggests Gayatri Spivak, such an approach relies on a colonialist model of "most efficient information retrieval."[43] It directs an objectifying gaze onto Third World writing, denying it any formal complexity in a way that sits comfortably with Western prejudice. In this aesthetic version of the "noble savage" motif, the Third World text is deemed to be authentic, uncomplicated, and transparent. It is culture rather than art, content rather than form, a handy and accessible window onto another world. Surveying the reception of Third World women writers in the West, Amal Amireh and Lisa Suhair Majaj object to this condescending treatment. "Instead of being received and read as literature, and assessed on literary grounds, Third World women's literary texts have been viewed primarily as sociological treatises granting Western readers a glimpse into the 'oppression' of Third World women."[44]

These authors' use of quotation marks is not, I think, intended to imply that women in non-Western countries are never oppressed. Rather, it expresses impatience at the ease with which imaginative writing is turned into sociological fodder for Western consumption, used to confirm stereotypes about non-Western women as backward, downtrodden victims. In discussing the transnational reception of well-known Egyptian writer Nawal El-Saadawi, Amireh argues that her novels are often read in this light in the United States, as straightforward documents of female bondage. Conversely, other Arab writers and critics are much more likely to look at the same works in terms of their literary qualities and their success as works of fiction. Novelist Ahdaf Soueif, it seems, speaks for many when she comments: "El Saadawi writes good scientific research, but she writes bad novels. It is unfair that the West thinks that what she writes represents Arab women's creative writing."[45] Whether or not one agrees with this evaluation, it underscores the patronizing nature of the assumption that there is no serious interest in aesthetic questions outside the West.

Trinh Min-ha is another writer who distrusts attempts to reduce art to a political tool. A well-known writer, filmmaker, and critic of Vietnamese origin, her own works are allusive, multilayered, and far from straightforward. In *Woman, Native, Other,* Trinh sketches out the terrain of debates over the political role of Third World art. Drawing on the ideas of African writer Ezekiel Mphahlele, she balks at the attempt to reduce literature to an instrument of advocacy. There is a deeply authoritarian impulse at work, she argues, in the attempt to subordinate form and style to the demands of a goal-oriented politics. When writing is used to instruct, impose, exhort, or redeem, it soon slides into dogma. The author, rather, should question the world by questioning writing, by wrestling with the distinctive qualities and formal properties of language. Trinh Min-ha calls for

> a conception of writing that can no longer naively be reduced to a *means* of expressing a reality or emitting a message. To lay emphasis on *expression* and on *message* is to forget that even if art is said to be a "window on the world," it is only "a sketched window" (V Shlovsky). And just as sketched windows have their own realities, writing as a system by itself has its own rules and structuring process. . . . Thus, writing constantly refers to writing, and no writing can ever claim to be "free" of other writings.[46]

In fact, Trinh Min-ha's call has been heard and attended to, perhaps with more fervor than she may have anticipated. The recent growth of postcolonial studies has helped inspire a very different vision of the literature of the non-Western world. This literature no longer stands for sober reportage and single-mindedness of purpose; it is no longer viewed as an instrument, a weapon, or a tool. Instead, it is hailed as a polyglot, hybrid, creole form teeming with multiple and conflicting voices. It is a hodge-podge, a polyphonic melange, a rich syncretic stew of styles and sources, drawing on diverse literary traditions and crossbreeding them in exciting and unexpected ways. Once seen as formally unadventurous, even dull, the postcolonial text is now on the cutting edge of aesthetic excitement. Elke Boehmer writes: "the postcolonial writer flamboyantly crosses, fragments and parodies different narrative styles and perspectives. . . . The writer introduces a noise of voices that resists easy decoding."[47] Here we see what looks like a dramatic reversal of perspective. Rather than a clarion call to justice, the writing of the non-Western world is now a thoroughly ambiguous melange of voices that is not easily deciphered.

One reason for this change of tune is a growing body of work by writers such as Salman Rushdie, Zadie Smith, and Anudhati Roy, whose novels draw promiscuously on diverse sources and traditions, espouse multivoicedness and many-sidedness, and engage in dazzling and erudite displays of verbal fireworks. These fictions of postmodern hybridity have been published in the West to great fanfare and acclaim. And yet it is not just that new forms of writing are changing the way people talk about authors of Third World origin, but also that the same works are being read differently. In the eyes of one critic, for example, it is obvious that a certain novel is buttonholing the reader, urging action, preaching a direct and forthright political message. From another perspective, however, the same novel may seem much more diffuse and inconclusive in its address. Where one reader finds partisanship, another finds ambiguity and hesitancy.

A good example of such a clash of viewpoints can be found in feminist responses to *The Joys of Motherhood*, a well-known novel by the African expatriate writer Buchi Emecheta. Emecheta tells the story of Nnu Ego, a woman living in Nigeria in the 1930s whose only desire is to become a mother, above all a mother of sons. After suffering from an inability to conceive and then undergoing the trauma of seeing her first son die in infancy, Nnu Ego is finally rewarded with many children. Yet her life is tarnished by disappointment, regret, and misfortune. Her life in Lagos is one of economic hardship and often acute poverty, so that her children are often malnourished. She submits to a joyless marriage with a negligent and often absent husband. Her sons, rather than supporting her in old age, leave home to study overseas.

Thus a pervasive theme of *The Joys of Motherhood* is the poignancy of lost dreams and unrealized hopes in the transition from tradition to modernity. "How was she to know," the heroine reflects at the end of the novel, "that by the time her children grew up the values of her country, her people and her tribe would have changed so drastically, to the extent where a woman with many children could face a lonely old age, and maybe a miserable death all alone, just like a barren woman?" In the final poignant pages, Nnu Ego dies alone and unattended by the side of the road, "with no child to hold her hand and no friend to talk to."[48]

Buchi Emecheta's work, as Cynthia Ward points out, has been a gold mine for critics seeking authentic representations of the African woman. Her novels are often read as feminist parables conveying a message about indigenous social conditions. Barbara Christian, for example, sees *The Joys of Motherhood* as the tragic story "of a victim who has yet to articulate her victimization, a necessary step for change. She is destroyed by this lack of consciousness and by the silence in her society where the personal lives of women and wider social change have yet to be related."[49] Juliana Nfah-Abbenyi agrees that "Nnu Ego therefore epitomizes that woman who enslaves and lets herself be enslaved not only by her gender but by her tradition as well."[50] Nancy Topping Bazin claims that Emecheta speaks for "millions of black African women" in her novels by describing what it is like to be female in patriarchal African cultures.[51]

These critics have no difficulty in envisioning an author at work behind the text, speaking confidently of Emecheta's purpose and intention. They see her novel as a work that is both realistic and exemplary: debunking romantic notions of motherhood in African novels by men, *The Joys of Motherhood* sheds light on what it really means to be a mother. Yet this truth-telling is not just a disinterested record but a realism that guides and instructs the reader. Emecheta's works are powerful allegories of gender oppression, speaking not just of the fictional fate of one woman but of the actual condition of African women as a whole.

Another group of female readers, however, is much more skittish about such acts of attribution. They point to the author's careful orchestration of multiple perspectives on the meaning of Nnu Ego's life and her refusal to sanction any one of them. They argue that the portrayal of African tradition in the novel is far from clear-cut. "Meaning can be wrested from the novel," concludes Cynthia Ward, "but never *can* a single authoritative voice be located and evoked to sanction that meaning."[52] Tuzyline Allan detects in Emecheta's work an authorial ambivalence and self-division not dissimilar to that which she finds in Virginia Woolf. "The case for Emecheta's radical feminism may well be overstated," she observes, "given the dialectic of repudiation and identification that characterizes her fiction."[53] And Katherine Fishburn recruits French feminist notions of an open-ended, subversive, feminine writing to show how Emecheta's fiction commingles many perspectives rather than laying down an ultimate truth: "Multiplicity. Ambiguity. Heterogeneity. Open-endedness. Surely all of these terms also describe

Buchi Emecheta's fiction. Could we not say, then, that the difference in her writing violates sexual, textual, *and cultural* boundaries—that she too is engaged in reconstituting the subject?"[54]

What are we to make of such disparate readings of the same author and indeed the same work? How can *The Joys of Motherhood* be simultaneously partisan and postmodern, incisive and indeterminate, engaged and evasive? And what are the stakes in this clash of interpretations? Is reading-for-complexity better than reading-for-a-message? Does it show greater respect for the literary qualities of the work and for Emecheta's achievements as a writer? Or do we blunt the political edge of Emecheta's fiction by assimilating it to a familiar Western preoccupation with ambiguity, irony, and indeterminacy? Is the literary value of Emecheta's work being increased at the expense of its political value?

There is surely something wrong with arguing that aesthetics does not matter in Third World literature by women, that there is only politics. This is to play straight into the hands of those who are convinced that this literature has no redeeming literary value, that it is nothing but confessional outbursts and strident acts of pamphleteering. It denies any aesthetic self-consciousness to the non-Western mind, ignoring the many writers who are exquisitely well informed in numerous literary traditions. It acts as if there were no literary intellectuals in the Third World, or as if the only possible role for such intellectuals were to serve as a mouthpiece for popular sentiment. It assumes, in other words, that the non-Western world is miraculously free of the complexities and contradictions of modernity, of the many tensions between art and politics, between intellectuals and others.

And yet it is also the case that writing from the Third World does sometimes retain an urgency of purpose that it has lost elsewhere. Surely there is a vital role for what is often disparaged as propagandistic art, for a writing that sacrifices subtlety for the burning clarity of conviction. In times of extremity, the need to end suffering may simply override all other concerns. Complexity and intricacy, Timothy Brennan reminds us, are much loved by literary intellectuals; their merits are far less obvious to those whose natural habitat is not the study or the seminar room. The wisdom of the flat, the brute, and the plain may be more compelling to the poor and disenfranchised, who do not have the time to ponder endlessly on the indeterminacy of the signifier.[55]

Literature, in other words, may speak to readers in ways that literary critics are often ill equipped to deal with. To recognize this fact, as well as the vastly differing interests of female readers, is to acknowledge once and for all the futility of trying to establish a single feminist scale of value. Critics who want to justify the study of Third World women's writing by extolling its formal ambiguity and aesthetic density often do not stop to consider that such qualities are not valued by everyone. Their only reference point is the ethos of professional criticism. Conversely, feminists critics who dismiss this ethos and who believe that rejecting scholarly and sophisticated techniques of reading is a way of expressing their solidarity with the oppressed are equally misguided. Feminist intellectuals do not help anyone by denying their own role as intellectuals.

Rather, any adequate approach to Third World women's writing means keeping in mind not only the miscellaneous genres and modes of writing in the non-Western world, but also the varying desires and expectations against which a work may be read. In this regard, equating the postcolonial with postmodern extravaganzas of verbal virtuosity is just as misleading as insisting that non-Western literature must always be dourly functional and anti-aesthetic. In the study of Third World literature, as elsewhere, such generalizations are dangerous; art and politics do not fall into such automatic and predictable alignment.

The Value of Value

I began this book by responding to critics who believe that art is art and politics is politics and ne'er the twain should meet. Because literature is immersed in society in so many different ways, this view cannot help but collapse under the weight of its own contradictions. Linking literature to politics is not a blunder, a lapse in judgment, or a category mistake. Rather, it returns us to a long tradition of seeing art as connected to the world, a tradition only briefly interrupted by an interlude of New Criticism and formalist analysis. And as our definition of politics has expanded to include not just putsches and polling booths but questions of identity and personal life, so literature becomes relevant in new and often unexpected ways.

We need, however, to distinguish between two versions of the claim that art is political. One version argues that art—even the most esoteric and hermetic art—is thoroughly embedded in the world and that our judgments of such art are never "pure" and free of social interests. Aesthetics is always mixed up with politics. The second version insists that art is just another word for ideology, that style, form, play, and imagination have no independent reality or significance, and that aesthetic judgments are nothing more than an endorsement of current power relations. Aesthetics is reduced to politics. This latter view is, I believe, demonstrably untrue; it does away with important distinctions in what people value, how they value, and why they value. And by "people," as I will explain below, I do not just mean teachers and students.

One of the fundamental tasks of anyone who teaches literature is to get across to her students that texts are mediated representations. They are, in other words, artful artifacts, not reflections of reality. This point, obvious enough in *The Waste Land* or *Tristram Shandy*, may be less apparent in other examples. The neophyte student may assume that *Oliver Twist* is an objective record of life in Victorian London or that *The Bell Jar* simply reflects what it was like to be a young, middle-class, white woman in 1950s America. Gradually, however, she learns to discern what was previously invisible and to identify the building blocks out of which texts are composed. She becomes aware of the powerful pressure of form: how point of view steers the reader's response, how the conventions of plot influence possible outcomes, and how the cadences of language achieve certain effects.

Studying literature, in this sense, is a different experience from just reading literature because it means puzzling out how texts work. This is one common meaning of the "aesthetic attitude": standing back from a literary work in order to figure out how it is put together. Formalist critics, of course, believe that this is the point at which interpretation stops. The well-wrought urn exists in splendid, self-confirming solitude, with the critic paying homage from a respectful distance. Other critics, however, see this stage as indispensable but incomplete; having made the detour through form, they want to explore the social implications of what they are reading. Feminist scholars, obviously, fall into the second camp.

Yet it is also true that paying attention to form will often have an impact on what you appreciate and why. Once you start looking at texts in terms of their artfulness, it soon becomes apparent that some are more artful than others. This is true of all works, not just canonical ones. A critic who devotes herself to studying AIDS novels or suffragette fiction or postcolonial poetry will soon find that some of the texts she encounters are more accomplished and successful at what they set out to do than others. The more books she reads, the more obvious these differences in achievement will become. Whatever criteria she chooses to work with, the laws of probability pretty much guarantee that not every work will meet these standards equally well.

Yet there is often a reluctance to admit this fact. As I have shown, feminist critics continue to make tacit value judgments about the works they read, yet they are often wary about spelling out the basis for such judgments for fear of being accused of elitism. What began as a stirring challenge to a sacred canon of great books has as its none-too-happy endpoint a paralyzing anxiety about any explicit act of evaluation. Value means hierarchy, in the simplest and most reductive version of this argument—and hierarchy means patriarchy.

This anxiety is bolstered by Pierre Bourdieu's well-known discussion of the "aesthetic attitude" as a product of class privilege. It is only the educated upper middle class, says Bourdieu, whose distance from the pressures of material need gives them the freedom to look at art in formal and aesthetic terms and to relate individual works to the history of art.[56] "Ordinary" people, by contrast, read for content, interpreting books in moral, religious, emotional, or political terms and relating them directly to their everyday life. They are like Rita, dismissing *Howards End* because of Forster's comments about the poor without realizing that it is possible to approach a novel as a work of art.

Bourdieu's work reminds us not only that people learn to read in different ways but that these differences are closely tied to education, status, and prestige. (Jonathan Frantzen's recent, widely publicized dismay at learning that his novel had been selected by Oprah's book club is a very good example of status anxiety and a worry about attracting the "wrong" kind of reading.) And yet Bourdieu tends at times to overemphasize these differences, writing as if ordinary people were fixated on content and never paid any attention to questions of form and technique. But as popular culture has grown ever more knowing and self-conscious, the aesthetic attitude has become much less rarified than it used to be. When characters in horror films spend much of their time making jokes about the conventions of horror films, it becomes hard for anyone in the audience to react only at the level of content.

Fan groups are one excellent example of interest in form in a nonacademic context. Enthusiasts who sit through hundreds of slasher films or read endless works of romance fiction are usually highly knowledgeable about the conventions of their favorite genres. Because of this expertise, they have no qualms about distinguishing between a classic and a flop, or between the so-so work that fulfills the rules of the genre and the outstanding work that transcends them. Fans often draw up lists of the ten best road movies of all time or the twenty greatest works of science fiction; they enthuse about the camera techniques of particular directors or the plots of preferred authors. They engage, in other words, in a discourse of aesthetic value.

This is not so very different from what goes on in a literature department. Canons are nothing more than lists of favorite books drawn up by people who read a lot of books. One important difference, of course, is that literary scholars often claim much greater authority for their judgments. Some critics who formed their taste on a restricted diet of literature by white men may have no qualms in insisting that these are the greatest works the world will ever know. The recent, vigorous critique of this misplaced confidence is, in my view, fully justified. One does not have to endorse the dubious notion of segregated canons organized by gender or race to recognize that expanding the circle of evaluators will influence the content of the list.

Lists, however, are inevitable. Given an infinity of books and a sadly finite amount of time, readers of literature are often desperately eager for advice about what is worth reading and what is not. It is important to realize that the demand for evaluation comes from below as much as from above. Just as someone who craves sushi or spaghetti consults a restaurant guide for ideas on where to eat, so too readers look to reviewers and critics for tips on what to look out for and what to avoid. Amazon.com, for example, gives us not just countless book reviews but also reviews of reviewers, allowing the voices of amateur readers to intermingle and compete with professional ones. Evaluators carry out a service for which there is a vast and inexhaustible demand.

For this reason, much of the talk about "exclusion" in feminist criticism strikes me as beside the point. The term is always used in a tone of righteous disapproval, as if the mere act of excluding anything were a heinous crime. Yet any useful piece of information leaves something out; the list that includes every possible member of the set is, for most purposes, an utterly worthless list. That works by women have been excluded from the canon is not in itself a good enough reason for putting all of them back in. Ninety-nine percent of works by men have also disappeared from the public record, and probably for good reason. Feminist critics are on much stronger ground when they offer positive justifications for their literary choices than when they lament the fact of exclusion.[57]

Of course, lists also vary. There is no single master list that includes all the books that are admired, taught, and written about. Rather, there are different lists for different purposes: the survey course, the graduate seminar, the textbook, the specialized monograph. There have always been scholars interested in obscure or lesser-known authors: the minor poets of the seventeenth century or the popular novelists of the 1920s. The acceleration of this trend is not just due to the splashy new enthusiasm for gender, race, and sexuality; it has a lot to do with soaring enrollments in higher education. Each year, many thousands of doctoral students scratch their heads in frustration as they frantically search for dissertation topics. It becomes ever harder to fulfill the requirement of original research by rereading an already exhausted trove of great books. Feminism appeared at the right time; it opened up unexpected angles on traditional works as well as making a range of lesser-known or forgotten texts newly interesting. Rather than destroying the field of literary study, feminism has reinvigorated it.

I want to return, finally, to *Educating Rita*. After banging her head against a brick wall for a very long time, Rita begins to make some progress. What was previously incomprehensible slowly starts to make sense. She gradually learns how to analyze a literary text and how to write a passable essay. At summer school, she discovers the poetry of William Blake; when Frank tries to introduce her to *The Songs of Innocence and Experience,* she is already one step ahead. Rita now knows how to talk about the erotic subtext of "The Blossom" rather than seeing it as just a poem about flowers. She knows about veins of concealed meaning and recognizing allusions. Responding to Frank's surprise at her essay on Blake, she shrugs nonchalantly: "It becomes a more rewarding poem when you see that it works on a number of levels" (*ER* 61).

Frank is heartbroken by this transformation. The bluntness and freshness of Rita's voice, he feels, have been replaced by the clichés of literary criticism. He mourns the Rita who has been lost and blames himself for having helped to change her. Her latest essay, he concedes, deserves a good grade, and yet it bespeaks a loss rather than a gain; "it's up to the minute, quite acceptable, trendy stuff about Blake, but there's nothing of you in there." Bored and disenchanted with academic life, Frank is only too happy to mock Rita's eagerness to be educated and her uncritical enthusiasm for her studies. "Found a culture, have you Rita? Found a better song to sing have you?" he asks sarcastically. "No— you've found a different song, that's all—and on your lips it's shrill and hollow and tuneless" (*ER* 69).

Rita responds, however, with a feisty challenge to Frank's casual disdain for a body of knowledge he is able to take for granted. She acerbically questions his patronizing view of the authentic charms of working-class life. She angrily defends her own desire for knowledge, her eagerness to change her life, her hunger for other worlds. No longer, she insists, will she play the role of the hapless naïf for her teacher's amusement: "I tell you what you can't bear, Mr Self-Pitying Piss Artist; what you can't bear is that I am educated now . . . I've got what you have an' y' don't like it because you'd rather see me as the peasant I once was; you're like the rest of them—you like to keep your natives thick because that way they still look charming and delightful" (*ER* 68). While blasé academics may be only too happy to mock the notion of education as self-improvement, things may look very different to first-generation college students who are suddenly exposed to an unimagined wealth of books, images, and ideas. Many of the current attacks on literature and the canon, as Jennifer Wicke points out, come from those who are themselves very well read.[58]

I admit to having a soft spot for Rita and not just because of the happy coincidence of our names. My own origins are one notch up from hers, but I too came to literary study from a relatively modest background. It is often hard for those who grew up in book-filled homes to appreciate how startling that first encounter with well-known works of art can be. For someone like myself, the impact of reading Beckett and Brecht, Kafka and Proust was little short of explosive. These writers intrigued and bewildered me; they opened up ways of thinking about the world that were dramatically different from anything I had previously encountered. Like Rita, I came to value literature not because it reflected my life, but precisely because it didn't.

In graduate school I came across the fields of feminist criticism and cultural studies. Here were new epiphanies, new ways of thinking. Some of my assumptions about literature were, it turned out, open to question, less clear-cut than they first appeared. But these fields were a way of enriching and expanding my earlier education rather than replacing it. How can anyone make a case for the distinctive qualities of women's writing without a grounding in the male literary tradition? And how can anyone make sense of the aesthetics and politics of popular culture without knowing something about its many connections to high art? Here again, there is no room for the logic of either/or.

Nowadays, of course, Rita would probably encounter works by women on her syllabus; she might even be encouraged to think about issues of class and gender in literature and to make some connections between her new life and her old. (Perhaps E. M. Forster's comments about the poor were not completely irrelevant after all!) Yet she would still passionately resist any attempt to fence her in, to suggest that the works of Blake, Ibsen, and Forster are inappropriate or irrelevant to a woman from a working-class background. Literature, for Rita, does not have an inherent or self-evident value; but it has acquired a value, a value that is all the more precious for being new and unexpected. She has indeed learned that there is more to life than she ever imagined. Feminist criticism, at its best, continues this opening up of new terrain, this enlargement of our horizons. Literature after feminism is an expanded field, not a diminished one.

NOTES

Introduction

1. Harold Bloom describes feminist scholars as "remorseless Puritans" in *The Western Canon: The Books and School of the Ages* (New York: Riverhead Books, 1994), 408. "Deconstruction and the activist social criticisms that have succeeded it, feminism and Marxism, appear like destroying angels, seeking the death of literature," says Alvin Kernan in *The Death of Literature* (New Haven, CT: Yale University Press, 1990), 145. Roger Kimball accuses feminist critics of assaulting the canon and debasing the curriculum in *Tenured Radicals: How Politics Has Corrupted Our Higher Education* (New York: Harper and Row, 1990). In *Literature Lost: Social Agendas and the Corruption of the Humanities* (New Haven, CT: Yale University Press, 1997), John Ellis describes feminist scholars as angry, resentful, and hostile, concluding that feminist "disparagement of the past has completely eclipsed a rational understanding of it" (65).

2. On women as agents rather than simply victims of power, see, e.g., Nancy Armstrong, *Desire and Domestic Fiction: A Political History of the Novel* (Oxford: Oxford University Press, 1987); Mary Poovey, *Uneven Developments: The Ideological Work of Gender in Mid-Victorian England* (Chicago: University of Chicago Press, 1988); Elizabeth Langland, *Nobody's Angels: Middle-Class Women and Domestic Ideology in Victorian Culture* (Ithaca, NY: Cornell University Press, 1995); Betsy Erkkila, *The Wicked Sisters: Women Poets, Literary History, and Discord* (Oxford: Oxford University Press, 1992). On the tensions as well as connections between aesthetics and politics, see Annette Kolodny, "Dancing through the Minefield: Some Observations on the Theory, Practice, and Politics of a Feminist Literary Criticism," Myra Jehlens, "Archimedes and the Paradox of Feminist Literary Criticism," and Lillian Robinson, "Treason Our Text: Feminist Challenges to the Literary Canon," all in *Feminisms: An Anthology of Literary Theory and Criticism,* ed. Robyn R. Warhol and Diane Price Herndl (New Brunswick, NJ: Rutgers University Press, 1997). See also my "Why Feminist Doesn't Need an Aesthetic (and Why It Can't Ignore Aesthetics)," in *Doing Time: Feminist Theory and Postmodern Culture* (New York: New York University Press, 2000). On female pleasure, see Rachel Brownstein, *Becoming a Heroine: Reading about Women in Novels* (New York: Viking, 1982); Patricia Yeager, *Honey-Mad Women: Emancipatory Strategies in Women's Writing* (New York: Columbia University Press, 1988); Janice Radway, *A Feeling for Books: The Book-of-the-Month Club, Literary Taste, and Middle-Class Desire* (Chapel Hill: University of North Carolina Press, 1997); Anna Quindlen, *How Reading Changed My Life* (New York: Library of Contemporary Thought, 1998); Marianne Noble, *The Masochistic Pleasures of Sentimental Fiction* (Princeton, NJ: Princeton University Press, 2000); *The Female Gaze: Women as Viewers of*

Popular Culture, ed. Lorraine Gamman and Margaret Marshment (London: The Women's Press, 1988); Ien Ang, *Watching Dallas: Soap Opera and the Melodramatic Imagination* (New York: Routledge, 1985); Jackie Stacey, *Star Gazing: Hollywood Cinema and Female Spectatorship* (London: Routledge, 1994); Jane Juffer, *At Home with Pornography: Women, Sex, and Everyday Life* (New York: New York University Press, 1998). Sympathetic feminist engagements with the writing of "dead white males" are countless, but on Greek tragedy, see, e.g., Froma I. Zeitlin, *Playing the Other: Gender and Society in Classical Greek Literature* (Chicago: University of Chicago Press, 1996), and for useful surveys of feminist work on Shakespeare, both critical and celebratory, see *Shakespeare and Gender: A History*, ed. Deborah Barker and Ivor Kamps (London: Verso, 1995), and *Shakespeare and Gender*, ed. Stephen Orgel and Sean Keilen (New York: Garland, 1999).

3. Judith Butler, *Gender Trouble: Feminism and the Subversion of Identity* (New York: Routledge, 1990), 3.

4. There are, of course, several surveys of feminist criticism intended primarily for classroom use. See, e.g., Toril Moi, *Sexual/Textual Politics: Feminist Literary Theory* (London: Methuen, 1985); Janet Todd, *Feminist Literary History* (London: Routledge, 1988); Jane Gallop, *Around 1981: Feminist Literary Theory* (New York: Routledge, 1989); and Ruth Robbins, *Literary Feminisms* (New York: St. Martin's Press, 2000).

5. I am thinking here of the blurbs adorning the back cover of John Ellis's *Literature Lost.* That Frank Kermode can describe this book as an example of "disinterested inquiry" suggests that he has lost some of his once impressive skills as a close reader.

6. Ellis, *Literature Lost,* 74.

7. Ibid., 239.

8. Jane Gallop cites various feminist critics who discuss the limits of criticizing sexual stereotypes in literature. For example, Elaine Showalter wrote in 1975: "Many essays of this type now have a tired air: they are only beating a dead pig." See Gallop, *Around 1981,* 101.

9. Ellis, *Literature Lost,* 54.

10. Gallop, *Around 1981,* 190.

11. Ellis, *Literature Lost,* 54.

12. For example, Ellis faults scholars in gay and lesbian studies for not acknowledging the "enormous prominence and influence" of homosexuals on Western culture (56). He seems not to have read the work of the most well-known figure in the field, Eve Kosofsky Sedgwick, whose work stresses precisely this point. See her *The Epistemology of the Closet* (Berkeley: University of California Press, 1990), 52.

13. Ellis, *Literature Lost,* 235 n. 15.

14. Robert Hughes, *Culture of Complaint: The Fraying of America* (London: Harvill Press, 1999), 92.

15. Ellis, *Literature Lost,* 35–36. Actually Ellis is quite wrong. The practice of pursuing minor themes through a variety of literary works, rather than focusing on a single work, is a traditional and well-respected form of literary scholarship. Has Ellis never heard of the study of topoi?

16. Wendy Steiner, *The Scandal of Pleasure: Art in an Age of Fundamentalism* (Chicago: University of Chicago Press, 1995).

17. Stanley Fish, *Professional Correctness: Literary Studies and Political Change* (Oxford: Clarendon, 1995), 69.

18. Barbara Maria Stafford, *Visual Analogy: Consciousness as the Art of Connecting* (Cambridge, MA: MIT Press, 1999), 2.

19. Ibid., 51.

20. George Steiner, *Antigones* (New Haven, CT: Yale University Press, 1996), 4.

21. Lionel Trilling, "Emma and the Legend of Jane Austen," in *Beyond Culture: Essays on Literature and Learning* (New York: Viking, 1965), 38. Trilling does see Jane Austen's characters as an important exception to this rule. More questionable to a contemporary sensibility is his claim that "we" do not even notice this impoverishment of female character in literature, for it corresponds to how things really are. Trilling writes, "Nor can we say that novels are deficient in realism when they present women as they do: it is the presumption of our society that women's moral life is not as men's. No change in the modern theory of the sexes, no advance in status that women have made, has yet contradicted this. The self-love that we do countenance in women is of a limited and passive kind, and we are troubled if it is as assertive as the self-love of men is permitted, and expected, to be" (39).

22. David Denby, *Great Books: My Adventures with Homer, Rousseau, Woolf, and Other Indestructible Writers of the Western World* (New York: Simon and Schuster, 1996), 431, 432, 443.

23. Ibid., 332.

24. K. Anthony Appiah, "Battle of the Bien-Pensant," *New York Review of Books* 47, 7 (April 27, 2000).

25. Hughes, *Culture of Complaint*, 95.

26. Griselda Pollock, *Differencing the Canon: Feminist Desire and the Writing of Art's Histories* (London: Routledge, 1999), 9.

27. See my essay, "The Role of Aesthetics in Cultural Studies," in *Aesthetics and Cultural Studies*, ed. Michael Bérubé (New York: Blackwell, 2003).

28. Eugene Goodheart, *Does Literary Studies Have a Future?* (Madison: University of Wisconsin Press, 1999), 34.

29. bell hooks, "An Aesthetic of Blackness: Strange and Oppositional," in *Yearning: Race, Gender, and Cultural Politics* (Boston: Southend Press, 1990), 109.

Chapter 1

1. Miguel de Cervantes, *Don Quijote*, trans. Burton Raffel (New York: Norton, 1996), 12.

2. Gustave Flaubert, *Madame Bovary* (New York: Norton, 1965), 63.

3. Ibid., 26.

4. Ibid., 211–12.

5. Emma, of course, tries to solve this problem by becoming more aggressive, adopting the masculine role in her affair with Leon. Mario Vargas Llosa's perceptive analysis is worth quoting. He writes, "Emma is forever doomed to frustration: as a woman, because the woman in the fictional reality is a subjugated being to whom the world of dreams and passion is forbidden; as a man, because she can reach that world only by turning her lover into a non-entity, incapable of arousing in her an admiration and a respect for the so-called *virile* virtues, which she has failed to find in her husband and seeks in vain in her lovers. This is one of the insoluble contradictions that make Emma a pathetic character. Heroism, daring, prodigality, freedom are, apparently, masculine prerogatives; yet Emma discovers that the males in

her life—Charles, Léon, Rodolphe—become weaklings, cowards, mediocrities, and slaves the moment she assumes a 'masculine' attitude (the only one that allows her to break the bonds of slavery to which those of her sex are condemned in the fictional reality. Thus there is no solution." See Vargas Llosa, *The Perpetual Orgy: Flaubert and Madame Bovary* (New York: Farrar, Straus and Giroux, 1986), 143–44.

6. Quoted in Kate Flint, *The Woman Reader, 1837–1914* (Oxford: Clarendon Press, 1993), 12.

7. Quoted in ibid., 219.

8. José Ortega y Gasset, *The Dehumanization of Art* (New York: Doubleday, 1956), 4, 25.

9. Ibid., 37.

10. Andreas Huyssen, "Mass Culture as Woman: Modernism's Other," in *After the Great Divide: Modernism, Mass Culture, Postmodernism* (Bloomington: Indiana University Press, 1986).

11. Mary Anne Doane, "Film and the Masquerade: Theorizing the Female Spectator," in *Femmes Fatales: Feminism, Film Theory, Psychoanalysis* (New York: Routledge, 1991), 27.

12. Judith Fetterley, *The Resisting Reader: A Feminist Approach to American Fiction* (Bloomington: Indiana University Press, 1978), viii, xii, xx.

13. See Adrienne Rich, "When We Dead Awaken: Writing as Re-Vision," in *On Lies, Secrets, and Silence: Selected Prose, 1966–1978* (New York: Norton, 1979).

14. Laura Mulvey, "Visual Pleasure and Narrative Cinema," in *Visual and Other Pleasures* (London: Macmillan, 1989), 16.

15. Martha Nussbaum, *Cultivating Humanity: A Classical Defense of Reform in Liberal Education* (Cambridge, MA: Harvard University Press, 1997).

16. Wendy Brown, *States of Injury: Power and Freedom in Late Modernity* (Princeton, NJ: Princeton University Press, 1995).

17. Wayne Booth, *The Company We Keep: An Ethics of Fiction* (Berkeley: University of California Press, 1988).

18. Shoshana Felman, *What Does a Woman Want? Reading and Sexual Difference* (Baltimore: Johns Hopkins University Press, 1993), 5–6.

19. See Carla Kaplan, *The Erotics of Talk: Women's Writing and Feminist Paradigms* (Oxford: Oxford University Press, 1996).

20. Patrocinio P. Schweickart, "Reading Ourselves: Toward a Feminist Theory of Reading," in *Gender and Reading,* ed. Elizabeth Flynn and Patrocinio P. Schweickart (Baltimore: Johns Hopkins University Press, 1986), 51.

21. bell hooks, "The Oppositional Gaze," in *Black Looks: Race and Representation* (Boston: Southend Press, 1992), 123. See also Jacqueline Bobo, *Black Women as Cultural Readers* (New York: Columbia University Press, 1995).

22. Terry Castle, *The Apparitional Lesbian: Female Homosexuality and Modern Culture* (New York: Columbia University Press, 1993), 11.

23. Jean Kennard, "Ourself behind Ourself: A Theory for Lesbian Readers," in *Gender and Reading,* ed. Flynn and Schweickart, 63.

24. On the lesbian reader, see also Bonnie Zimmerman, "What Has Never Been: An Overview of Lesbian Feminist Criticism," in *Making a Difference: Feminist Literary Criticism,* ed. Gayle Greene and Coppelia Kahn (London: Methuen, 1985); Alison Hennegan, "On Becoming a Lesbian Reader," in *Sweet Dreams: Sexuality,*

Gender, and Popular Fiction, ed. Susannah Radstone (London: Lawrence and Wishart, 1988).

25. bell hooks, *Wounds of Passion: A Writing Life* (New York: Henry Holt, 1997); Jeanette Winterson, *Art Objects: Essays on Ecstasy and Effrontery* (New York: Knopf, 1996); Angela Carter, *Shaking a Leg: Collected Writings* (New York: Penguin, 1997); Kathy Acker, *Bodies of Work* (London: Serpent's Tail, 1997); "Doris Lessing," "Germaine Greer," and "Buchi Emecheta," in *The Pleasures of Reading,* ed. Antonia Fraser (London: Bloomsbury, 1992); Alice Walker, *In Search of Our Mothers' Gardens: Womanist Prose* (New York: Harcourt Brace Jovanovich, 1983).

26. Jamaica Kincaid, *The Autobiography of My Mother* (New York: Plume, 1997).

27. Anne Fadiman, *The Spirit Catches You and You Fall Down: A Hmong Child, Her American Doctors, and the Collision of Two Cultures* (New York: Farrar, Straus and Giroux, 1997).

28. Anne Friedberg, "A Denial of Difference: Theories of Cinematic Identification," in *Psychoanalysis and Cinema,* ed. E. Ann Kaplan (London: Routledge, 1990), 45.

29. See Christine Gledhill, "Pleasurable Negotiations," in *Female Spectators,* ed. Deirdre Pribram (London: Verso, 1988), and Judith Mayne, "Paradoxes of Spectatorship," in *Cinema and Spectatorship* (London: Routledge, 1993).

30. Wolfgang Iser, *The Act of Reading: A Theory of Aesthetic Response* (London: Routledge and Kegan Paul, 1978), 155. For one discussion of how "minority literature" may refuse rather than court the reader, see Doris Sommer, *Proceed with Caution, When Engaged by Minority Writing in the Americas* (Cambridge, MA: Harvard University Press, 1999).

31. Minrose Gwin, *The Woman in the Red Dress: Gender, Space, and Reading* (Urbana: University of Illinois Press, 2002), 52.

32. Virginia Woolf, *A Room of One's Own* (San Diego: Harcourt, Brace, 1981), 74.

33. Winterson, *Art Objects,* 110.

34. Vanessa Thorpe, "'Women's Books' That Turn Men Off," *The Observer* (March 19, 2000), 8. Thorpe writes: "The first survey into the impact of gender on reading habits, published tomorrow, will show that men instinctively flinch from any book that they consider a 'women's read.' Never mind what the book is about: male readers are unduly influenced by the sex of the author, by the look of the cover and by the use of emotional words in the title. . . . In contrast to men, women are shown to read openly and widely. Although they do identify certain novels as being targeted at men, they are quite likely to read them anyway."

35. See Diana Fuss, "Reading as a Feminist," in *Essentially Speaking* (New York: Routledge, 1989), and *Identification Papers* (New York: Routledge, 1995).

36. Eve Kosofsky Sedgwick, *Tendencies* (Durham, NC: Duke University Press, 1993); Wayne Koestenbaum, *The Queen's Throat: Opera, Homosexuality, and the Mystery of Desire* (New York: Poseidon Press, 1993); Hennegan, "On Becoming a Lesbian Reader."

37. Carolyn Heilbrun, *Reinventing Womanhood* (New York: Norton, 1979); Mayne, *Cinema and Spectatorship.*

38. Martha Nussbaum, *Poetic Justice: The Literary Imagination in Public Life* (Boston: Beacon, 1995).

39. Elaine Showalter, "Critical Cross-Dressing: Male Feminists and the Woman of the Year," in *Men in Feminism*, ed. Alice Jardine and Paul Smith (New York: Methuen, 1987); Ann duCille, "The Occult of True Black Womanhood," in *Skin Trade* (Cambridge, MA: Harvard University Press, 1996).

40. Kim Chabot Davis, "Sentimental Postmodernism and the Politics of Identification" (Ph.D. dissertation, University of Virginia, 2000). See also Sara Mills, "Reading as/like a Feminist," in *Gendering the Reader*, ed. Sara Mills (Brighton: Harvester Wheatsheaf, 1994).

41. Janice Radway, *Reading the Romance: Women, Patriarchy, and Popular Literature* (Chapel Hill: University of North Carolina Press, 1984).

42. Ien Ang, *Watching Dallas: Soap Opera and the Melodramatic Imagination* (New York: Methuen, 1985).

43. Anna Quindlen, *How Reading Changed My Life* (New York: Library of Contemporary Thought, 1998), 38.

44. See Janice A. Radway, *A Feeling for Books: The Book-of-the-Month Club, Literary Taste, and Middle-Class Desire* (Chapel Hill: University of North Carolina Press, 1997); Lynne Pearce, *Feminism and the Politics of Reading* (London: Arnold, 1997); Lynne Sharon Schwartz, *Ruined by Reading* (Boston: Beacon Press, 1996); Rachel Brownstein, *Becoming a Heroine: Reading about Women in Novels* (New York: Viking, 1982); Anne Fadiman, *Confessions of a Common Reader* (New York: Farrar, Straus and Giroux, 1998). Interesting work on reading and feeling by male scholars includes Alberto Manguel's learned yet engagingly personal *A History of Reading* (New York: Viking, 1996) and Mario Vargas Llosa's wonderful description of his "unrequited passion" for Emma Bovary in *The Perpetual Orgy*.

45. Radway, *A Feeling for Books*, 13.

46. Gwin, *Woman in the Red Dress*, 32.

Chapter 2

1. The two relevant essays are Roland Barthes, "The Death of the Author," in *Image, Music, Text*, trans. Stephen Heath (New York: Hill and Wang, 1977), and Michel Foucault, "What Is an Author?" in *Language, Counter-Memory, Practice*, ed. Donald F. Bouchard (Ithaca, NY: Cornell University Press, 1977).

2. Peggy Kamuf, "Replacing Feminist Criticism," and Nancy Miller, "The Text's Heroine: A Feminist Critic and Her Fictions," *Diacritics* 12, 2 (1982): 42–53.

3. Toril Moi, *Sexual/Textual Politics: Feminist Literary Theory* (London: Methuen, 1985), 63.

4. See Anthony Appiah, "Is the Post- in Postmodernism the Post- in Postcolonial?" *Critical Inquiry* 17 (1991): 336–57; James Clifford, "Histories of the Tribal and the Modern," in *The Predicament of Culture: Twentieth-Century Ethnography, Literature, and Art* (Cambridge, MA: Harvard University Press, 1988).

5. Lynn Schwarz, *Ruined by Reading: A Life in Books* (Boston: Beacon Press, 1996), 118.

6. Barthes, "The Death of the Author," 147.

7. See Nancy Miller, *Subject to Change: Reading Feminist Writing* (New York: Columbia University Press, 1988).

8. Barthes, "The Death of the Author," 143.

9. Susan Gilbert and Sandra Gubar, *The Madwoman in the Attic: The Woman*

Writer and the Nineteenth-Century Literary Imagination (New Haven, CT: Yale University Press, 1979), 77. The quotation I give here refers to the work of Mary Elizabeth Coleridge but works equally well as a summary of Gilbert and Gubar's approach to *Jane Eyre*.

10. Elaine R. Hedges, "Afterword to 'The Yellow Wallpaper,' Feminist Press Edition," in *The Captive Imagination: A Casebook on "The Yellow Wallpaper,"* ed. Catherine Golden (New York: Feminist Press, 1972), 131.

11. Gilbert and Gubar, *Madwoman in the Attic*, 78.

12. Hedges, "Afterword," 124.

13. Gilbert and Gubar, *Madwoman in the Attic*, 83.

14. Paula A. Treichler, "Escaping the Sentence: Diagnosis and Discourse in 'The Yellow Wallpaper,'" in *The Captive Imagination*, 196; Hedges, "Afterword," 132.

15. Gilbert and Gubar, *Madwoman in the Attic*, 89; Annette Kolodny, "A Map for Rereading: Or, Gender and the Interpretation of Literary Texts," in *The Captive Imagination*, 162.

16. Gayatri Chakravorty Spivak, "Three Women's Texts and a Critique of Imperialism," in *"Race," Writing, and Difference*, ed. Henry Louis Gates Jr. (Chicago: University of Chicago Press, 1986), 270. On race in *Jane Eyre*, see also Suvendrini Perera, *Reaches of Empire: The English Novel from Edgeworth to Dickens* (New York: Columbia University Press, 1991); and Susan Meyer, *Imperialism at Home: Race and Victorian Women's Fiction* (Ithaca, NY: Cornell University Press, 1996).

17. See, e.g., Nancy Armstrong, *Desire and Domestic Fiction: A Political History of the Novel* (Oxford: Oxford University Press, 1987); Mary Poovey, *Uneven Developments: The Ideological Work of Gender in Mid-Victorian England* (Ithaca, NY: Cornell University Press, 1988); Elizabeth Langland, *Nobody's Angels: Middle-Class Women and Domestic Ideology in Victorian Culture* (Ithaca, NY: Cornell University Press, 1995); and Judith Walkowitz, *City of Dreadful Delight: Narratives of Sexual Danger in Late-Victorian England* (Chicago: University of Chicago Press, 1992).

18. Mary Jacobus, "An Unnecessary Maze of Sign-Reading," in *The Captive Imagination*; Susan S. Lanser, "Feminist Criticism, 'The Yellow Wallpaper,' and the Politics of Color in America," *Feminist Studies* (1989): 415–41.

19. Colette, "The Hidden Woman," in *The Collected Stories of Colette* (New York: Farrar, Straus and Giroux, 1983), 235–36. All further page references appear in the text.

20. Helene Cixous, "The Laugh of the Medusa," *Signs: Journal of Women in Culture and Society* 1, 4 (1976): 887.

21. Ibid., 879.

22. Ibid., 884.

23. See, e.g., Joan Riviere, "Womanliness as a Masquerade," and Stephen Heath, "Joan Riviere and the Masquerade," both in *Formations of Fantasy: Pleasure*, ed. Victor Burgin et al. (London: Methuen, 1986). My use of the term "masquerading women" differs slightly from the idea of "femininity as masquerade," which focuses specifically on the performance of femaleness by women. Rather, "masquerading women" highlights a growing interest in discussing how female authors can perform both masculinity and femininity in their writing.

24. Judith Butler, "Imitation and Gender Insubordination," in *Inside/Out: Lesbian Theories, Gay Theories*, ed. Diana Fuss (New York: Routledge, 1991), 21.

25. Mary Jacobus, "Reading Woman (Reading)," in *Reading Woman: Essays in Feminist Criticism* (New York: Columbia University Press, 1986), 22–23.

26. Angela Carter, *Nights at the Circus* (London: Chatto and Windus, 1986), 103.

27. Jeanette Winterson, *Written on the Body* (New York: Vintage, 1992). For pertinent discussions of Winterson, see "The Erupting Lesbian Body: Reading *Written on the Body* as a Lesbian Text," in *"I'm Telling You Stories": Jeanette Winterson and the Politics of Reading*, ed. Helen Grice and Tim Woods (Amsterdam: Rodopi, 1998); Elizabeth Langland, "Sexing the Text: Narrative Drag as Feminist Poetics and Politics in Jeanette Winterson's *Sexing the Cherry*," *Narrative* 5, 1 (1997): 99–107; and "Teledildonics: Virtual Lesbians in the Fiction of Jeanette Winterson," in *Sexy Bodies: The Strange Carnalities of Feminism*, ed. Elizabeth Grosz and Elspeth Probyn (London: Routledge, 1995). On Angela Carter, see, e.g., Anne Fernihough, "'Is She Fact or Is She Fiction?': Angela Carter and the Enigma of Woman," *Textual Practice* 11, 1 (1997): 89–108.

28. Langland, "Sexing the Text," 106.

29. Alvina E. Quintana, *Home Girls: Chicana Literary Voices* (Philadelphia: Temple University Press, 1996), ix.

30. Barbara Smith, "Introduction," *Home Girls: A Black Feminist Anthology* (New York: Kitchen Table/Women of Color Press, 1983), xxii.

31. Mary Helen Washington, "I Sign My Mother's Name: Alice Walker, Dorothy West, and Paule Marshall," in *Mothering the Mind: Twelve Studies of Writers and Their Silent Partners*, ed. Ruth Perry and Martine Watson Brownley (New York: Holmes and Meier, 1984), 161.

32. Smith, "Introduction," xx.

33. Paule Marshall, "Shaping the World of My Art," *New Letters* 40 (1973), 103–4.

34. Smith, "Introduction," li.

35. Alice Walker, "In Search of Our Mothers' Gardens," in *In Search of Our Mothers' Gardens: Womanist Prose* (New York: Harcourt Brace Jovanovich, 1983), 240.

36. Washington, "I Sign My Mother's Name," 148.

37. Paule Marshall, "From the Poets in the Kitchen," *New York Times Book Review* (January 9, 1983), 3.

38. Walker, "In Search of Our Mothers' Gardens," 234, 239.

39. bell hooks, "An Aesthetics of Blackness: Strange and Oppositional," in *Yearning: Race, Gender, and Cultural Politics* (Boston: Southend Press, 1990), 105–6. See also Barbara Christian, "The Highs and the Lows of Black Feminist Criticism," in *Feminisms: An Anthology of Literary Theory and Criticism*, ed. Robyn R. Warhol and Diane Price Herndl (New Brunswick, NJ: Rutgers University Press, 1997).

40. Marshall, "From the Poets in the Kitchen," 3.

41. Ibid., 34.

42. Susan Willis, *Specifying: Black Women Writing the American Experience* (Madison: University of Wisconsin Press, 1987).

43. Toni Morrison, "Rooted: The Ancestor as Foundation," in *Black Women Writers, 1950–1980: A Critical Evaluation*, ed. Mari Evans (New York: Doubleday, 1984), 341.

44. Alice Walker, "Everyday Use," in *Stories of Love and Trouble* (New York: Harcourt Brace Jovanovich, 1973), 57.

45. Houston A. Baker Jr. and Charlotte Pierce-Baker, "Patches: Quilt and Community in Alice Walker's 'Everyday Use,'" in *Everyday Use*, ed. Barbara Christian (New Brunswick, NJ: Rutgers University Press, 1994), 161, 163.

46. Valerie Smith, "Authenticity in Narratives of the Black Middle Class," in *Not Just Race, Not Just Gender: Black Feminist Readings* (New York: Routledge, 1998). See also J. Martin Favor, *Authentic Blackness: The Folk in the New Negro Renaissance* (Durham, NC: Duke University Press, 1999).

47. Mary Helen Washington, "An Essay on Alice Walker," in *Everyday Use*, ed. Christian, 103.

48. See Deborah E. McDowell, *"The Changing Same": Black Women's Literature, Criticism, and Theory* (Bloomington: Indiana University Press, 1995).

49. Hazel Carby, *Reconstructing Womanhood: The Emergence of the African-American Woman Novelist* (Oxford: Oxford University Press, 1987); Ann duCille, *The Coupling Convention: Sex, Text, and Tradition in Black Women's Fiction* (Oxford: Oxford University Press, 1993); Hortense Spillers, "Afterword," in *Conjuring: Black Women, Fiction, and Literary Tradition*, ed. Marjorie Pryse and Hortense Spillers (Bloomington: Indiana University Press, 1989), and "The Crisis of the Negro Intellectual: A Post-Date," *Boundary 2* 21, 3 (1994): 65–116; and Smith, *Not Just Race, Not Just Gender*.

50. Carole Boyce Davies, *Black Women, Writing, and Identity: Migrations of the Subject* (London: Routledge, 1994).

51. Gloria Anzaldúa, *Borderlands/La Frontera: The New Mestiza* (San Francisco: Spinsters/Aunt Lute, 1987), 19–20. See also Sonia Saldivar-Hull, *Feminism on the Border: Chicana Gender, Politics, and Literature* (Los Angeles: University of California Press, 2000).

52. Marianne Noble, *The Masochistic Pleasures of Sentimental Literature* (Princeton, NJ: Princeton University Press, 2000), 5.

53. Judith Newton and Deborah Rosenfelt, "Towards a Materialist Feminist Criticism," in *Feminist Criticism and Social Change*, ed. Judith Newton and Deborah Rosenfelt (New York: Methuen, 1985), xxix–xxx.

54. Poovey, *Uneven Developments*.

55. Susan Stanford Friedman, *Mappings: Feminism and the Cultural Geographies of Encounter* (Princeton, NJ: Princeton University Press, 1998), 26–27.

56. Cheryl Wall, "Feminist Literary Criticism and the Author," *Critical Inquiry* 16, 3 (1990): 560.

57. Elaine Showalter, *Sister's Choice: Tradition and Change in American Women's Writing* (Oxford: Clarendon, 1991), 18.

58. Betsy Erkkila, *The Wicked Sisters: Women Poets, Literary History, and Discord* (Oxford: Oxford University Press, 1992), 15.

59. Toril Moi, "I Am a Woman," in *What Is a Woman? And Other Essays* (Oxford: Oxford University Press, 1999), 204–5.

Chapter 3

1. Carolyn Steedman, *Landscape for a Good Woman: A Story of Two Lives* (London: Virago, 1986).

2. A. S. Byatt, "Old Tales, New Forms," in *On Histories and Stories: Selected Essays* (Cambridge, MA: Harvard University Press, 2000), 132.

3. Wendy Doniger, *The Implied Spider: Politics in Theology and Myth* (New York: Columbia University Press, 1998).

4. George Steiner, *Antigones* (New Haven, CT: Yale University Press, 1984), 122.

5. Franco Moretti, *Modern Epic: The World-System from Goethe to Garcia-Marquez* (London: Verso, 1996), 38.

6. Simone de Beauvoir, *The Second Sex* (London: Picador, 1988), 318.

7. Nancy K. Miller, "Emphasis Added: Plots and Plausibilities in Women's Fiction," *PMLA* 96, 1 (1981): 47.

8. Ian Watt, *Myths of Modern Individualism: Faust, Don Quixote, Don Juan, Robinson Crusoe* (Cambridge: Cambridge University Press, 1996), 125.

9. Sandra M. Gilbert and Susan Gubar, *The Madwoman in the Attic: The Woman Writer and the Nineteenth-Century Literary Imagination* (New Haven, CT: Yale University Press, 1979), 50.

10. Joanna Russ, "What Can a Heroine Do? Or, Why Women Can't Write," in *Images of Women in Fiction: Feminist Perspectives*, ed. Susan Koppelman Cornillon (Bowling Green, OH: Bowling Green University Press, 1972), 6.

11. Ibid., 7.

12. Ibid., 9.

13. Joseph Allen Boone, *Tradition counter Tradition: Love and the Form of Fiction* (Chicago: University of Chicago Press, 1987), 74.

14. See Susan Fraiman, *Unbecoming Women: British Women Writers and the Novel of Development* (New York: Columbia University Press, 1993); Nancy Miller, *The Heroine's Text: Readings in the French and English Novel, 1722–1782* (New York: Columbia University Press, 1980); Patricia Meyer Spacks, *Desire and Truth: Functions of Plot in Eighteenth-Century English Novels* (Chicago: University of Chicago Press, 1990); Rachel Blau du Plessis, *Writing beyond the Ending: Narrative Strategies of Twentieth-Century Women Writers* (Bloomington: Indiana University Press, 1985).

15. Russ, "What Can a Heroine Do?" 8.

16. Rita Felski, "Judith Krantz, Author of The Cultural Logics of Late Capitalism," in *Doing Time: Feminist Theory and Postmodern Culture* (New York: New York University Press, 2000).

17. Ferdinand Mount, "Why Men Can't Write for Toffee," *The Guardian* (February 24, 2001).

18. Ellen G. Friedman and Miriam Fuchs, "Contexts and Continuities: An Introduction to Women's Experimental Fiction in English," in *Breaking the Sequence: Women's Experimental Fiction*, ed. Ellen G. Friedman and Miriam Fuchs (Princeton, NJ: Princeton University Press, 1989), 7.

19. Judith Roof, *Come as You Are: Sexuality and Narrative* (New York: Columbia University Press, 1996), xxvi.

20. See Teresa de Lauretis, *Alice Doesn't: Feminism, Semiotics, Cinema* (Bloomington: Indiana University Press, 1984).

21. "Doesn't every narrative lead back to Oedipus?" asks Roland Barthes. See *The Pleasure of the Text* (New York: Hill and Wang, 1975), 47.

22. Margaret Homans, "Feminist Fictions and Feminist Theories of Narrative," *Narrative* 2, 1 (1994): 5.

23. See, e.g., Elizabeth Wanning Harries, *Twice upon a Time: Women Writers and the History of the Fairy Tale* (Princeton, NJ: Princeton University Press, 2001).

24. Alison Booth, "Introduction," *Famous Last Words: Changes in Gender and Narrative Closure*, ed. Alison Booth (Charlottesville: University Press of Virginia, 1993), 4.

25. Patricia Yaeger, *Honey-Mad Women: Emancipatory Strategies in Women's Writing* (New York: Columbia University Press, 1988), 185.

26. See Janice Radway, *Reading the Romance: Women, Patriarchy, and Popular Literature* (Chapel Hill: University of North Carolina Press, 1984). See also Tania Modleski, *Loving with a Vengeance: Mass-Produced Fantasies for Women* (New York: Routledge, 1982).

27. Ann duCille, *The Coupling Convention: Sex, Text, and Tradition in Black Women's Fiction* (Oxford: Oxford University Press, 1993), 14.

28. See Susan Stanford Friedman, *Mappings: Feminism and the Cultural Geographies of Encounter* (Princeton, NJ: Princeton University Press, 1998), esp. chap. 9.

29. Doniger, *The Implied Spider*, 95.

30. See Maria Pia Lara, *Moral Textures: Feminist Narratives in the Public Sphere* (Berkeley: University of California Press, 1988).

31. Jane DeLynn, *Don Juan in the Village* (New York: Painted Leaf Press, 1998), henceforth cited as *DJ* in the text; Michelle Tea, *Valencia* (Seattle: Seal Press, 2000), henceforth cited as *V* in the text, and *The Passionate Mistakes and Intricate Corruption of One Girl in America* (New York: Semiotext(e), 1998); Sarah Schulman, *Girls, Visions, and Everything* (Seattle: Seal Press, 1999), henceforth cited as *G* in the text, and *After Delores* (New York: Plume, 1989); Eileen Myles, *Cool for You* (New York: Soft Skull Press, 2000).

32. See, however, Nicki Hastie's discussion of *Don Juan* as a picaresque novel in *Lesbian Excursions: Journeying through the Personal Narrative* at http://www.nickihastie.demon.co.uk/chaptwo.htm.

33. For an excellent discussion of the "new American picaresque," see Rowland A. Sherill, *Road-Book America: Contemporary Culture and the New Picaresque* (Urbana: University of Illinois Press, 2000).

34. Steiner, *Antigones*, 130.

35. Sally R. Munt, *Heroic Desire: Lesbian Identity and Cultural Space* (New York: New York University Press, 1998), 45.

36. Bonnie Zimmerman, *The Safe Sea of Women: Lesbian Fiction, 1969–1989* (London: Onlywomen Press, 1992). See also Paulina Palmer, *Contemporary Lesbian Writing: Dreams, Desire, Difference* (Buckingham: Open University Press, 1993).

37. Judith Halberstam, *Female Masculinity* (Durham, NC: Duke University Press, 1998), 5.

38. Marilyn R. Farwell, *Heterosexual Plots and Lesbian Narratives* (New York: New York University Press, 1996).

39. Maxine Hong Kingston, *The Woman Warrior: Memoirs of a Girlhood among Ghosts* (New York: Vintage, 1975), henceforth cited as *WW* in the text; Amy Tan, *The Joy Luck Club* (New York: Vintage, 1989), henceforth cited as *JLC* in the text, and *The Kitchen God's Wife* (New York: Ballantine, 1992); Fae Myenne Ng, *Bone* (New York: HarperCollins, 1993); Mei Ng, *Eating Chinese Food Naked: A Novel* (New York: Washington Square Press, 1998).

40. Adrienne Rich, *Of Woman Born: Motherhood as Experience and Institution* (London: Virago, 1977), 237.

41. Margaret Atwood, *The Blind Assassin* (New York: Random House, 2000), 94.

42. Marianne Hirsch, *The Mother-Daughter Plot* (Bloomington: Indiana University Press, 1989).

43. Quoted in King-Keok Chung, *Articulate Silences: Hisaye Yamamoto, Maxine Hong Kingston, Joy Ogawa* (Ithaca, NY: Cornell University Press, 1993), 85.

44. Wendy Ho, *In Her Mother's House: The Politics of Asian-American Mother-Daughter Writing* (Walnut Creek, CA: Altamira Press, 1999), 166.

45. Caroline Rody, *The Daughter's Return: African-American and Caribbean Women's Fictions of History* (Oxford: Oxford University Press, 2001).

46. Leslie Bow, *Betrayal and Other Acts of Subversion: Feminism, Sexual Politics, Asian American Women's Literature* (Princeton, NJ: Princeton University Press, 2001), 71.

47. See Sharon Rose Wilson, *Margaret Atwood's Fairy-Tale Sexual Politics* (Jackson: University Press of Mississippi, 1993).

48. "Address to the American Booksellers Association Convention," *Book Group Companion to Margaret Atwood's "The Robber Bride"* (New York: Doubleday, 1994), 11.

49. Gayle Greene, *Changing the Story: Feminist Fiction and the Tradition* (Bloomington: Indiana University Press, 1991), 207, 210, 213.

50. Jean Wyatt, "I Want to Be You: Envy, the Lacanian Double, and Feminist Community in Margaret Atwood's *The Robber Bride*," *Tulsa Studies in Women's Literature* 17, 1 (1998): 51.

51. Margaret Atwood, *The Robber Bride* (New York: Doubleday, 1993), 457; henceforth cited as *RB* in the text.

52. Quoted in Karen F. Stein, *Margaret Atwood Revisited* (New York: Twayne, 1999), 99.

53. Margaret Atwood, *Alias Grace* (New York: Doubleday, 1996). See also Magali Cornier Michael, "Rethinking History as Patchwork: The Case of Atwood's *Alias Grace*," *Modern Fiction Studies* 47, 1 (2001): 421–47.

54. Lynn Hunt, "'No Longer an Evenly Flowing River': Time, History, and the Novel," *American Historical Review* 103, 5 (1998): 1517–21.

55. Jonathan D. Spence, "Margaret Atwood and the Edges of History," *American Historical Review* 103, 5 (1998): 1524.

56. Quoted in J. Brooks Bouson, "Slipping Sideways into the Dreams of Women: The Female Dream Work of Power Feminism in Margaret Atwood's *The Robber Bride*," *Literature, Interpretation, Theory* 6 (1995): 149–66.

57. Amanda Craig, "Have Our Literary Darlings Lost the Plot?" *London Sunday Times* (July 15, 2001).

58. B. R. Myers, "A Reader's Manifesto," *Atlantic Monthly* (July–August 2001).

Chapter 4

1. Pierre Bourdieu, *Distinction: A Social Critique of the Judgement of Taste* (Cambridge, MA: Harvard University Press, 1984).

2. Willy Russell, *Educating Rita* (London: Longman, 1991), 3; henceforth cited as *ER* in the text.

3. Gerald Graff, *Professing Literature: An Institutional History* (Chicago: University of Chicago Press, 1987), 255.

4. Richard Rorty, "The Inspirational Value of Great Works of Literature," *Raritan* 16, 1 (1996): 16.

5. George Levine, "Introduction: Reclaiming the Aesthetic," *Aesthetics and Ideology* (New Brunswick, NJ: Rutgers University Press, 1994), 2–3, 4, 3. Levine's account of the demise of the aesthetic strikes me as exaggerated. The work of many influential and often cited critics—Adorno, Bakhtin, and Kristeva come immediately to mind—are very much concerned with questions of aesthetics and poetics.

6. Rorty, "Inspirational Value," 13.

7. Ibid., 15.

8. There is, I am well aware, an incongruity in these three categories, an incongruity that reflects the current state of feminist scholarship. I would wager that more criticism has been published on Woolf than on most of the women writers of the Third World put together.

9. Barbara Herrnstein Smith, *Contingencies of Value: Alternative Perspectives for Critical Theory* (Cambridge, MA: Harvard University Press, 1988), 69.

10. Terry Eagleton, *Literary Theory: An Introduction* (Oxford: Blackwell, 1983), 11.

11. See Harold Bloom, *The Western Canon: The Books and School of the Ages* (New York: Riverhead Books, 1994).

12. Brenda R. Silver, *Virginia Woolf Icon* (Chicago: University of Chicago Press, 1999), xv.

13. Bloom, *Western Canon*, 405.

14. James Naremore, *The World without a Self: Virginia Woolf and the Novel* (New Haven, CT: Yale University Press, 1973), 242.

15. Geoffrey Hartman, "Virginia's Web," in *Virginia Woolf: A Collection of Critical Essays*, ed. Margaret Homans (Englewood Cliffs, NJ: Prentice-Hall, 1993), 43, 44.

16. Virginia Woolf, *To the Lighthouse* (Harmondsworth: Penguin, 1964), 96; henceforth cited as *L* in the text.

17. Virginia Woolf, "Women and Fiction," in *A Woman's Essays*, ed. Rachel Bowlby (London: Penguin, 1992), 49.

18. Pamela L. Caughie, *Virginia Woolf and Postmodernism* (Urbana: University of Illinois Press, 1991), 10.

19. Toril Moi, *Sexual/Textual Politics: Feminist Literary Theory* (London: Methuen, 1985), 13.

20. Margaret Homans, "Introduction," *Virginia Woolf: A Collection of Critical Essays* (Englewood Cliffs, NJ: Prentice-Hall, 1993), 3.

21. Joseph Allen Boone, *Tradition counter Tradition: Love and the Form of Fiction* (Chicago: University of Chicago Press, 1987), 201.

22. See, e.g., Rachel Blau du Plessis, *Writing beyond the Ending: Narrative Strategies of Twentieth-Century Women Writers* (Bloomington: Indiana University Press, 1985).

23. Homans, "Introduction," 9.

24. Rachel Bowlby, *Feminist Destinations and Further Essays on Virginia Woolf* (Edinburgh: Edinburgh University Press, 1997), 15.

25. Nina Baym, "Melodramas of Beset Manhood: How Theories of American

Fiction Exclude Women Authors," in *Feminism and American Literary History* (New Brunswick, NJ: Rutgers University Press, 1992), 7.

26. Lilian S. Robinson, "Treason Our Text: Feminist Challenges to the Literary Canon," in Robyn R. Warhol and Diane Price Herndl, *Feminisms: An Anthology of Literary Theory and Criticism* (New Brunswick, NJ: Rutgers University Press, 1997), 120.

27. Jane Tompkins, *Sensational Designs: The Cultural Work of American Fiction, 1790–1860* (New York: Oxford University Press, 1985), 186–87.

28. Ibid., 193.

29. Ellen Moers, *Literary Women* (New York: Oxford University Press, 1976), 91.

30. Patricia Meyer Spacks, *Desire and Truth in Narrative: Functions of Plot in Eighteenth-Century English Novels* (Chicago: University of Chicago Press, 1990), 159–60.

31. Quoted in Eugenia C. DeLamotte, *Perils of the Night: A Feminist Study of Nineteenth-Century Gothic* (Oxford: Oxford University Press, 1990), 4.

32. Coral Ann Howells, *Love, Mystery, and Misery: Feeling in Gothic Fiction* (London: Athlone Press, 1978), 5.

33. Mary Poovey, "Ideology and *The Mysteries of Udolpho*," *Criticism* 21, 4 (1979), 321.

34. Michelle A. Massé, *In the Name of Love: Women, Masochism, and the Gothic* (Ithaca, NY: Cornell University Press, 1992). See also Tania Modleski, *Loving with a Vengeance: Mass-Produced Fantasies for Women* (New York: Routledge, 1982).

35. Claire Kahane, "The Gothic Mirror," in *The (M)other Tongue: Essays in Feminist Psychoanalytic Interpretation*, ed. Shirley Nelson Garner, Claire Kahane, and Madelon Sprengnether (Ithaca, NY: Cornell University Press, 1985).

36. Terry Castle, *The Female Thermometer: Eighteenth-Century Culture and the Invention of the Uncanny* (Oxford: Oxford University Press, 1995).

37. Moers, *Literary Women*, 90–91.

38. Mariama Bâ, quoted in Mineke Schipper, "Women and Literature in Africa," in *Unheard Words: Women and Literature in Africa, the Arab World, Asia, the Caribbean, and Latin America*, ed. Mineke Schipper (London: Alison and Busby, 1985), 50.

39. Barbara Harlow, *Resistance Literature* (New York: Methuen, 1987), xvii, 98.

40. See, e.g., Carole Boyce Davies, "Writing off Marginality, Minoring, and Effacement," *Women's Studies International Forum* 14, 4 (1991): 249–63.

41. Florence Stratton, *Contemporary African Literature and the Politics of Gender* (New York: Routledge, 1994), 4.

42. Susan Andrade, review of *Contemporary African Literature and the Politics of Gender*, *Researches in African Literatures* 26 (1995): 193–94.

43. Gayatri Spivak, "Introduction to 'Draupadi,' by Mahsweta Devi," in *In Other Worlds: Essays in Cultural Politics* (New York: Methuen, 1987), 179.

44. Amal Amireh and Lisa Suhair Majaj, "Introduction," *Going Global: The Transnational Reception of Third World Women Writers* (New York: Garland, 2000), 7.

45. Amal Amireh, "Framing Nawal El Saadawi: Arab Feminism in a Transnational World," *Signs: Journal of Women in Culture and Society* 26, 1 (2000): 236.

46. Trinh T. Min-ha, *Woman, Native, Other: Writing Postcoloniality and Feminism* (Bloomington: Indiana University Press, 1989), 21.

47. Elleke Boehmer, *Colonial and Postcolonial Literature* (Oxford: Oxford University Press, 1995), 206.

48. Buchi Emecheta, *The Joys of Motherhood* (London: Heinemann, 1979), 219, 224.

49. Barbara Christian, "An Angle of Seeing: Motherhood in Buchi Emecheta's *Joys of Motherhood* and Alice Walker's *Meridian,*" in *Black Feminist Criticism: Perspectives on Black Women Writers* (New York: Pergamon Press, 1985), 243.

50. Juliana Makuchi Nfah-Abbenyi, *Gender in African Women's Writing: Identity, Sexuality, and Difference* (Bloomington: Indiana University Press, 1997), 46.

51. Nancy Topping Bazin, "Feminist Perspectives in African Fiction: Bessie Head and Buchi Emecheta," *Black Scholar* (March–April 1986): 39.

52. Cynthia Ward, "What They Told Buchi Emecheta: Oral Subjectivity and the Joys of 'Otherhood,'" *PMLA* 105, 1 (1990): 96.

53. Tuzyline Jita Allan, *Womanist and Feminist Aesthetics: A Comparative Review* (Athens: Ohio University Press, 1995), 106.

54. Katherine Fishburn, *Reading Buchi Emecheta: Cross-Cultural Conversations* (Westport, CT: Greenwood Press, 1995), 128.

55. Timothy Brennan, *At Home in the World: Cosmopolitanism Now* (Cambridge, MA: Harvard University Press, 1997).

56. See Bourdieu, *Distinction.*

57. On this point, see also John Guillory, *Cultural Capital: The Problem of Literary Canon Formation* (Chicago: University of Chicago Press, 1993).

58. Jennifer Wicke, "Great-Enough Great Books," http://bodoni.village.virginia.edu/text-context/.

Acker, Kathy, 42

Adorno, Theodor, 183n. 5

aesthetic appreciation, link to social class, 136–38, 165

aesthetic attitude, 164

aesthetic distance, 85

aesthetic experience: and aesthetic value, 139; feminist critics on, 142

aesthetic pleasure, as enemy of feminism, 35

aesthetics, of everyday life, 83

aesthetic value, 139–41. *See also* literary value

African American women. *See* black female authors; black female readers

African literature, 157

After Delores (Shulman), 113

Alias Grace (Atwood), 131

Allan, Tuzyline, 161

Allison, Dorothy, 47

American Historical Review, 131

Amireh, Amal, 158

analogy, 16–17

Andrade, Susan, 157

anecdote, 83

Ang, Ien, 54

Animal Husbandry (Zigman), 102

Antigone, 17

antiromance, 25

Anzaldúa, Gloria, 87–88

Appiah, Anthony, 19

Arnold, Matthew, 14

art: challenge to universality of, 13–18; gender as a product of, 75–79; humanist view of, 50; and politics, 19–20, 79, 163–64

Asian American women, literature by, 123

The Assassin's Tale (Atwood), 125

Atlantic Monthly, 133

Atwood, Margaret, 124–31; *Alias Grace,* 131; *The Assassin's Tale,* 125; *Cat's Eye,* 126; *The Edible Woman,* 124–25; on female villains, 125–26; moral sympathy of, 103; objections to feminist misreadings, 92; revision of fairy-tale motifs, 125; *The Robber Bride,* 102, 127–31

Austen, Jane: feminist rereadings of, 57; *Pride and Prejudice,* 18; Trilling on, 173n. 22

author: death of, 57–59, 62; as nonneutral label, 61–62; as a projection, 64. *See also* female authors

authorship: anonymous, 60–61; male perspective on, 58–59. *See also* black female authors; female authorship

Autobiography of My Mother (Kincaid), 44

Bâ, Mariama, 156

backlash, and feminism, 5

Baker, Houston, 85

Bakhtin, Mikhail, 183n. 5

Barthes, Roland, on authorship, 57, 58–59, 60, 62, 63

Bataille, Georges, 42

Baudelaire, Charles, 113

Baym, Nina, 149

Bazin, Nancy Topping, 161

Beauvoir, Simone de, 97

Beer, Gillian, 95

Beloved (Morrison), 102

Bernhard, Thomas, 44

bias, degrees of, 10

Bildungsroman, 108

bisexuality, 74, 75
Bishop, Elizabeth, 92
bi-textuality, 49
black female authors: in debates about the canon, 18–19; discourse on, 81; home as an essential source for, 81–83; and marriage plot, 107; and maternal lineage, 80, 84; as "migratory subjects," 87; noncommodified relationship to language, 83–84; presence of in speech, 84; and themes of separation and connection, 84
black female readers, as resisting to texts by and about white women, 40–41
black feminism, 79
black feminist criticism: and black women writers, 81; and division between "high" and "low," 83; and maternal lineage, 80
black women, and television and film, 40
Bloom, Harold: attacks on feminism, 1, 3; theory of poetic creation, 66; The Western Canon, 143
Blue Highways (Least Heat-Moon), 110
Boehmer, Elke, 159
bohemianism, French tradition of literary, 113
Bone (Ng), 117
Boone, Joseph Allen, 100, 147
Booth, Alison, 106
Booth, Wayne, 37
border crosser, woman of color as, 87–88
The Bostonians (James), 36–37
Bourdieu, Pierre, 135, 136, 138, 165
Bovary, Emma, 23, 24, 54
Bow, Leslie, 123
Bowlby, Rachel, 148
Bradford, Barbara Taylor, 101
Brennan, Timothy, 162
Bridget Jones's Diary (Fielding), 102
Brontë, Charlotte, Jane Eyre, 64–65, 88
Brookner, Anita, 103
Brown, Wendy, 37
Burroughs, William, 42

Butler, Judith, 4, 75–76, 88
Byatt, A. S., 96, 125

Campion, Jane, 52
Camus, Albert, 44
canon: and black female authors, 18–19; critique of, 166
Carby, Hazel, 87
Carter, Angela, 42, 77, 125
Castle, Terry, 41, 155
Cat's Eye (Atwood), 126
Caughie, Pamela, 146
Cervantes, Miguel de, Don Quixote, 23, 24, 25–29
"chick flicks," 48
Chinese American female authors, 117, 118, 124
Chodorow, Nancy, 118
Christian, Barbara, 161
Cixous, Hélène, "The Laugh of the Medusa," 73–75
Colette, "The Hidden Woman," 71–73
Collins, Jackie, 101
A Confederacy of Dunces (Toole), 110
cross-dressing, 49
cross-gender identification, 49–51
cultural studies, 20, 21, 46, 138
The Culture of Complaint (Hughes), 10, 19

Darrieussecq, Marie, Pig Tales: A Novel of Lust and Transformation, 102
daughterly return, romance of, 122
Davidson, Robyn, Tracks, 102
Davies, Carole Boyce, 87, 157
Davis, Kim Chabot, 52
de la Motte, Eugenia, 152
de Lauretis, Teresa, 104
DeLynn, Jane, Don Juan in the Village, 109, 110–13
Denby, David, Great Books, 17–18
Dickens, Charles, 43
Dickinson, Emily, 42, 57
Dirty Weekend (Zahavi), 102
disinterestedness, 10, 53, 142
Divine Secrets of the Ya-Ya Sisterhood (Wells), 102
Doane, Mary Ann, 33

documentary realism, 100
Doniger, Wendy, 96, 108
Don Juan, myth of and lesbian picaresque, 111
Don Juan in the Village (DeLynn), 109,
110–13
Don Quixote (Cervantes), 23, 24, 25–
29
Dostoyevsky, Fyodor, 43
double vision, 21–22
drag, 75–76, 77
duCille, Ann, 51, 87, 107
du Plessis, Rachel Blau, 100
Dworkin, Andrea, 3

Eagleton, Terry, 142
Eating Chinese Food Naked (Ng), 117
The Edible Woman (Atwood), 124–25
Educating Rita (Russell), 135–38, 167–
69
Eliot, George, 30
Eliot, T. S., 42
Ellis, John: attacks on feminism, 3; *Lit-
erature Lost*, 6–12, 15, 172n. 5
El-Saadawi, Nawal, 158
Emecheta, Buchi, 43; *The Joys of Moth-
erhood*, 160–62
enclosure, imagery of, 67
Erkkila, Betsy, 92
escapism, 53, 54, 55
Even Cowgirls Get the Blues (Robbins),
110
"Everyday Use" (Walker), 84–87
experimental writers, 79, 104

Fadiman, Anne, *The Spirit Catches You
and You Fall Down*, 44–45, 46
fairy tales, 125
fan groups, 166
fantasy, 49, 54
Farwell, Marilyn, 116
A Feeling for Books (Radway), 56, 107
Felman, Shoshana, 38
female, as embodiment of difference, 14
female authors: African American, 18–
19, 80–84, 87; Chinese American,
117, 118, 124; covert meanings in
texts by, 69; as creating new mean-

ings from old myths, 132; discomfort of male students with, 18; objection to labeling, 92; as rebutting
current theories of gender and narrative, 132; sentimental, 89
female authorship: allegories of, 64–93;
and allegory of the home girl, 79–
88; and allegory of the madwoman
in the attic, 64–71; and allegory of
the masquerading woman, 71–79;
feminine writing, 73–74
female *Bildungsroman*, 100
female heroes, lack of in Western culture, 97–98
female identity: Cixous's theory of ex-
ploding versus discovering, 73–74;
and the mother, 118; stereotypes of,
74
The Female Man (Russ), 100
female paranoia, and the Gothic novel,
152
female readers: black, as resisting texts
by and about white women, 40–41;
lesbian, 41–42; male representation
of, 33; pleasure in reading, 29, 53–
54; of romance novels, 25, 48, 53;
twentieth-century view of, 31. *See
also* reading
female villains, 125, 126–29
feminism: attacks on, 1, 3; black, 79; and
the mother figure, 117–18, 124
feminist criticism: and aesthetic experience, 142; allegory of the home girl,
79–88; allegory of the madwoman
in the attic, 64–71; allegory of the
masquerading woman, 71–79; approaches to authorship, 57–59, 62;
attacks upon, 1–2, 3; on Atwood's
fiction, 126–27; on black women's
writing, 51; caricatures of, 2–3; and
cross-gender identification, 51;
early views of the female author,
68; either/or arguments against, 6–
13; as an established institution, 5;
evaluation anxiety in, 165; "exclusion" in, 166–67; on female texts,
39; fragmentation, 2, 3–4; on gender effects on reading, 34, 47–48;

feminist criticism (*continued*)
  and Gothic fiction, 151–55; and lesbian readers, 41; and literary value,
  141–51; and male authorship, 91;
  on modernist and postmodernist
  fiction, 76–79; and opposition of art
  and politics, 19–20; on the pleasure
  of reading, 53–56; on plot, 96, 99–
  101, 103–6; on Shakespeare's female characters, 8; success of, 149;
  "third position," 91; and Third
  World women's writing, 155–63;
  on Virginia Woolf, 143–49
feminist film theory, 40
feminist reader, as resisting reader, 34–
  38
Fetterley, Judith, *The Resisting Reader*,
  33, 34, 38
Fierce Attachments (Gornick), 102
Fish, Stanley, *Professional Correctness:
  Literary Studies and Political
  Change*, 13, 14
Fishburn, Katherine, 161–62
Flaubert, Gustave, 11; *Madame Bovary*,
  23, 24, 26–29, 54, 173n. 5
Flint, Kate, 29
folk tales, 106
form: and aesthetic value, 164–66; gen-
  der and narrative, 104; nonacademic
  interest in, 166; Woolf's attention
  to, 147–48
formalist analysis, 163, 164
Forster, E. M., *Howards End*, 136
Foucault, Michel, on authorship, 57, 58,
  60, 62, 63
Fraiman, Susan, 100
Frantzen, Jonathan, 165
Freudian thought, and the Gothic
  novel, 154–55
Friedberg, Anne, 45
Friedman, Ellen, 104
Friedman, Susan Stanford, 91, 108
Fuchs, Miriam, 104
Fuss, Diana, 49

Gallop, Jane, 7–8, 172n. 8
Gasset, José Ortega y, 31–32
gender: effects on reading, 29, 47–49,

175n. 34; and literary value, 140;
  literature as saturated by, 11–12;
  and narrative form, 104; as perfor-
  mance, 75–79; and plot, 104–5; as
  product of art, 75–79
Gilbert, Sandra, 7, 65–68, 69, 70, 80, 98
The Gilda Stories (Gomez), 102
Gilman, Charlotte Perkins, "The Yellow
  Wallpaper," 64–65, 67, 68
*The Girl's Guide to Hunting and Fish-
  ing* (Banks), 102
Girls, Visions, and Everything (Schul-
  man), 113
Gogol, Nikolai, 43
Gomez, Jewelle, *The Gilda Stories*, 102
Goodheart, Eugene, 22
Gordon, Mary, *Spending*, 102
Gothic novel, 141, 149–55
Graff, Gerald, 137
Grafton, Sue, 101
Greek myths, 96–97
Greene, Gayle, 126
Greer, Germaine, 43
Gubar, Susan, 7, 65–68, 69, 70, 80, 98
Gwin, Minrose, *The Woman in the Red
  Dress*, 23, 46–47, 56

Halberstam, Judith, 115
Hamilton, Jane, 103
Haraway, Donna, 7
Harlow, Barbara, *Resistance Literature*,
  156–57
Hartman, Geoffrey, 144
Hedges, Elaine, 66
Hegel, G. W. F., 17, 97
Heilbrun, Carolyn, 50
Hennegan, Alison, 50
hermeneutic circle, 9, 47
heroes: American, as male fantasies, 15;
  female, lack of in Western culture,
  97–98
heterosexual imperative, 76
"The Hidden Woman" (Colette), 71–73
Hirsch, Marianne, 118
Ho, Wendy, 121
Homans, Margaret, 105, 147, 148
home, and black female writing, 81–83
home girls, 79–88

Home Girls (Smith, ed.), 79, 80, 81
hooks, bell, 22, 40, 42, 83
Housekeeping (Robinson), 110
Howards End (Forster), 136
Howells, Coral Ann, 153
How Reading Changed My Life
    (Quindlen), 55
Hughes, Robert, *The Culture of Com-
    plaint,* 10, 19
Hunt, Lynn, 131
Hurston, Zora Neale, 87, 143
Huyssen, Andreas, 32

Ibsen, Henrik, 102
identification, 49–52
identity, female: Cixous's theory of ex-
    ploding versus discovering, 73–74;
    and the mother figure, 118
identity politics, 51
imitation, as irony, 75
"In Search of Our Mothers' Gardens"
    (Walker), 81, 82–83
intellect, as separate from emotion, 54–
    55
interpretation, 46; tradition of, 35; un-
    certainties of, 16
Iser, Wolfgang, 46

Jacobs, Harriet, 47
Jacobus, Mary, 70, 77
James, Henry, *The Bostonians,* 36–37
Jane Eyre (Brontë), 64–65, 88
The Joy Luck Club (Tan), 102, 117,
    121–23, 124
The Joys of Motherhood (Emecheta),
    160–62

Kafka, Franz, "The Metamorphosis,"
    15, 16
Kahane, Claire, 154
Kamuf, Peggy, 59
Karenina, Anna, 24
Kennard, Jean, 41
Kernan, Alvin, 3
Kerouac, Jack, 110, 113
Kincaid, Jamaica, 46; *Autobiography of
    My Mother,* 44

Kingston, Maxine Hong, *The Woman
    Warrior,* 117, 119–21, 123, 124
The Kitchen God's Wife (Tan), 117
Kitchen Table/Women of Color Press,
    81
Koestenbaum, Wayne, 50
Kolodny, Annette, 68
Krantz, Judith, 101
Kristeva, Julia, 183n. 5

language: belief in absolute power of,
    60; black female authors and, 83–
    84; the mother as source of, 82; or-
    dinary, 83
Lanser, Susan, 70
Lara, Maria Pia, 108
"The Laugh of the Medusa" (Cixous),
    73–75
Lawrence, D. H., 42
Leavis, F. R., 14, 148
lesbian fiction, 104
lesbianism, feminist view of, 76
lesbian picaresque, 109–16; in contrast
    to coming-out novel, 114–15; pro-
    sex stance, 112; sources of, 113; tra-
    ditionally masculine plots and,
    115–16
lesbian readers: cross-identification,
    41–42; and ingenuity, 41
lesbian sexuality, debates about, 111
Lessing, Doris, 42–43
Levine, George, 138–39, 183n. 5
linguistic subversion, and politics and
    art, 79
literary bohemianism, 113
literary value, 135–38; and feminist
    criticism, 141–51; and form, 164–
    66; gendered, 140; inspirational,
    138–39; and political value, 142,
    155–63
literature: modern, underlying myths
    of, 97; as saturated with social
    meanings, 12–13; study of, 164
Literature Lost (Ellis), 6–12, 15, 172n.
    5
Llosa, Mario Vargas, 173n. 5
logocentrism, 73
Lorde, Audre, 42

love story, 99–102
Lyotard, Jean-François, 148
lyricism, 100

MacKinnon, Catharine, 3, 7
Madame Bovary (Flaubert), 23, 24, 26–29, 54, 173n. 5
madness, as response to constraints on women, 65–70
The Madwoman in the Attic (Gilbert and Gubar), 7, 65–68
Majaj, Lisa Suhair, 158
male universal, 14
Man of La Mancha, 24
Mansfield, Katherine, 42
Marks, Grace, 131
Marlowe, Philip, 113
marriage plot, changing politics of, 107
Marshall, Paule, 81, 83
masculinity, feminist interest in, 91
masquerading women, 71–79, 177n. 23
mass culture, association with stereotypical feminine traits, 32
Massé, Michelle, 154
mass-market fiction, 61
materialist-feminist perspective, 90
McDowell, Deborah, 87
Medea (Euripides), 97
"The Metamorphosis" (Kafka), 15, 16
"migratory subject," black woman writer as, 87
Miller, Henry, 113
Miller, Nancy, 59, 98, 100
modernism, 31–32, 91
modern literature, underlying myths of, 97
Moers, Ellen, 155
Moi, Toril, 59, 92–93, 146
Moretti, Franco, 97
Morrison, Toni, 42, 47; *Beloved*, 102; on emotional power of black art, 84; "Rootedness: The Ancestor as Foundation," 81
mother-daughter plots, 116–24
mother figure: and female identity, 118; and feminism, 117–18, 124; as source of language, 82
Mount, Ferdinand, 102–3

Mphahlele, Ezekiel, 159
Muller, Marcia, 101
Mulvey, Laura, 35
Munt, Sally, 113
museum display, politics of, 60
Myers, B. R., "Reader's Manifesto," 133
Myles, Eileen, 109
The Mysteries of Udolpho (Radcliffe), 152, 153–54
mystery fiction, 101
myths: Greek, 96–97; Oedipal, as founding myth of Western culture, 104; as shape-shifters, 96–97; as underlying modern literature, 97

Naremore, James, 144
narrative plot, as patriarchal form, 104, 105
Naylor, Gloria, 43
negotiation, interaction of reader and text as, 46
New Criticism, 163
Newton, Judith, 89–90
Nfah-Abbenyi, Juliana, 161
Ng, Fae Myenne, *Bone*, 117
Ng, Mei, *Eating Chinese Food Naked*, 117
Nights at the Circus (Carter), 77
Noble, Marianne, 89
Northern Exposure, 52
novel: coming-out, 114; confessional, 108; Gothic, 141, 149–55
novel-reading, dangers to women, 29–30
Nussbaum, Martha, 35–36, 50

Oates, Joyce Carole, 92
O'Connor, Flannery, 43
Oedipal story, as founding myth of Western culture, 104
Orlando (Woolf), 77
"over-feminization," 91, 92

Paley, Grace, 42
paranoia, female, and Gothic novel, 152
Paretsky, Sara, 101
parody: as dependency, 97; as way of exposing artificiality of gender, 75–79

performance, gender as, 75–79
The Piano, 52
picaresque, 109–10
Pierce-Baker, Charlotte, 85
Pig Tales: A Novel of Lust and Trans-formation (Darrieussecq), 102
Plath, Sylvia, 63, 129
Platonism, 140
pleasure, in reading, 29, 54–55
plot: feminist case against, 96, 99–106; gendered, 104–5; of lesbian picaresque, 115–16; in literary fiction, 132–33; marriage, changing politics of, 107; mother-daughter, 116–24; narrative, as patriarchal form, 104, 105; patterns in contemporary fiction, 101–2; as playground, 106
Poe, Edgar Allan, 42
poetic creation, theory of, 66
political value, and literary value, 155–63
politics: and art, 19–20, 79, 163–64; and literature, 6–13, 19
Poovey, Mary: on the Gothic, 154; *Uneven Developments: The Ideological Work of Gender in Mid-Victorian England*, 90
popular culture, 54
postcolonial studies, 159, 163
postmodernism, 148
poststructuralism, 79, 148
Poulet, Georges, 47
Pound, Ezra, 97
Pride and Prejudice (Austen), 18
Professional Correctness: Literary Studies and Political Change (Fish), 13, 14
psychoanalysis, 105, 154

queer theory, 49–50, 76, 77
Quindlen, Anna, *How Reading Changed My Life*, 55
Quintana, Alvina, 79

Radcliffe, Ann: and the Gothic novel, 151; *The Mysteries of Udolpho*, 152, 153–54

Radway, Janice: *A Feeling for Books*, 56, 107; *Reading the Romance*, 53, 107
readers, resisting, 34–38. *See also* female readers
"Reader's Manifesto" (Myers), 133
reading: academic and nonacademic compared, 32, 53, 54; as coauthorship, 34; in *Don Quixote*, 26–27; and ethnicity, 40–41; experience of, 18; foolish, 23, 25, 29; and gender, 29, 47–49, 175n. 34; and identification, 49–52; in *Madame Bovary*, 27–29; as a mutual encounter, 47; of novels, and dangers to women, 29–30; passionate involvement, 54–56; pleasure in, 29, 54–55; across race, gender, and sexuality, 42–43; as rape, 39; rethinking, 47–56; roles of for women in Victorian England, 30–31; and romance, 24–33; skeptical strategy for, 35–36
Reading the Romance (Radway), 53, 107
rereading, 34
Resistance Literature (Harlow), 156–57
resistance narrative, 157
The Resisting Reader (Fetterley), 33, 38
reviews, 166
Rich, Adrienne, 34, 117
Ricoeur, Paul, 35
Rilke, Rainer Maria, 42
The Robber Bride (Atwood), 102, 127–31
"The Robber Bridegroom," 128, 130
Robinson, Lilian S., 150
Rody, Caroline, 122
romance novels: as heroic quest, 24; women readers of, 25, 48, 53; and women's fantasies, 107
romance of daughterly return, 122
Roof, Judith, 104
"Rootedness: The Ancestor as Foundation" (Morrison), 81
Rorty, Richard, 138, 139–40
Rosenfelt, Deborah, 89–90
Roy, Anudhati, 159–60
Rushdie, Salman, 159–60

Russ, Joanna: *The Female Man,* 100; "What Can a Heroine Do? Or, Why Women Can't Write," 99–101

Russell, Willy, *Educating Rita,* 135–38, 167–69

Sade, Marquis de, 42

sadomasochism, gender politics of, 112

Sartre, Jean-Paul, 43

Schulman, Sarah, 116; *After Delores,* 114; *Girls, Visions, and Everything,* 113; lesbian picaresque, 109

Schwarz, Lynn, 62

Schweickart, Patricinio, 38–40

science fiction, 100

Scoppetone, Sandra, 101

Scott, Walter, 155

Sedgwick, Eve Kosofsky, 49, 172n. 12

self, 59–60

Sensational Designs: The Cultural Work of American Fiction, 1790–1860 (Tompkins), 150

Sex and the City, 102

sexual ambiguity, 72–73, 74–75

Shakespeare, William, 7–8, 18

Shields, Carol, 103

Showalter, Elaine, 51, 91–92, 172n. 8

Smith, Barbara, *Home Girls,* 79, 80, 81

Smith, Barbara Herrnstein, 142

Smith, Valerie, 86, 87

Smith, Zadie, 103, 159–60

Soueif, Ahdaf, 158

Spacks, Patricia Meyer, 100, 152

Spence, Jonathan, 131

Spending (Gordon), 102

Spillers, Hortense, 87

The Spirit Catches You and You Fall Down (Fadiman), 44–45, 46

Spivak, Gayatri, 70, 158

Stafford, Barbara, 16

Steedman, Carolyn, 96

Steiner, George, 14, 17, 96–97, 111

Steiner, Wendy, 12

Stendhal, 43

storytelling: distrust of, 103; and feminist presence in the public sphere, 108; and maternal legacy, 119–21; as remembrance, 130; and sexual difference, 104

Stratton, Florence, 157

subversive mimicry, 75

suffragette movement, encouragement of reading, 31

surrealism, 95

Tan, Amy: *The Joy Luck Club,* 102, 117, 121–23, 124; *The Kitchen God's Wife,* 117

Tea, Michelle, *Valencia,* 109, 112, 114

Third World, writing by women, 141, 155–63

Thorpe, Vanessa, 175n. 34

Times Literary Supplement, 102

Tompkins, Jane, *Sensational Designs: The Cultural Work of American Fiction, 1790–1860,* 150

To the Lighthouse (Woolf), 144–49

Tracks (Davidson), 102

transvestism, 49, 50

Trilling, Lionel, 14, 17, 173n. 22

Trinh Min-ha, *Woman, Native, Other,* 158–59

Two Girls Fat and Thin (Gaitskill), 102

"under-feminization," 92

Uneven Developments: The Ideological Work of Gender in Mid-Victorian England (Poovey), 90

universal, male as, 14

universality of art, challenge to, 13–18

Updike, John, 43

Valencia (Tea), 109, 112, 114

value. *See* aesthetic value; literary value; political value

Victorian women: authors, as protofeminists, 66–67; race and class differences, 69–70; roles of reading for, 30–31

villains, female, 125, 126–29

Waiting to Exhale (McMillan), 102

Walker, Alice, 43; "Everyday Use," 84–87; "In Search of Our Mothers' Gardens," 81, 82–83

Walker, Cheryl, 91
Ward, Cynthia, 160, 161
Washington, Mary Helen, 80, 82, 86
Watt, Ian, 98
Weaver, Sigourney, 101
The Western Canon (Bloom), 143
Wharton, Edith, 149
"What Can a Heroine Do? Or, Why Women Can't Write" (Russ), 99–101
What Girls Learn (Cook), 102
White, Edmund, 42
white feminists, commentary by on black women's writing, 51
Wicke, Jennifer, 135, 168
Willis, Susan, 83
Winfrey, Oprah, 165
Winterson, Jeanette, 42, 49, 79, 88, 92; *Written on the Body*, 77–78
Wollstonecraft, Mary, 30
The Woman in the Red Dress (Gwin), 23, 46–47, 56
Woman, Native, Other (Trinh Min-ha), 158–59

The Woman Warrior (Kingston), 117, 119–21, 123, 124
women: as embodiment of difference, 14; in fiction, 17. *See also* female readers; Victorian women
Woolf, Virginia, 18, 48, 100, 141; attention to language and form, 147–48; as canonical woman writer, 143; feminist readings of, 143–49; *Orlando*, 77; *To the Lighthouse*, 144–49
Written on the Body (Winterson), 77–78
Wyatt, Jean, 126

Xena the Warrior Princess, 101

Yeager, Patricia, 106
"The Yellow Wallpaper" (Gilman), 65–66, 67, 68, 70

Zahavi, Helen, *Dirty Weekend*, 102
Zimmerman, Bonnie, 114